Interpretation for the
21st Century

Fifteen Guiding Principles
for Interpreting Nature and Culture

Larry Beck
Ted T. Cable

SAGAMORE PUBLISHING

Champaign, IL 61820

Book design: Susan M. McKinney
Cover design: Julie L. Denzer

ISBN: 1-57167-133-1
Printed in the United States.

Sagamore Publishing
804 N. Neil
Champaign IL 61820
http://www.sagamorepub.com

*Grateful acknowledgment is made to the following for permission to use
lengthy quotations from previously published material:*

*Excerpt from **Crow and Weasel** by Barry Lopez, with illustrations by Tom
Pohrt. Text Copyright (c) 1990 by Barry Holstun Lopez. Illustration Copyright
(c) 1990 by Tom Pohrt. Reprinted by permission of North Point Press, a
division of Farrar, Straus & Giroux, Inc.*

*Excerpts from **PrairyErth: a Deep Map**. Copyright (c) 1991 by William Least
Heat-Moon. Reprinted by permission of Houghton Mifflin Co. All rights
reserved.*

*From **The National Parks** by Freeman Tilden. Copyright 1951 by Alfred A.
Knopf, Inc. Reprinted by permission of the publisher.*

*From **The Diversity of Life** by Edward O. Wilson. Copyright (c) 1992 by Edward
O. Wilson. Reprinted by permission of Harvard University Press.*

For our sons:

Spencer and Benjamin
—L.B.

Tim, Eric and Scott
—T.C.

Aye, starry-eyed did I rejoice
  With marvel of a child,
And there were those who heard my voice
  Although my words were wild:
So as I go my wistful way,
  With worship let me sing,
And treasure to my farewell day
  God's Gift of Wondering.

—Robert Service

CONTENTS

About the Authors

Larry Beck and Ted T. Cable have each won awards as interpreters, educators, and scholars. Both have published widely in the fields of natural resource management and interpretation. They co-authored, with Doug Knudson, the textbook *Interpretation of Cultural and Natural Resources.* Both authors teach coursework in interpretation at their respective universities.

Larry Beck, Ph.D., is on the faculty in the Department of Recreation, Parks, and Tourism at San Diego State University. He worked as an interpreter for the National Park Service at Denali National Park and Preserve (Alaska), Glen Canyon National Recreation Area (Arizona/Utah), and Cabrillo National Monument (California). Professor Beck serves as an associate editor of the *Journal of Interpretation Research.* He lives with his wife, Andréa, and two sons in La Mesa, California.

Ted T. Cable, Ph.D., is on the faculty in the Department of Horticulture, Forestry, and Recreation Resources at Kansas State University. He worked as an interpreter for Cook County Forest Preserve District (Illinois) and for Lake County Parks and Recreation Department (Indiana). Professor Cable is editor of the *Journal of Interpretation Research.* In 1996, he received the distinguished "Master of Interpretation" award from the National Association for Interpretation. He lives with his wife, Diane, and three sons in Manhattan, Kansas.

ACKNOWLEDGMENTS

The following individuals provided information, reviewed chapters, or in some other way helped us in writing this book: Michele Baumer, Deborah Beringer, James Bigley, Stephen Bitgood, Rob Bixler, John Doerner, Bob Loudon ,Scott Maxey, Bill McGowan, Mark Morgan, Jay Miller, Greg Schumaker, Lois Silverman, Gerry Snyder, Jane Welch, and Ron Zimmerman. We are also grateful for the editing expertise of Dan Dustin.

FOREWORD

by Tim Merriman, Ph.D.

One sunny Saturday, years ago, I led the weekly guided trail hike up into the narrow canyons of sandstone, the Giant City Nature Trail, 10 miles south of Carbondale, Illinois. My group was the usual—25 or so adults and children, parents with young children, seniors, and empty nesters—all clustered around me for Stop Three, one of my favorites.

"What does this look like to you?" I asked.

"A face," someone answered. "An Indian face!" another offered.

"Yes, a petroglyph. A face carved by native people who lived here. Do you see the feathers carved above the face?"

They did. I explained that an archaeologist told me that the carving of the face was probably one thousand years old or older but the feathers were recent. Someone who knew Indians only from television added the feathers—an act of vandalism. The people were transfixed by the stone face. The petroglyph hovered in time and space within their minds. Physically it was just above waist height to an adult, on a square corner of Mississippi sandstone, an ancient river sandbar.

Then a young girl asked. "Where are the others?"

"What others?" I answered with my own question, a little too quickly.

"There must be others."

"In my five years of walking this trail," I pontificated, "I've never seen others."

She was sure I was wrong, and asked my permission to look for them. I might have thought she was a pest for being so insistent that day. I hope I didn't, but I might have.

Much to her delight and my surprise, she found four more before we finished the one-mile hike. She believed there were more. They had hidden meanings to her that I had missed in my hundreds of trips on the very same trail. In the three years that followed I found three more, after she had opened my eyes. As I led people on that same trail each week, I began seeing and feeling new things among the familiar.

You have just opened a book that takes us to familiar places in the field of interpretation. And it asks us to see it all differently with a look into the next century, the coming millennium. While Freeman Tilden's book, *Interpreting Our Heritage*, established a firm foundation with six principles of interpretation, Larry Beck and Ted Cable remind us that others like Enos Mills, Bill Lewis, Grant Sharpe, Sam Ham, Terry Tempest Williams, Doug Knudson, and many others have written about the principles of interpretation or about being a better observer of this planet, and the universe. Their influence on the profession has been significant.

Beck and Cable relate the parallels between Tilden's words and those of Enos Mills. Mills left us incredible stories of his time and all times as he wrote of his experiences on Long's Peak in the Rockies and of his travels. A little more than a decade ago, Enda Mills Kiley, the daughter of Enos Mills, gave me a copy of his book, *The Story of a Thousand Year Old Pine*. Reading it caused me to look at every tree differently, with more interest in its personal story. I have shared the story of the ancient pine with young interpreters who have not heard of Enos Mills or his wonderful books.

The authors have taken on an awesome task and have done it very well. Those of us who have studied, practiced, and taught interpretive principles over the past 30 years have rightfully paid regular homage to Tilden. He spoke to the profession so clearly and eloquently that it became the standard, almost unquestioned. We say "Tilden's six principles of interpretation" as if there could be no more. Who would dare look for more of them?

The authors even find Tilden's principles in need of a tuneup. It seems like a sacrilege. It is not. Like the girl looking for carved faces from the past, we must continue probing our profession for deeper understandings, principles learned from practice, and new challenges. We must provoke ourselves to learn more in both familiar and unfamiliar settings.

It is time to take a different look at the conceptual landscape of interpretation. The extension of the six principles into fifteen is interesting. I can almost hear the discussions among lumpers and splitters about the rightness of the "fifteen." I silently applauded the work of Beck and Cable while reading each chapter. They document very well the many contributors to our knowledge and beliefs about the art and science of interpretation. I find no argument with the number of principles they chose. Their reasons are very well stated. They have created a new teaching and training aid of great value.

Cable and Beck frame their guiding principles around the work of Mills and Tilden, but they also take them into critical new areas for the 21st century. From basic communication techniques to high technology, they have addressed the importance of all forms of communication.

They even point out the political realities of our profession in Chapter 12, "Attracting Support and Making Friends." Over the past 30 years, it has been sad to watch good programs die under the "downsizer's" knife because they were merely good. These programs had not found relevance to organizational goals, built essential income sources, or developed advocates who would throw their political might behind the program. In this new century and millennium, our business and political skills will be tested along with our interpretive abilities.

Beck and Cable have been good interpreters as well. They will lead you through their thought processes with knowledge, challenges, and thought-provoking stories and ideas. They have studied diverse scholars and interpreters before them in developing the foundation of their principles. *Interpretation for the 21st Century* will provoke you to think in new ways about this very ancient profession. May we never think we have found the only truths, the one set of principles about our profession. There will always be more to know, and change is one of several immutable rules of life. One day in the future, someone else will build from their ideas to reframe the principles of interpretation again. That is as it should be.

When I was a park interpreter, I experimented with my work with naivete, foolish courage, and passion. I remember first reading Tilden's book and feeling like I had discovered the Holy Grail. It gave this young interpreter with limited experience six general guidelines that helped me to improve. I encourage all interpreters who love to learn and grow to read this book and study Beck and Cable's guiding principles. We must all search the trail ahead. There are many more faces to find and stories to tell.

—Tim Merriman, Ph.D.
Executive Director
National Association for Interpretation
Fort Collins, Colorado, 1997

PREFACE

Interpretation is an educational activity that aims to reveal meanings about our cultural and natural resources. Through various media—including talks, guided tours, and exhibits—interpretation enhances our understanding, appreciation, and, therefore, protection of historic sites and natural wonders. Interpretation is an informational and inspirational process that occurs in parks, forests, wildlife refuges, zoos, museums, and cultural sites—places like the Grand Canyon, Yellowstone, Gettysburg National Military Park, the Smithsonian Museums, Yosemite, Mt. Rushmore, Colonial Williamsburg, and Thomas Jefferson's Monticello in the United States. Well-known international sites include Canada's Banff National Park, the Great Barrier Reef, the Egyptian pyramids, the Tower of London, and the Great Wall of China. This book is intended to contribute to an evolving philosophy of interpretation.

Enos Mills was an interpretive guide in what is now Rocky Mountain National Park from the late 1880s to the early 1920s. He wrote *Adventures of a Nature Guide and Essays in Interpretation* which was published in 1920. Mills eloquently put forth a number of principles that laid a philosophical foundation for effective interpretation. He wrote, "A nature guide [i.e., interpreter] is a naturalist who can guide others to the secrets of nature."[1] He believed in the importance of first-hand, experiential learning. Mills observed, "He who feels the spell of the wild, the rhythmic melody of falling water, the echoes among the crags, the bird songs, the winds in the pines, and the endless beat of waves upon the shore, is in tune with the universe."[2]

Mills presented a poetic interpretation of the facts of nature. Being less interested in dry information, he sought to make his topics meaningful by compiling material from "nature's storybook" in the form of its "manners and customs, its neighbors and its biography."[3] Mills developed his principles based upon his own professional experience as an interpreter.

The next landmark contribution to a philosophy of interpretation was Freeman Tilden's *Interpreting Our Heritage*, initially published in 1957. Tilden's six "principles of interpretation" are parallel to those principles championed by Mills. Yet it is Tilden who is far better known and who is often credited with first formulating a philosophy of interpretation.

Within the interpretive profession Tilden's six principles are still embraced and practiced. *Interpreting Our Heritage* has been widely adopted at colleges and universities that offer coursework in cultural and environmental interpretation. Educational sessions at interpretation conferences and workshops still address application of Tilden's principles. His writing continues to be extensively cited in the interpretive literature.

Although the wisdom of Tilden's principles continues to be useful, a need exists to relate his work to the present and to look forward to the issues of the 21st century. Subsequent editions of Tilden's book were paced a decade apart; the second edition in 1967 and the third edition in 1977. So, Tilden himself recognized that this area of study and practice would, like all disciplines, evolve over time. In the Preface to the second edition, Christopher Crittenden wrote, "It [*Interpreting Our Heritage*] is not the final word, as the author and his associates would be the first to admit."[4]

Over the course of the past 25 years there have been many solid contributions to the body of knowledge about interpretation. In 1976, a veteran National Park Service interpreter, Russell Grater, wrote an influential techniques book titled *The Interpreter's Handbook: Methods, Skills, and Techniques*.[5] The first comprehensive text on the various facets of interpretation was *Interpreting the Environment* by Grant Sharpe, also published in 1976.[6] This book, with a second edition in 1982, became the definitive text for use in university curricula.

The 1980s saw publication of an introductory handbook designed primarily for national park interpreters titled *Interpreting for Park Visitors* by William Lewis.[7] A sourcebook for interpreters, docents, and tour guides useful for interpretive training programs was *The Good Guide* by Alison Grinder and E. Sue McCoy.[8] Gary Machlis, Don Field, and their associates contributed a series of essays on the application of sociology to interpretation in *On Interpretation*.[9] Another collection of essays focused on evaluating interpretation in the National Park Service was *Interpretive Views*, edited by Gary Machlis.[10] In the late 1980s, Michael Gross, Ronald Zimmerman, and their associates began editing the "Interpreter's Handbook Series." This series consists of several publications aimed at teaching interpretive approaches and techniques.[11]

The early 1990s saw a revised edition of *On Interpretation* with several new essays. Sam Ham contributed a practical book for "people with big ideas and small budgets" in *Environmental Interpretation*.[12] Next came a planning text on the design of interpretive facilities and services titled *Interpretive Master Planning* by John Veverka.[13] Most recent is a comprehensive book designed to cross the boundaries between theory and practice—*Interpretation of Cultural and Natural Resources*.[14]

The books listed above are major contributions directly related to the field of interpretation. As an indicator of the *overall* growth of resources available to interpreters and environmental educators, the *Acorn Naturalists* 1997 Catalog lists more than 3500 books, field guides, science kits, nature puzzles, and other natural science curriculum supplements.[15]

However, Tilden's *Interpreting Our Heritage* has remained the standard in terms of an interpretive philosophy. Aspects of Tilden's interpretive principles are timeless and we recognize his quintessential contribution to an evolving philosophy of interpretation. Like so many others, we were inspired by his wisdom. However, elements of his philosophy can benefit from a current perspective.

For example, Tilden's third principle of interpretation suggests that interpretation is an art—knowledge treated imaginatively. We agree. However, Tilden continued by noting that interpreters should not "read poems, give a dramatic performance, deliver an oration . . . or anything as horribly out of place as these." Yet these same delivery methods have become increasingly popular in a broad array of settings that offer interpretive services because they have proven to be appealing and effective. As another example, in Tilden's discussion of "gadgetry" there is no mention of today's computer technology and its application in interpretive venues.

In this book we restructure Tilden's treatment of interpretation to fit today's world. We update and build upon his well-established six interpretive principles. Then we add nine principles, many of which are grounded in the work of Mills, Tilden, and many other pioneering champions of our heritage such as John Muir and Robert Marshall, and current spokespersons such as Barry Lopez and Terry Tempest Williams. What we present is intended to be a stepping stone in an evolving philosophy of interpretation.

Interpretation for the 21st Century is written for a broad audience. Students and educators may find it valuable as a supplement to traditional, more comprehensive interpretive textbooks. The book should also be useful to field interpreters and managers at parks, forests, wildlife refuges, museums, zoos, aquaria, historic areas, nature centers, and tourism sites.

Finally, this book is meant to guide general readers who want to explore their cultural and natural legacy. For those who enjoy visiting places that commemorate their heritage, an understanding of interpretation offers the means for evaluating interpretive services and interpreting resources personally. To that end we hope all readers find our treatment of an interpretive philosophy useful in their own lives.

INTRODUCTION

Interpreting Interpretation

The legacy of any nation is encompassed by its natural land-scapes, its wildlife, its historic sites, its culture. As Aldo Leopold stressed, we are *members* of a *community* that includes the whole environment.[1] Pride in our country—an understanding of our past, a concern for the present, and a vision for our future—stems from a close attachment to the land and our cultural roots.

In the Preface we acknowledged the contributions of Enos Mills (see Box 1) and Freeman Tilden (see Box 2) to an evolving interpretive philosophy. We also defined interpretation as an informational and inspirational process designed to enhance understanding, appreciation, and protection of our cultural and natural legacy.

Box 1
Enos Mills

Enos Mills grew up on a farm in Kansas. In 1884, at the age of 14, he began building a log cabin at the base of Long's Peak in Colorado. In his career he led more than 250 parties of "flatlanders" up the 14,255-foot Long's Peak. He developed a life-long friendship with John Muir who helped him broaden his commitment as a crusader for parks and wilderness. Mills was a naturalist, mountain guide, author, and lecturer. He served on the committee that wrote the guiding mandate of the National Park Service Act of 1916: "To conserve the scenery and the natural and historic objects and the wildlife therein ... as will leave them unimpaired for the enjoyment of future generations." Perhaps the accomplishment in which Mills took the greatest pride was the establishment of Rocky Mountain National Park. In addition to establishing standards of nature guiding and principles of interpretation, Mills developed a vision of the world in which people live in harmony with their environment and with each other. Enos Mills died in 1922.

Box 2
Freeman Tilden

Freeman Tilden was a native of Massachusetts. He quit a successful career as a writer of fiction and plays to devote himself to conservation, with particular emphasis on the symbolism of national parks in American culture. His best-known work, in interpretive circles, is the classic *Interpreting Our Heritage*. He also wrote *The National Parks* (a comprehensive book that covered the natural, historical, and recreational areas of our national park system) and *The Fifth Essence* (an eloquent book about the important role of private donations in protecting our national parks). Freeman Tilden served as a consultant to four directors of the National Park Service. He lived on his farm in Warren, Maine until his death in 1980.

However, other more familiar meanings of the word "interpretation" confuse the general public and create controversy within the profession. Tilden observed that the word interpretation has several special implications—translation of a foreign language, for example. [2] For our purposes interpretation is to give meaning to a "foreign" landscape or event from the past or present. What is being translated (say, glaciation of Yosemite Valley, ecosystem dynamics at Yellowstone, or events surrounding the battle at Gettysburg) may well be "foreign" to substantial numbers of visitors. The interpreter elucidates technical information about the geology, ecology, or history of an area in a straightforward, understandable, and engaging manner. Mills observed that the effective interpreter has "the faculty of being entertaining, instructive, watchful, and commanding, all without his party realizing it." [3]

Tilden stated the role of interpretation eloquently in a small book titled *The Fifth Essence*:

> Vital to any administrative program that envisages the fullest and
> finest use of [our] Parks—whether areas of solacing wilderness
> or historic shrines—is the work of creating understanding. It is

true that each preserved monument "speaks for itself." But unfortunately it speaks partly in a language that the average visitor cannot comprehend. Beauty and the majesty of natural forces need no interlocutor. They constitute a personal spiritual experience. But when the question is "why?" or "what?" or "how did this come to be?" [interpretive] people must have the answers. And this requires both patient research and the development of a program fitted to a great variety of needs.[4]

Each interpreter should strive to communicate a sense of place or a sense of historic meaning in a personal, individualized manner. The many facets of interpretation are part of what makes it so fascinating. The most effective interpreters orchestrate their interpretation to elicit a response from the audience: astonishment, wonder, inspiration, action, sometimes tears. In describing those who are being interpreted to, Mills observed, "They are not in a hurry, they are in a mood to be human."[5]

Interpretation is a process, a rendering, by which visitors see, learn, experience, and are inspired firsthand. Interpreters must be skilled in communication and knowledgeable in natural and cultural history consistent with their site's mission.

At best, interpreters promote enriched recreational experiences that turn to magic, where everything comes together, where there is unencumbered delight in knowledge and experience—a greater joy in living, a better understanding of one's place in the overall scheme, a positive hope for the future. Through interpretation visitors may be provoked to initiate a long-term path of exploration and learning related to cultural or natural history, or both.

Interpretation is important to federal land managing agencies such as the National Park Service, U.S. Forest Service, U.S. Fish and Wildlife Service, and the Bureau of Land Management. Through interpretation of the landscape comes a better understanding of agency policies. Similarly, state, regional, and county natural resource agencies employ interpretation to explain their policies and to protect their sites.

Visitors may learn through interpretation about wise use of our natural resources and ways to minimize our impact on the environment. Good interpretation encourages a greater sensitivity to one's surroundings, a heightened ecological and cultural awareness, and a meaningful link to the past and future.

Interpretation Helps People to See

Interpretation tells the story behind the scenery or history of an area. It is a process that can help people see beyond their capabilities. Perhaps it is best illustrated in the following tale conveyed to Tilden by a naturalist at Crater Lake National Park in Oregon. The account is documented in Tilden's *The National Parks*.

To facilitate understanding of Crater Lake the observation center, which overlooks the lake, is equipped with exhibits, field glasses fixed on key interest areas, and a large relief model of the great volcanic cone. A park naturalist, on duty at the observation center, was approached by a man who was totally blind. The man asked, "Will you describe Crater Lake for me?"

The naturalist was aware of the challenge before him as this man had come to *see* Crater Lake. The naturalist led the man to the relief map and recounted the incident as follows:

> I took his hands and moved them around the crater model in relief, trying to convey through his sensitive fingertips and through his quick, eager mental perception the general shape of the crater and the variations of its rim skyline. By putting his thumbtips together, with hands extended, the little fingers accomplished the scaled diameter of the lake. I asked him if he had an idea of distances. He said that he could relate distances to those he experienced in walking. It was obvious that when he knew the scale spanned by his hands, he could sense the great expanse covered by the crater and its water. Then we moved the fingertips up the modeled face of Llao Rock, the two inches on the model representing the sheer face of almost twenty-two hundred feet of drop. He understood that there were two thousand more feet of the crater below the surface of the water. His fingers told him the conical shape of Wizard Island. The tiny depression at the summit of the cone gave him not only that special feature, but the type of many other craters too. He could *see*, through his fingers, the lava flows that extend from the base of the island cone. And then we traced out the U-shaped glacial valleys and compared them with the V-shaped stream-cut valleys in other parts of the park.

This episode continues with other revelations until the blind man is finally led away. The naturalist observed:

He went away with a smile on his face. And I shall not forget that smile. He had not only seen Crater Lake. He had extended his power of seeing—which was an achievement beyond price.[6]

So *this* is interpretation. Helping people to see. For even those with eyesight discern only a portion of the total scene. Mills wrote, "A day with a nature guide may help to train the eyes and all of the senses."[7] Interpreters, in sum, help convey a fuller appreciation and understanding of the site.

Modes of Interpretation

Interpretation is offered in many forms. Personal interpretation refers to programs in the form of talks, demonstrations, puppet shows, living history, storytelling, nature walks, and tours. These may occur in auditoriums, outdoor arenas (as with the traditional national park campfire program), along a trail, or following a route inside a historic building. Nonpersonal interpretation encompasses everything from Traveler Information Station (TIS) radio broadcasts as a visitor enters a park, to signs and exhibits, to self-guided trails and interactive computers.

Clarifying the Meaning of Interpretation

Interpretation encompasses so many possibilities in so many different places the public is often confused about what interpretation is or what interpreters do. This confusion has been a source of frustration to interpreters since the term gained widespread application to the profession in the late 1930s.[8] In an effort to distinguish this field, a slightly altered spelling of the word interpreter ("interpretor") has been used, although this seems unworkable.[9]

Is there another word that captures the mission of those who bring forth to the public our heritage? Tilden offered the following from *Interpreting Our Heritage*:

Because of the fear of misconception arising from conflicting definitions of the word, and also because some have thought it a pretentious way of describing what they believe to be a simple activity, there has been objection to the use of the word "interpretation" even among those engaged in this newer device of education. For myself I merely say that I do not share this objection. I have never been able to find a word more aptly descriptive of what we ... are attempting to do. [10]

To paraphrase a comment that Winston Churchill made about democracy as a form of government, "interpretation" is probably the worst word for "what we ... are attempting to do," except for all the others.

If we agree that another word will not suffice, and that changing the spelling isn't the answer, is it the destiny of interpreters to have a perpetual identity crisis? We don't think so. Several strategies which, if applied with a concerted effort over time, could lead to a general adoption and understanding of the word, as we use it in this book, by the public.

One useful practice would be to simply precede "interpreter" with the resource being interpreted (e.g., park interpreter, zoo interpreter, museum interpreter, historic site interpreter, and so on). This practice is common in the sciences where, for example, the generic "biologist" is specified as a microbiologist, an evolutionary biologist, or a wildlife biologist.

Likewise, to enhance public understanding interpreters could, where the program is appropriate, announce what they are called, what it is they do, why they do it, and the traditional confusion with the job title. This type of introduction to a program could be educational, and perhaps humorous, depending on the interpreter's own personal experiences.

Furthermore, signs at visitor centers, as well as other publicity, could capture what interpretation is and what interpreters have to offer. This might be put forward in conjunction with a concise interpretive mission statement for the site—widely available to the visiting public.

Of course, there is also the matter of various interpretive position titles within organizations including rangers, guides, naturalists, and recreation planners. Until members of the profession consistently call themselves interpreters, they can't expect the public to do so. Interpreters and professional organizations representing interpreters (such as the National Association for Interpretation) should encourage agencies to reassess these myriad titles and adopt a uniform title—interpreter—that reflects the unity of the profession.

In this case the challenge is to interpret to the public what interpreters do. In so doing interpreters may foster support both for the intricacies of the profession and the settings where interpretation is provided. Interpreters, for the sake of clarity, should be interpreting interpretation.

Evolution of an Interpretive Philosophy

Mills was among the first to use the term "interpret" to describe his nature guiding at Long's Peak, Colorado. He presented various philosophical principles in *Adventures of a Nature Guide and Essays in Interpretation* in 1920. Tilden wrote the first edition of *Interpreting Our Heritage* in 1957. The guiding principles of Mills and Tilden are strikingly similar. To track, and credit, the evolution of an interpretive philosophy we present Tilden's six principles of interpretation along with consistent observations from Mills.

Tilden's First Principle is, "Any interpretation that does not somehow relate what is being displayed or described to something within the personality or experience of the visitor will be sterile."[11] And Enos Mills observed, "The nature guide is at his best when he discusses facts so that they appeal to the imagination and reason [of those interpreted to]."[12] He continued, "The nature guide who understands human nature and possesses tact and ingenuity is able to hold divergent interests . . ."[13]

Tilden's Second Principle is, "Information, as such, is not interpretation. Interpretation is revelation based upon information. But they are entirely different things. However, all interpretation includes information."[14] And Enos Mills determined, "A nature guide . . . has been rightfully associated with information and some form of education. But nature guiding, as we see it, is more inspirational than informational. The nature guide arouses interest by dealing in big principles—not with detached and colorless information."[15] Mills continued, "The aim is to illuminate and reveal the alluring world."[16]

Tilden's Third Principle is, "Interpretation is an art, which combines many arts, whether the materials presented are scientific, historical or architectural. Any art is in some degree teachable."[17] Similarly, Mills described a female colleague as having "a purpose—a vision. Daily she accumulated experience and information. These she handled like an artist . . . Our [interpreter] had the art and the vision which enabled her to make these outings permanent, purposeful, growth-compelling experiences."[18]

Tilden's Fourth Principle is, "The chief aim of interpretation is not instruction, but provocation."[19] And Mills observed, "This new occupation [interpretation] is likely to be far-reaching in its influences; it is inspirational and educational . . . and possess[es] astounding possibilities for arousing the feelings and developing the unlimited resources of the mind."[20]

Tilden's Fifth Principle is, "Interpretation should aim to present a whole rather than a part, and must address itself to the whole man rather than any phase."[21] And Mills quoted Liberty H. Bailey as follows: "This man [the recipient of good interpretation] will see first the large and significant events; he will grasp relationships; he will correlate; later, he will consider the details."[22]

Tilden's Sixth Principle is, "Interpretation addressed to children (say, up to the age of twelve) should not be a dilution of the presentation to adults, but should follow a fundamentally different approach. To be at its best it will require a separate program."[23] And Mills suggested, "This childish desire to know, to learn, will assure mental development if information be given in a way that appeals . . . The experiences these children have and their reflections concerning the things seen give them the ability to reason, and develop their observation and imagination."[24]

The Fifteen Principles

Out of respect for the work of Tilden and Mills, and particularly because of the familiarity so many interpreters have with Tilden's six principles, our framework of principles begins with a re-statement of Tilden's. (See Box 3 for insights about Tilden's perspectives and beliefs.) Note that the principles have been re-worded to better reflect their treatment in the chapters that follow. In addition to these six principles we offer nine new principles that provide a more elaborate interpretive philosophy.

Box 3
Travels with Freeman

As a student-trainee in the Old Faithful area of Yellowstone for the summer, about to return to Texas A & M for his last semester of studies, Walter Dabney received a letter with the prospect of a special assignment upon graduation. In sum, the proposed job was to serve as an aide to Freeman Tilden in an excursion throughout the national park system.

Walter was 23 at the time and Freeman was 87. They traveled some 30,000 miles together from Florida to Canada and from Hatteras to San Francisco. Walter carried Freeman's typewriter and suitcase, drove the car, and provided interpretation program observations to Harpers Ferry Center. Freeman spent his time writing, talking to park staffs, and teaching. Walter kept a journal and captured some of his companion's wit and wisdom in the following subject areas.

Freeman Tilden On . . .

Interpretation: I've been working with the concepts of interpretation for about 25 years, and I still don't know what it is, though I've got some ideas, and I've written a lot of definitions. But I was never completely satisfied with them.

Park Education: We should expand our emphasis on education. Our parks are the greatest natural classrooms available. We must use them to teach people the basics of ecology. We've been doing this for a long time but we've got to do it on a better and on a bigger scale.

Knowledge: As you get older and maybe after reaching some prominence, people begin to attribute to you knowledge that you simply do not possess.

Adapted from Walter Dabney, 1988, "Travels with Freeman."

Mills and Tilden offer precious counsel. Still, times have changed dramatically since their principles were first conceived. We aim to sculpt and elaborate upon their contributions.

Here, then, are the 15 principles:

1. To spark an interest, interpreters must relate the subject to the lives of visitors.

2. The purpose of interpretation goes beyond providing information to reveal deeper meaning and truth.

3. The interpretive presentation—as a work of art—should be designed as a story that informs, entertains, and enlightens.

4. The purpose of the interpretive story is to inspire and to provoke people to broaden their horizons.

5. Interpretation should present a complete theme or thesis and address the whole person.

6. Interpretation for children, teenagers, and seniors—when these comprise uniform groups—should follow fundamentally different approaches.

7. Every place has a history. Interpreters can bring the past alive to make the present more enjoyable and the future more meaningful.

8. High technology can reveal the world in exciting new ways. However, incorporating this technology into the interpretive program must be done with foresight and care.

9. Interpreters must concern themselves with the quantity and quality (selection and accuracy) of information presented. Focused, well-researched interpretation will be more powerful than a longer discourse.

10. Before applying the arts in interpretation, the interpreter must be familiar with basic communication techniques. Quality interpretation depends on the interpreter's knowledge and skills, which should be developed continually.

11. Interpretive writing should address what readers would like to know, with the authority of wisdom and the humility and care that comes with it.

12. The overall interpretive program must be capable of attracting support—financial, volunteer, political, administrative— whatever support is needed for the program to flourish.

13. Interpretation should instill in people the ability, and the desire, to sense the beauty in their surroundings—to provide spiritual uplift and to encourage resource preservation.

14. Interpreters can promote optimal experiences through intentional and thoughtful program and facility design.
15. Passion is the essential ingredient for powerful and effective interpretation—passion for the resource and for those people who come to be inspired by the same.

A New National Park Service Model and the 15 Principles

The National Park Service's Interpretive Development Program is a training initiative to develop interpretive excellence.[25] The program identifies 11 essential competencies for park interpreters to attain and demonstrate as they progress to higher levels within the agency. The Interpretive Development Program uses an "Interpretive Equation" as a framework to present the "how and why" of interpretation. We believe this framework will be a solid contribution to the interpretation of National Park Service sites and that it can also be useful generically for other interpretive settings as well. As indicated below, the chapters in this book will speak to the variables found in this equation (see Box 4).

The equation is $(Kr + Ka) + AT = IO$ where:

Kr = Knowledge of the resource. Interpreters must know the facts. In addition they must be aware of the many tangible, intangible, and universal concepts the resources represent. The challenge to interpreters is to find connections between the tangible aspects of the site (artifacts, structures, wildlife, trees) and the intangible ideas associated with those resources. For example, the Liberty Bell is a tangible product. Yet when people see the bell they make personal connections to intangible ideas such as courage, freedom, and quality of life.[26] Likewise, the tangible resource of wilderness also represents intangible ideas such as harmony, self-sufficiency, wholeness, and spirituality.

Interpreters must know how past and contemporary issues relate, understand controversies related to the site, and be able to espouse differing points of view. This part of the equation is relevant to the second, third, fifth, ninth, eleventh, and thirteenth principles.

Ka = Knowledge of the audience. Interpreters must know about their audience. Beyond demographic characteristics, this

Box 4
The National Park Service Equation
and the 15 Principles

NPS Equation: $(Kr + Ka) + AT = IO$	15 Principles
Kr = Knowledge of the resource	2
	3
	5
	9
	11
	13
Ka = Knowledge of the audience	1
	6
	7
	12
AT = Appropriate Technology	8
IO = Interpretive Opportunity	4
	10
	14
	15

variable includes knowledge of audience motivations, desires, and needs. Without knowledge about the audience it is difficult, if not impossible, to reach out in an efficient and meaningful way. This portion of the equation is covered primarily in our discussion of the first principle. It is also relevant to the sixth, seventh, and twelfth principles.

AT = Appropriate Technology. Interpreters must select the best delivery technique to communicate the message. This can only occur after the interpreter has satisfactorily determined "Kr" and "Ka" and knows the theme and desired outcomes of the message. This interpretive variable is covered primarily under the eighth principle, although there is overlap with several of the other principles as well.

IO = Interpretive Opportunities. Interpreters have no guarantee that their work will have the desired effect with each visitor. Some visitors may resist or want to avoid interpretation entirely. The best that can be done is to create various opportunities and favorable circumstances to affect visitors in a positive way. The motives and design for creating interpretive opportunities are addressed in the fourth, tenth, fourteenth and fifteenth principles.

Note that the principles listed for each of the NPS variables are those principles *most* associated with that portion of the equation. In addition, there is widespread overlap of the principles as they relate to the NPS equation, as well as considerable overlap among the principles themselves. That is, if you pick out any one of the principles you will find it linked and intertwined with the others. And if you wrap them up, all together, then it is our determination that interpretation is "a gift" (see Conclusion).

An Interpreter Is . . .

. . . someone who works with people to convey the meaning of our cultural and natural landscapes and the features that make up these landscapes. An interpreter is invested in a life-long quest of learning and experience, and in sharing that accumulated wisdom. He or she is familiar with and practices effective communication techniques and strives to create meaningful and provocative stories. An interpreter has a grounding in the liberal arts, and keeps current with the news (local, regional, national, international), to better relate to a diverse consortium of visitors.

An interpreter can communicate excitement for the resource and inspire a response. An interpreter is deeply concerned with the welfare of visitors—their safety, their dignity—the quality of their experiences. He or she interprets imaginatively by knowledge and personal example.

An interpreter acts out of authority and humility; confidence and compassion; respect for others and one's own integrity; stability and enthusiasm; and joy. An interpreter treats others with kindness.

An interpreter respects the moral worth of visitors and their potential for growth. The interpreter is enthused and energetic about the place, the visitors who come there, and the work at hand. An interpreter embraces the wonder and beauty of life.

■ *Chapter One* ■

LIGHTING A SPARK

To spark an interest, interpreters must relate the subject to the lives of visitors.

No man can reveal to you aught but that which already lies half asleep in the dawning of your knowledge. The teacher who walks in the shadow of the temple, among his followers, gives not of his wisdom but rather of his faith and his lovingness. If he is indeed wise he does not bid you enter the house of his wisdom, but rather leads you to the threshold of your own mind.

—Kahlil Gibran

As Kahlil Gibran reflected, receiving information is a deep and personal matter. The knowledge and experiences we gain make up who we are. Interpreters must relate to the people they interpret to if they wish to lead them to the "thresholds" of their minds.

People choose when, where, what, and how to learn based on their interests. Richard Saul Wurman wrote, "Learning can be seen as the acquisition of information, but before it can take place, there must be interest; interest permeates all endeavors and precedes learning. In order to acquire and remember new knowledge, it must stimulate your curiosity in some way ... Learning can be defined as the process of remembering what you are interested in." [1]

Freeman Tilden suggested that the "chief" interests of visitors to sites of natural beauty and historical significance are in whatever touches their personalities, experiences, or ideals.[2] This is the backbone of effective interpretation; taking information about cultural and natural resources and making it relevant to the audience.

Interpretive messages must be *interesting* to capture attention, *meaningful* so that people care, and *compelling* so that people no longer think or act the same after hearing them. By identifying interests of particular audiences, the interpreter has, at least, a broad target to aim at. To paraphrase what R.J. Mall observed about teachers, three kinds of interpreters exist: those you can listen to, those you can't listen to, and those you can't help but listen to. Applying this first principle is the first step to becoming one of the latter.

The First Principle in Theory

Tilden's dictum to relate information to the visitors' "chief" interests may have been intuitive, but it is grounded in solid theory. For years educational psychologists and theorists have been suggesting that people learn by integrating and storing information in the context of their past experience. One such theorist, Jean Piaget, suggested that "to understand, we have to invent, or, that is, reinvent, because we can't start from the beginning again . . . anything is only understood to the extent that it is reinvented."[3]

Cognitive Map Theory

William Hammitt analyzed Tilden's interpretive principles in the context of cognitive map theory, a widely adopted view of how people process information.[4] This theory suggests that people receive information, code it into simplified units, and then store it in relationship to other existing information. As information continues to be stored in this way a network of informational units form, linked by pathways of commonality. These units and pathways collectively form cognitive maps—a person's structure of storage and organization of information. Subsequent stimuli "trigger" the internal model that best matches them.

Effective interpretation produces external stimuli that trigger existing maps, thereby allowing the audience to "get it" and store the information in relation to other information they already possess. If the interpreter expresses irrelevant or completely unfamiliar information, then existing maps will not be triggered. We should, ideally, be aware of the cognitive maps held by an audience relative to the topic of interpretation. With this awareness we may target messages to trigger existing maps and to build on that scaffolding.[5]

Another important factor with implications for interpreters is that when a map is triggered, people can perceive more than what actually exists in the immediate environment. Hammitt suggested that "few individuals who have caught trout and cooked them over a campfire cannot view a photograph of such a scene without visualizing the landscape, smelling the smoke and feeling the warmth of the fire, and even tasting the fish." [6]

The External-Internal Shift

Consistent with cognitive map theory, brain researchers have delved into how our brains determine which stimuli are attended to and which are ignored. Scientists have identified a process, called the "external-internal shift," which explains how people attend to communication that relates to their experiences. [7]

Before focusing attention, the brain stem passively receives many sensory stimuli from our sense organs. The brain cannot process all the information so it actively scans the stimuli searching for anything that requires immediate attention. It ignores or merely monitors other stimuli. During this search the brain is constantly switching its focus between external events and internal memories and interests.

For example, while an interpreter is telling the audience how to react if they encounter a bear, a listener may recall a childhood observation of a bear. The listener's attention shifts to the personal bear story and he or she merely monitors the presentation while processing the personal story. In fact, since we can think six to seven times faster than people can talk, most of the time we are "talking" (that is, thinking) to ourselves. This explains the ease in tuning a speaker out, *especially* if the information is not relevant to one's interests or past experiences.

Such mental shifts between external and internal events seem to be an important factor in maintaining and updating long-term memory. Recalling memories strengthens neural networks that contain and process them. Most important for interpreters is the knowledge that people tend to seek out stimuli and situations (e.g., movies, books, trips, conversations) that will trigger these memories and build on them. Educators Robert Sylvester and Joo-Yun Cho observed, "When we consciously seek such specific information, our attention system primes itself in anticipation. It increases the response levels of the networks that process that information, and it inhibits other networks."[8]

Individuals in this primed mental state are receptive to the information presented. Capitalizing on this receptive mood is the interpreter's challenge.[9]

Relating the message to the knowledge and experiences of the audience teaches new information, reinforces memories, and gives the audience satisfying personal experiences.

"Meaning-Making"

In recent years, a new communication paradigm has been developed called constructivism or "meaning-making." In essence, this new paradigm redefines communication. No longer is communication considered merely a linear sender-receiver process. Instead, meaning-making conceptualizes communication as a negotiation process between parties whereby information is *created* rather than transmitted. Individuals receiving the information *shape the meaning* based on their store of past knowledge and experiences.[10] Because visitors actively create meaning through the contexts they bring to the interpretive site, being aware of their perspectives, knowledge, and past experiences is essential for successful interpretation.

The First Principle in Practice: Knowing the Audience

Regardless of the theory used to conceptualize communication, interpreters must know about their visitors. Knowing the audience is important in any communication whether by a preacher, professor, or politician. Many interpretive agencies now realize the importance of knowing the needs and wants of their customers. They conduct visitor surveys to assess the characteristics of their clientele in an attempt to determine what is meaningful to them.

Demographics

Most visitor surveys focus on identifying the visitors' demographic characteristics. Whether the audience is local or transient, old or young, educated or less educated, foreign or domestic—all have ramifications for targeting interpretive messages. To the interpreter this means carefully considering these characteristics and choosing approaches, metaphors, anecdotes, and stories that will match visitor interests.

Interpreting to different ages—children, teenagers, and older persons—is the focus of Chapter Six. Box 1 provides examples of how other distinct factors could affect efforts to relate to the audience's "chief" interests. Additional visitor characteristics that might affect the interpretive approach include gender, race, educational levels, and whether visitation is local, non-local, or mixed. Sometimes the ethnic or religious background of the audience is important, particularly in developing countries where ethnic and religious beliefs strongly affect how people perceive the use of natural and cultural resources.

Box 1
Relating to Distinct Audiences

Repeat vs. Non-repeat Visitors

If a site has many repeat visitors, interpreters must change interpretive offerings more frequently or schedule special events to recapture interest continually. With repeat visitors, interpreters can offer a sequence of programs with increasing sophistication of topics, thereby allowing visitors to advance to progressively higher levels of understanding. If a site has mostly first time, non-repeat visitors, programs do not have to be changed as frequently. Then program offerings should be broad and present the "compelling story" of the site.

Rural vs. Urban Visitors

Most adult visitors have some level of rural and urban experiences, regardless of where they live. With children, however, this may not be as likely. For example, those who interpret to school groups need to know whether they are coming from rural or inner-city school systems. Using subways and high rise apartments as metaphors for burrows and nesting colonies would miss the mark for farm kids. On the other hand, city kids might not know the source of their water or food. Many, for example, think that bread originates from the grocery store.

Foreign vs. Domestic Visitors

Foreign audiences may require language translations or background information to provide frameworks that already exist in the minds of domestic visitors. Furthermore, history is understood differently by Americans and many foreigners. Mexicans may have a different view of Texas settlement and Europeans may view "new world" colonization differently. The Japanese have a different perspective than Americans on events leading to the end of World War II.

Beyond Demographics

A study conducted at the Ronald V. Jensen Living Historical Farm, in Utah, found that the staff intuitively knew the demographics of their visitors. However, despite high levels of staff-visitor contact, interpreters did not understand visitors' motivations and satisfactions.[11]

Most visitor studies have merely documented visitor characteristics and participation patterns. According to the Jensen Farm research, in cases where the staff is in regular contact with visitors, such studies may not even be necessary. Interpreters seem to grasp quickly (within about two months) general audience demographics.[12]

However, to respond to visitors fully, research should concentrate on visitors' values, motivations, attitudes, and satisfactions. Indeed, knowing these traits allows us to predict the demographics that likely accompany them—though we usually assume that only the reverse is true.[13]

Targeting Motivations

Research designed to assess the visitors' motivations allows interpreters to more successfully apply this first principle. Understanding what an audience already knows and what motivates them permits interpreters to present more interesting, pertinent, and challenging information.

It is not only important to understand who is interested in what subjects, but also *why* they are interested in those subjects. The reasons may be surprising and provide clues for presenting information in interesting ways. For example, visitors could be interested in an old locomotive because their fathers or grandfathers worked for the railroad. Or visitors could be interested in the same locomotive because they are fascinated by how steam powered machines work. Or they could be interested because they have a passion for American history and the westward expansion. Or they may have been enamored with trains as kids. The differences are critical to interpreters in determining how to present a program.

If we know the *reason* for the interest in a particular subject, then we can structure the content of the interpretation to fit that interest. This means we must ask visitors why they are interested in various interpretive possibilities. Such research may be conducted formally using questionnaires or structured interviews or informally in conversation.

We should also be aware of whether visitors *want* to learn and, if so, *how* they want to learn. Ross Loomis reviewed social psychological studies that suggested visitors vary in their "need for cognition" and in how they process information.[14] Some visitors may not *want* to learn. Interpreters should know that and be able to accept it, or try to do something about it. Although this appears to be a matter of leading the horse to water, but not being able to make it drink, if interpreters know that the visitor lacks a desire to learn, they may be inspired to create interpretation that will make "the horse" thirsty.

Targeting Learning Styles

To enhance interest and effectiveness, some interpretation researchers identify visitors' learning styles and then match exhibits to these specific learning preferences. A study at the Milwaukee Public Museum used the popular Myers-Briggs Type Indicator as an instrument to identify learning styles of visitors. As a consequence of this research a rainforest exhibit was modified and it was determined that matching learning styles with exhibit presentation can result in increased learning.[15]

Barriers to Participation

Interpreters also should know why people do not visit interpretive sites so that those barriers may be broken down. Knowing who is absent, and why, may be as pertinent as knowing who attends. Fear and negative perceptions are two widespread and powerful barriers to visitation to, and interest in, natural areas. Researchers have found that many people find wildland settings to be scary, disgusting, and uncomfortable.[16] Likewise, many people hold images of museums as being formal, stuffy, and elitist. We can strive to correct misconceptions and structure interpretive possibilities so that they are "accessible" to those who are otherwise inhibited. For example, personal comfort, esteem, and security are "chief" interests of these potential visitors and interpretation can be adjusted accordingly (see Chapter Five).

Knowing and addressing the visitors' interests does not mean pandering to any desire of the audience. For example, part of what makes natural settings attractive is the contrast they provide to civilization. Some aspects of the setting should not be compromised. But, when the interests of the audience are appropriate for the site and consistent with management objectives, then interpreters are wise to attend to those interests. Those may be the only messages that the audience will receive.

How to Capture "Chief" Interests

Even if the visitors' interests are correctly identified, poor delivery will cause attention to wane. Effective interpretive delivery must be mastered and applied (see Chapter Ten). The following is a discussion of some general considerations for delivering messages in a manner that will capture and maintain interest.

The first task is to capture the visitor's attention. This is a prerequisite for receiving information as previously noted. Attention is limited and many stimuli constantly compete for it. Mihalyi

Csikszentmihalyi and Kim Hermanson wrote, "Even though we are surrounded by increasing waves of information, the amount of it that any person actually notices and then retains in memory may be less than it was in the days of our cave-dwelling ancestors, and it certainly cannot be much more."[17] We can capture attention by using movement, noise, bright colors, unusual objects, or with startling statements, either written or spoken.

After attention is captured, the task becomes one of maintaining interest. Poor mechanics can derail the interpretation. Can the speaker be clearly heard? Is the exhibit text easily read? Are visuals comprehensible? If not, interest vaporizes and audiences escape—mentally, if not physically.

We can make interpretation more interesting by using personal language. The word "you" immediately makes the audience members think of themselves. This is a key component in implementing this first principle because the self-referencing quickly engages and involves the audience—it creates an inviting opportunity for them to relate to the information. Other personal words such as "your," "we," and "our" can be similarly effective.

Posing relevant questions is a good technique for maintaining interest. People will try to answer questions, even rhetorical ones. Asking personalized questions such as "What would you have done?" with reference to a historical event connects the person with the subject. Visitors immediately imagine what their own conduct would have been under the historical circumstances.

History

We are all historians.[18] Although far removed from the dates, famous names, and places taught in history classes, people engage in history-related activities all the time. We make photographic records of our personal and family histories through snapshots and videos. Our homes become museums filled with baby books, scrapbooks, and yearbooks. Diaries and journals provide a personal historical record. We are also history makers.[19] History is the composite of innumerable personal biographies.

Although we are all historians and history makers, people generally consider "history" to be dry, impersonal, and serious—something remote and distant from their lives.[20] Yet, people consider the term "the past" to be relevant and personal. People connect with "the past," whereas "history" conjures up images of obscure Presidents and wars. The challenge for interpreters is to present information in such a way so that people may "personalize the past."[21]

Discovery

Most people enjoy the sense of accomplishment that comes from making "discoveries." Discovery-oriented programs in interpretive settings allow people to gain new insights and to see previously known facts in new ways.

Discovery approaches have been popular in formal science education settings for many years. One science educator noted, "Discovery has become a big word in science education ... discovery and rediscovery appear more and more to be essential elements of learning experiences ... "[22]

Discovery lends itself to the application of this first principle because information is personally revealed to the individual investigator. Discovery carries with it elements of suspense and surprise. Interactive exhibits increase personal involvement and can provide mental challenges through puzzles or games that lead people to discover new facts or relationships (see Chapter Eight). By providing discovery situations interpreters provoke interest and connect the subject matter with the audience.

Enthusiasm

Humor and novelty may also contribute to capturing and maintaining interest, but the most powerful force is enthusiasm. Since enthusiasm is contagious, so is interest. William Everhart, former director of the National Park Service, when asked what it took to become an interpreter would reply, "There [are] few essentials. You have to be a genuine enthusiast, almost impelled to share your knowledge with others."[23]

Interpreters should not only stimulate curiosity and capture interest for the duration of someone's visit to an interpretive site, but should provoke continued interest as well (see Chapter Four).

This can be accomplished by initially relating to the visitor's "chief" interests. From there, visitors may be self-motivated to new horizons. Anatole France wrote, "Do not try to satisfy your vanity by teaching a great many things. Awaken people's curiosity. It is enough to open minds; do not overload them. Put there just a spark. If there is some good inflammable stuff, it will catch fire."[24]

Interpreters must know the visitor's "chief" interests to determine where and how to place the spark. We must strive to understand the "inflammable stuff." Delivering the message effectively ensures that the inflammable stuff will ignite. When fires of curiosity burn, the interpreter has successfully applied this first principle and has led the visitors to the thresholds of their own minds where learning and inspiration occur.

■ Chapter Two ■

INTERPRETING IN THE INFORMATION AGE

T he purpose of interpretation goes beyond providing information to reveal deeper meaning and truth.

When I heard the learn'd astronomer,
When the proofs, the figures, were ranged in columns before
me,
When I was shown the charts and diagrams, to add, divide,
and measure them,
When I sitting heard the astronomer where he lectured with
much applause in the lecture room,
How soon unaccountable I became tired and sick,
Till rising and gliding out I wandered off by myself,
In the mystical moist night air, and from time to time,
Looked up in perfect silence at the stars.

—Walt Whitman

Some interpreters are like the "learn'd astronomer." They possess and present detailed information that misses the larger point. Enos Mills understood this: "From personal experience I would say that the chief errors likely to be made by a nature guide are: to become too booky, to follow academic methods, to compel, like the school teacher, the learning of lessons. There has been altogether too much of this dulling lesson business."[1]

This second principle speaks to using information properly and distinguishing between information and interpretation. Mills suggested the interpreter "is at his best when he discusses facts so that they appeal to the imagination and to the reason."[2] Of course, all interpretation includes information.[3]

If there is no information imparted then the program is, at best, entertainment. For example, some interpreters show cartoons, on occasion, in campground amphitheaters. Others entertain with magic or games. The appropriateness of such activities is not in question here—this could be great entertainment. However, without information these activities do not qualify as interpretation.

Furthermore, providing information does not automatically mean interpretation is taking place. Interpreters on "information duty" at visitor centers and entrance stations efficiently communicate considerable amounts of information to large numbers of people. We give weather reports, communicate road conditions, and direct people to restrooms, trailheads, and lodges. Although the information is important to those who receive it, none of this qualifies as interpretation. Interpretation must be more than information.

Freeman Tilden stated, "Information, as such, is not interpretation. Interpretation is revelation based upon information."[4] Interpreters on "information duty" have an opportunity to interpret. A question about a recent forest fire provides a chance not only to give a straight answer, but to explain the role of fire in the ecosystem. A question about poisonous snakes offers a chance not only to give appropriate warnings, but to do some public relations work on behalf of all snakes. A question about regulations provides an opportunity to interpret the reason for the rule, thereby enhancing the probability of compliance.

We should warn that discretion needs to be used when interjecting interpretation into "information duty." A harried visitor wanting to know the time does not want to know how to build a clock. Interpreters will try the visitor's patience and increase their anxiety by launching into an impromptu interpretive program. Yet, if we sense the state-of-mind and interest of the visitor to be receptive, then we should seize opportunities to *interpret* requested information.

The charge for interpreters, here, is to *reveal* information about our cultural and natural history in meaningful ways. Revealing information about the subject may be accomplished in formal programs (see Box 1), exhibits (see Box 2), or interpretive publications (see Box 3). (Also see Box 1 in Chapter 13 for examples of how to reveal information about the nature and heritage of tallgrass prairie.)

Here is a simple example: On the back of a bag of Lay's™ potato chips you may find the following: "In a year, Americans purchase on average 329,000,000 pounds of Lay's™ brand Potato Chips. That's over 901,000 pounds a day, 625 pounds a minute and 10 pounds a second!" Think about it. In the time it takes to read this paragraph, Americans will consume almost 250 pounds of potato chips. If Lay's™ can interpret the consumption of potato chips, think of the possibilities for interpreting our nation's cultural and natural wonders!

Box 1
Revealing Information Via Local Landmarks

At Sandridge Nature Center near Chicago, the visitors are almost exclusively local. Audiences are asked by interpreters to think about major intersections in the surrounding area. When approaching intersections with major east-west highways, travelers go up a gentle hill. Audience members can easily visualize these specific intersections. Interpreters then explain that each of these roads, running parallel to the southern shore of Lake Michigan, traverse the tops of ancient sand dunes formed as the lake receded after the last glaciation. Interpreters relate that bison, Native Americans, fur trappers, and others used these high and dry ridges as their highways too. These roads, driven daily, take on new meaning as people learn about local geology, ecology, and history.

Box 2
Interpreting Gray Whales

- The annual gray whale migration route, of approximately 10,000 miles, is the *longest* of any mammal.

- The distance traveled over the lifespan of a gray whale is equivalent to the distance to the moon and back.

- Nine 32-gallon trash cans lined up as if full of amphipods (small "shrimp-like" organisms the whales consume) represent how much an adult gray whale eats in a day.

- A baby gray whale drinks 50 gallons of milk and, consequently, gains 60 to 70 pounds—*a day*.

Derived from interpretive displays at the Stephen Birch Aquarium and Museum, Scripps Institution of Oceanography, La Jolla, California.

Box 3
Interpreting Tropical Rain Forest Depletion

By 1989 the tropical rain forests of the world had been reduced to about 8 million square kilometers, or slightly less than half of the prehistoric cover. They were being destroyed at the rate of 142,000 square kilometers a year, or 1.8 percent of the standing cover, nearly double the 1979 amount. The loss is equal to the area of a football field every second. Put another way, in 1989 the surviving rain forests occupied an area about that of the contiguous forty-eight states of the United States, and they were being reduced by an amount equivalent to the size of Florida every year.

From Edward O. Wilson, 1992, The Diversity of Life. By permission.

The Raw Material

Like all raw materials, information must be found and collected. Unlike other raw materials, information is an inexhaustible resource. New information about every conceivable topic is being produced at unprecedented rates. The following statistics illustrate why this period in history is being called the "Information Age."

- More new information has been produced in the last 30 years than in the previous 5,000 years.
- A weekday edition of the *New York Times* contains more information than the average person was likely to come across in a lifetime in 17th century England.
- The English language contains about 500,000 words—more than five times the number of words when Shakespeare wrote.
- About 1,000 new books are published internationally each day.
- About 9,600 different periodicals are published each year in the United States alone.[5]

According to statistical forecasts, information will have doubled four times between 1993 and 2000—the class of 2000 will be exposed to more new information in that year than their grandparents experienced in their lifetimes.[6]

What does this exploding body of information mean to interpreters? It means that we have a daunting task of keeping up. A *Dilbert* comic, by Scott Adams, vividly captures the challenge. As they walk, Dogbert tells Dilbert:

> People are getting stupider every day, relatively speaking. The complexity of the world is increasing geometrically. But your ability to learn is at the same slow trickle it has always been. Information is gushing toward your brain like a firehose aimed at a teacup. You're at a crossroads in history. Even the smartest among you has become "functionally stupid." Your only hope is to choose a leader whose vision can penetrate the thick fog of human incompetence.[7]

Dogbert concludes, "Dogbert for supreme ruler of Earth!!" For our purposes, Adams provided vivid imagery: information is gushing toward us like a firehose aimed at a teacup!

Because people are constantly being bombarded with more and more information, we must be diligent in providing quality opportunities to compete for their attention. We must ensure that our information is among that which ends up in the "teacup."

Keeping Up

It may be especially challenging for interpreters to stay abreast of new information because so many of us are generalists. Furthermore, we often interpret many facets of a park or historic site. At Cabrillo National Monument, in California, park interpretive topics include the voyage and discoveries of Juan Rodríguez Cabrillo, the history of the Old Point Loma Lighthouse, the migration of gray whales, tidepool ecology, coastal sage scrub ecology, and military history of the San Diego harbor. All of this on 144 acres!

Some interpreters respond to the swelling body of information by exhibiting what Richard Saul Wurman calls "information bulimia."[8] Like the diet disorder characterized by binge eating, those who fear being uninformed begin "manic subscribing" by sending off for every journal that is remotely relevant. However, soon a pile of publications forms on the desk demanding to be read. Wurman observed that nothing could make us feel as guilty as an unread magazine.[9] The pile that was to save us from being uninformed becomes another reminder of just how uninformed we are. Then comes the purge—we hide everything under the bed or throw it away.

The Internet, "the information superhighway," offers yet another outlet for gaining information and it will only continue to expand. Although we must be kept informed and be thoroughly accurate in what we interpret, there are perils with spending too much time reading or "surfing the Net." Time spent travelling "the information superhighway" is time away from experiencing the resource.

How can we prevent becoming overwhelmed when faced with trying to keep up? We can eliminate junk information, just as we try to eliminate junk food. By subscribing to only the best journals and news groups we can consume information with little waste of time. We might ask, "Will the information enrich my life? Is it necessary for excellence in my work?"

Unfortunately, instead of assisting people to broaden themselves, the information boom may cause some people to narrow their interests. This becomes the classic case, as some pundits have noted, of people learning more and more about less and less until they know everything about nothing.

Interpreters should remember, both for their own sanity and their acceptance of others, that everyone is ignorant, only in different subjects, as Will Rogers observed. It is a relief to us when we realize we don't have to know all the answers. Interpreters who respect their audience, and themselves, will readily admit not knowing the answer to a question. Rather than attempting to fool anyone, we should thank visitors for their questions and assure them we will try to find the answer. Speculation and guesses should be clearly identified as such.

Getting Through

Another challenge faced by interpreters from the information explosion is the task of getting a message through to the audience without it being deflected or buried by other stimuli. In one year, an average American will look at 100 newspapers, 36 magazines, and 3,000 forms or notices. The average American will watch 2,463 hours of television, listen to 730 hours of radio, and read three books.[10] Interpreters provide only a tiny segment of the public's total information intake. The way in which information is delivered will determine whether it will break through the competing stimuli.

As noted in the previous chapter, the brain constantly selects its focus, attending to the important and ignoring the unimportant. Our brains have a built-in bias for noticing high-contrast stimuli, novelty, and emotion. Interpreters may respond to this insight by using catchy and provocative titles for programs, by composing attractive publications, by designing colorful and dynamic exhibits, by offering unusual presentations, and by appealing at the level of the visitor's emotion.

Other factors influence the brain's selection process as it affects our attention. Cyclical fluctuations in the efficacy of neurotransmitter molecules chemically regulate attention.[11] These fluctuations occur about every 90 minutes throughout the day. At about 6:00 a.m. many people experience a rise in these attention molecules, causing them to wake up. The average level of molecules remains high in the morning and tends to decline during the afternoon. This means it is easiest to maintain attention in the morning and more difficult to maintain it later in the day. Typically, if we have a choice, we do what is most demanding in the morning when attention is greatest. This implies that interpreters might be wise to schedule programs which teach skills, identification techniques, and other tasks requiring rapt concentration in the morning and schedule less demanding, more socially engaging programs in the afternoon.

Scientists have also determined that our brains are designed to respond to immediate dangers. Yet, interpreters attempt to communicate *gradual* processes that over time may reach crisis proportions such as deforestation and species extinction. Educators suggest that the most challenging aspect of teaching is to help people consciously manage aspects of their attentional system that aren't preprogrammed to enhance survival.

> In the modern era, human life is more than attending to immediate survival. It is now vital to attend to the quality of our lives and to the potential gradual erosion of that quality. It's important we teach ... how to appreciate a fine work of art without asking how much it costs, how to simply observe a sunset. The energy released by the plants that surround a rocket launch site is at least as socially meaningful as the energy used to launch the rocket. Although we attend to the televised blast-off, we now have to learn how to attend to the equally important gentle growth of the plants in the background of the televised sequence. [12]

To reveal this deeper meaning is one of the tasks that interpreters face and we will touch on it again in Chapter Five.

The Finished Product

If information is the "raw material," then interpretation is the finished product. Interpreters equipped with good information can produce a finished product that transcends merely informing people of facts to revealing deeper meanings and truth.

What is involved in this process? Interpreters must make sure the collected raw material is accurate and that sufficient quantity has been collected. Tremendous damage can be done to the credibility of the individual and organization if misinformation is given out to the public. Misinformation can also be confusing or harmful to those who have received it. When working with the media, the distinction between facts, opinions, and editorial comments becomes especially critical. When convinced the raw material is suitable, the interpreter can begin to shape it into interpretation.

We can touch people by revealing not only information about the subject, but by having the courage (and humility) to reveal something of ourselves. Interpreters can and should share personal perspectives, insights and testimonies related to the subject matter. Audiences are generally appreciative of these personal touches. These efforts make us seem more human as we bridge the gap between "expert" and audience. A saying in the field of education suggests that students don't care what the teacher knows, they just want to know that the teacher cares.

To Enjoy Understandingly

The joy of knowing can be stimulating. Mihalyi Csikszentmihalyi stated, "Great thinkers have always been motivated by the enjoyment of thinking rather than by the material rewards that could be gained by it."[13] So, cognitive learning can produce positive outcomes.

John Burroughs, in an essay titled, "The Gospel of Nature," struck a balance between the importance of knowledge about, and appreciation of, nature. Both are important and the end result is to "enjoy understandingly":

> All that science has to tell me is welcome, is indeed, eagerly sought for. I must know as well as feel. I am not merely contented, like Wordsworth's poet, to enjoy what others understand. I must understand also; but above all things, I must enjoy. How much of my enjoyment springs from my knowledge I do not know. The joy of knowing is very great; the delight of picking up the threads of meaning here and there, and following them through the maze of confusing facts, I know well. When I hear the woodpecker drumming in the woods, and know what it is all for, why, that knowledge, I suppose, is part of my enjoyment. The other part is the associations that those sounds call up as voicing the arrival of spring; they are the drums that lead the joyous procession. To enjoy understandingly, that, I fancy, is the great thing to be desired.[14]

We can encourage visitors to "enjoy understandingly" through interpretation that reveals deeper meanings. Enos Mills concluded, "People are out for recreation and need restful, intellectual visions, and not dull, dry facts."[15]

Emily Dickinson wrote of one who "has the facts but not the phosphorescence of learning."[16] The interpreter's aim is to use the raw material of information to produce interpretation that will instill in people not only the facts, but the "phosphorescence of learning." We must strive to construct our interpretation so that it has the potential for people to "enjoy understandingly." Thoughtful and well-designed interpretation can lead to exhilarating visitor experiences in which one may exclaim, "Ah-ha! Suddenly I see everything in a different light!"[17]

> *Education is much more than intellectual taxidermy—the scooping out of the mind and the stuffing in of facts—is worthless. The human mind is not a deep-freeze for storage but a forge for production; it must be supplied with fuel, fired, and properly shaped.*
>
> —William A. Donaghy

▪ *Chapter Three* ▪

IMPORTANCE OF THE STORY

The interpretive presentation—as a work of art—should be designed as a story that informs, entertains, and enlightens.

> *After the listening you become accountable for the sacred knowledge that has been shared. Shared knowledge equals power. Energy. Strength. Story is an affirmation of our ties to one another.*
>
> —Terry Tempest Williams

Enos Mills wrote about the "poetic interpretation" of nature and compared the nature guide to an artist.[1] Mills himself was an accomplished storyteller (see Box 1). Freeman Tilden identified interpretation as "an art, which combines many arts."[2] The use of "art" in interpretation refers to the creative process of putting together the interpretive story. It also refers to various arts employed in interpretation from drama to music to dance.

The *story* must somehow relate to something within the personality or experience of the visitor as stated in the first principle. Furthermore, information, as such, is not interpretation. The *story* offers revelation based upon information as noted in the second principle. Within this principle is also the seed of the fourth principle, that the purpose of the interpretive *story* is to inspire; to provoke people to broaden their horizons.

Box 1
Enos Mills: Storyteller

Through the encouragement of John Muir, Enos Mills began "lecturing" and writing. However, storytelling is a more appropriate term to describe Mill's presentation style. He did not use a lectern or notes. Newspaper reviews of his talks consistently stressed how he was animated, exciting, and spellbinding. Indeed, during a private presentation at the White House, President William Howard Taft refused to leave for an official appointment until Mills finished his story about bears. Mills was a master at creating suspense and drama, and then adding just the right amount of humor. He walked around as his stories unfolded and his hands were constantly in motion. Although he spoke frequently to prestigious groups, he believed his most important audiences were children.

Adapted from the Foreword, by Tom Danton, 1990, to *Adventures of a Nature Guide and Essays in Interpretation.*

The Meaning of Story

What makes interpretation provocative is a meaningful story. To assemble an effective story requires a great deal of research, thought, organization, and care.

At one level, presenting an interpretive story encompasses the orchestration of a solid introduction, body, and conclusion—the story is circular. The interpreter tells the audience what he or she is going to do, does it, and then tells the audience what he or she has done. This is the standard format of an oral presentation (see Chapter Ten). Various strategies, such as the use of examples or anecdotes, are incorporated to add interest. The story, even at this basic level, is an act of creativity.

At another level is story as myth, legend, tale, historic event, or elaborate personal experience. Depending upon the circumstances and intent, the story may be fictional or nonfictional. One full historical account or Native American story of nature may constitute the entire presentation. Or perhaps shorter vignettes may be weaved into the larger whole of a program. Or the interpretive presentation may be like Matriochka dolls, with stories one inside the other.

The interpretive storyteller may speak to an audience or interact with people who both listen and participate as the story unfolds. Responsive participation is especially effective with children. This method demands the listener's presence and fully reveals the intimacy, immediacy, and excitement of storytelling.

Keeping the Story Pertinent and On Track

Consider the tale of a traveler passing through and spending the night in a small midwest town. He joined a group of men sitting on the porch of the general store. After several futile attempts to initiate a conversation he asked, in exasperation, "Is there a law against talking in this town?"

"No law against it," said one old-timer. "We just like to make sure it's an improvement on silence."

Interpreters must, first of all, be certain that their interpretation is an improvement on silence. Furthermore, we must be sure that we eliminate unnecessary details and sidetracks that will detract from the message. Tilden suggested, "The artist ruthlessly cuts away all the material that is not vital to his story." [3]

We are all familiar with well-meaning accounts that drag on with various unimportant tangents until the narrative finally bogs down in an abundance of details that no longer remotely relate to the start of the tale. The reader's own experiences are sufficient here to make the point.

The skilled and considerate interpreter knows precisely where he or she is going. If there happens to be a divergence it will be found to be an integral slice of the overall story. As a book title of several years back made clear, *If You Don't Know Where You're Going, You'll Probably End Up Somewhere Else.*

Note that we are not suggesting that interpretation be inflexible. On the contrary, the very command of the material and structure advocated here allows *for* flexibility—a thoughtful reaction to

an unusual occurrence or an intelligent and appropriate response
to the particular nuances of the audience.

Treating Knowledge Imaginatively

Tilden suggested that interpreters treat knowledge imaginatively and Mills admonished them to reveal the "biography" of the
place.[4] A number of strategies may be employed to make the story
more personal, meaningful, and interesting. These tactics can be
used to bridge the familiar with the unfamiliar or to vary the presentation for more impact. Here are some possibilities:

Examples: Use concrete illustrations to assist the audience to understand and relate to the message.
Cause-and-Effect: Show relationships—people are interested in
what things cause other things to happen.
Analogies: Explain a point by making a comparison to something
similar that is more familiar to the audience.
Exaggerate the Time Scale: Make information more meaningful by
exaggerating the scale of time (i.e., the history of the Earth
condensed into a 24-hour day to explain geological features).
Similes: Use the words "like" or "as" to relate characteristics of two
things.
Metaphors: Give a word or phrase that is usually used to describe
something different to fuel interest.
Anecdotes: Use concise personal sketches that relate to the theme
of the presentation to lend interest. ‹little story›
Quotations: Quote others to add color to the message. People are
interested in the observations of others. deflated balloon
Humor: Use appropriate humor to engage an audience. Humor
may be especially useful in the early stages of the presentation to loosen up the audience.   its all about survival
Repetition: Repeat key phrases to create memorable messages.
Current News Events: Incorporate current events into the presentation to make a related point.[5]

These strategies can be purposefully used in various combi-
nations to orchestrate meaningful and effective interpretation.

Stories in Our Lives

Stories are omnipresent in our lives. "Man lives surrounded by his stories and the stories of others," Sartre told us, "he sees everything that happens to him through them."[6] Indeed, we are encircled by stories. Yet the interpretive contribution of storytelling is anything but mundane. Unlike many stories that we meet elsewhere, those offered in interpretive settings are designed to inform and enlighten us—to do us good.

As noted in the previous chapter, we are bombarded by a constant stream of information from the advertising industry and other forms of mass media that offer little in substance. The assumption (a fair one if the product is well-crafted) is that the telling of an interpretive story can change people in beneficial and enduring ways. We seldom expect the same from most of the stories that we casually encounter elsewhere. [7]

A broken connection with landscape and our history has been a compelling factor in the modern mindset in which detachment seems to dominate over collective and meaningful interaction. Jeremy Rifkin notes that in oral cultures—closely tied to the land—most language is stored in the mind, wisdom is cherished above all else, and that by their very nature these cultures are intimate and sensual.[8] Information is not merely retrieved, it is recalled for the good of the community.

Interpreters can benefit from an understanding of the intricacies of oral cultures. For example, one function of a story is to entertain people. Another, the epistemological function of a story, is to serve an educational purpose—to equip people with knowledge. A third possibility is the transformative function of a story whereby people are motivated to form a more balanced relationship to the Earth and other people.[9]

According to storyteller Susan Strauss, Native American folklore is particularly useful because the stories are indigenous to the landscape, natural history information is weaved into the story fabric, and certain "totem" qualities are often embodied such as courage and endurance. [10]

Story and the Proper Use of the Arts

The many avenues for treating knowledge imaginatively constitute one aspect of creating story as an art form. In addition, every interpreter is capable of some level of artistic talent. Tilden exclaims, "You have been so frustrated by the curatorship of unimportant details that you have forgotten your inborn talent." [11] Furthermore, when interpreters use art to create story they will find that they are among people who have the capacity to appreciate and understand their efforts. Interpreters, therefore, must be bold in seeking, practicing, and using the various arts in interpretation.

According to Tilden, the effective telling of an interpretive story implies the use of art. However, he goes on to apparently contradict the original premise:

> I am sure that what I am saying will not be misconstrued to mean that the interpreter should be any sort of practicing artist: that he should read poems, give a dramatic performance, deliver an oration, become a tragic or comic thespian, or anything as horribly out of place as these. Nothing could be worse, except perhaps to indulge in an evangelical homily. [12]

The State of the Arts

Over the past two decades the field of interpretation has witnessed an elaborate expression of story through poetry, dramatic performance, storytelling, puppetry, music, dance, and visual art. This mode of interpretive programming has been tremendously effective in its power to attract and move people. It offers broad appeal to visitors who might otherwise forego more traditional interpretive opportunities. Furthermore, this type of programming may attract members of the local community who may have previously shown minimal interest in interpretation.

The Power of Dramatic Performances

The actor, Lee Stetson, who portrays John Muir at Yosemite National Park, notes that dramatic performances offer a vitality to the listener, provide a sharing of one another's truth, and "reaffirm the possibility of Creation." [13] Stetson explained to one of the authors:

I am passionately convinced that art can serve to enhance our moral sensibilities and to promote in many a sense of environmental integrity. It used to be that our place on this planet was well claimed by the feelings of the people who lived here. Indigenous peoples, once naturally contained and nourished by the environment, integrated and celebrated that environment in their art, dance, music, community rituals. Their daily art evoked their values, aspirations, understanding, and their thoughts. The things we still need to learn are very old things we once knew well.[14]

Evangelism

As for evangelistic interpretation, it is telling that Guy Kawasaki was the keynote speaker at the 1992 National Association for Interpretation conference. He wrote *Selling the Dream: How to Promote Your Product, Company, or Ideas—and Make a Difference—Using Everyday Evangelism*. Kawasaki defines evangelism as the process of convincing people to become as passionate about your cause as you are. The book is written for people, like interpreters, who want to make a difference.

According to Kawasaki, evangelism "is the purest form of selling because it involves sharing ideas, insights, and hope in contrast to exchanging goods or services for money."[15] The goal of evangelism is sharing, not promotion for personal gain. Is this not what interpretation is all about—sharing a story that is revealing, penetrating, and affirming?

Yes, interpretation is an evangelistic art which combines many arts. The basic principles for creating and presenting an effective story also apply to any of the arts used in whole or combination: drama, poetry, puppetry, storytelling, music, and dance.[16] The possibilities are endless and the final product is a function of the individual interpreter's knowledge, talents, experiences, imagination, organizational care, and presentation skills (see Box 2).

The Power of Story

The following discussion suggests the potential power of perceiving interpretation as the development and application of story. It is a brief, philosophical discussion that considers story, in its broadest meaning, as an integral and prominent component of

Box 2
Excert from *Crow and Weasel* by Barry Lopez

Weasel began to speak.

"My friend," said Badger. "Stand up, stand up here so you can express more fully what you have seen."

Weasel stood up, though he felt somewhat self-conscious in doing so. He began to speak about the people called Inuit and their habit of hunting an unusual white bear.

"Wait, my friend," said Badger. "Where were you when this happened?"

"We were in their camp. They told us."

"Well, tell me something about their camp."

Weasel described their camp, and then returned again to the story of hunting the bear.

"But, my friend," interrupted Badger, "tell me a little first of who these people are. What did they look like?"

Badger's words were beginning to annoy Weasel, but Crow could see what Badger was doing, and he smiled to himself. Weasel began again, but each time he would get only a little way in his story before Badger would ask for some point of clarification. Weasel was getting very irritated.

Finally Crow spoke up.

"Badger," he said, "my friend is trying very hard to tell his story. And I can see that you are only trying to help him, by teaching him to put the parts together in a good pattern, to speak with a pleasing rhythm, and to call on all the details of memory. But let us now see if he gets your meaning, for my friend is very smart."

"That is well put," said Badger, curious.

"Weasel," continued Crow, "do you remember what that man said before he began to tell us stories about Sedna and those other beings?" He said, 'I have put my poem in order on the threshold of my tongue.' That's what this person Badger, who has taken us into her lodge, is saying. Pretend Badger and I are the people waiting back in our village. Speak to us with that kind of care."

Badger looked at Crow with admiration. Weasel, who had been standing uneasily before them, found his footing and his voice. He began to speak with a measured, fetching rhythm, painting a picture of the countryside where they had been, and then drawing the Inuit people and the others, the caribou, up into life, drawing them up out of the ground.

When Weasel finished, Badger nodded with gratitude, as though she had heard something profound.

From Barry Lopez, 1990, *Crow and Weasel*. By permission.

our lives. Story, as discussed here, is an ideal to strive for in interpretation.

We are proposing what Robert Coles suggested as "a respect for narrative as everyone's rock-bottom capacity, but also as the universal gift." [17] Terry Tempest Williams wrote, "We have all been nurtured on stories. Story is the umbilical cord that connects us to the past, present, and future." [18] In a live performance a visceral and intimate connection between the teller and the listeners can be far more powerful than the intervention of electronic media. Yet, we live in a culture that is increasingly dominated by impersonal communication.

Interpretation, along with education and religion, retains the tradition of oral communication. People learn in settings where instructors speak to them and are available to answer questions. Similarly, people prefer to worship in settings where they are preached to and where they participate in the service. Oral communication has traditionally been, and can continue to be, a distinguishing feature of natural and cultural history interpretation. Although interpretation need not be entirely dependent on live performance, it should be a prominent and critical dimension of the overall interpretive mix.

Barry Lopez suggested that listening to stories may be exhilarating and can renew a sense of purpose in one's life:

This feeling, an inexplicable renewal of enthusiasm after storytelling, is familiar to many people...I think intimacy is indispensable—a feeling that derives from the listener's trust and a storyteller's certain knowledge of his subject and regard for his audience. This intimacy deepens if the storyteller tempers his authority with humility, or when terms of idiomatic expression, or at least the physical setting for the story, are shared. [19]

Story, then, entertains, enlightens, and enriches our existence. It is structured and offered with the hope that the listener will find something of personal value. It is essential that we know our subject; otherwise a tentativeness in tone may be detected. Furthermore, our authority must be tempered by humility; otherwise, the message, however valuable, may be thwarted, lost in the arrogant atmosphere of the presentation.

The depth of what is being interpreted is made vivid through story. The story must be relevant to the visitor and it must reveal the deeper meanings the place holds. The interpreter creates a whole, yet focused message that is provocative, an inspirational message designed for the audience at hand. With these ingredients considered and fulfilled, the interpreter's story becomes that of his or her listeners as well. They will carry it with them. This is the exemplar we strive for.

> *Stories that instruct, renew, and heal provide a vital nourishment to the psyche that cannot be obtained in any other way. Stories . . . provide all the vital instructions we need to live a useful, necessary, and unbounded life—a life of meaning, a life worth remembering.*
>
> —Clarissa Pinkola Estes

■ *Chapter Four* ■

PROVOCATION

The purpose of the interpretive story is to inspire and to provoke people to broaden their horizons.

Let us probe the silent places,
let us seek what luck betide us;
Let us journey to a lonely land I know.
There's a whisper on the night-wind,
there's a star agleam to guide us,
And the Wild is calling, calling ... let us go.
—Robert Service

The purpose of the interpretive story, whether oral or written, is to prompt the listener or reader toward broadening his or her horizons and then acting on that new found breadth. Most visitors to interpretive settings are interested and eager to learn the deeper truths of the places they have self-selected to experience.

One task of the art of interpretation is to peel away layer after layer of mystery from the natural and cultural world. Of course diminishing the mystery need not limit the sense of wonder. Certainly, enjoyment, knowledge, and inspiration can increase together. Anyone can rejoice in a spectacular vista and this, in and of itself, is worthy. However, interpretation can add an intellectual spice to a basic emotion and can motivate yet further experiences and knowledge. Provocation through interpretation spans a broad spectrum from an interpreter serving as a role model to the tackling of controversial issues. At its most powerful level interpretation can result in changed perspectives and behavior.

Inspiration by Example

Interpreters entice visitors to learn more about the cultural and natural history of an area through their own passion for the place. Messages presented by example are highly motivational.[1]

People are inspired by representative aspects of those they admire. As role models, interpreters present their quality of life as a consequence of staying close to the landscape—the physical landscape for natural history interpreters and the landscape of human conduct for those who interpret cultural history.

The relationship of the interpreter to his or her subject, marked by a depth of knowledge and a sense of wonder, serenity, and fulfillment, is something that visitors will notice. They may inquire, on a personal level, how the interpreter can achieve these qualities in life and they may, ultimately, try to emulate them. [2]

Promoting the Place

As noted in previous chapters, many people are swamped by information yet removed from meaningful stories. Likewise, many are removed from their natural and cultural roots. We are becoming, more and more, a society that appreciates history and nature, from secondary sources: television, books, magazines, videos, the Internet, a day at the zoo.

Even when people plan trips to places of natural or cultural significance they often isolate themselves from the resource itself. Terry Tempest Williams bemoans "a society of individuals who only observe a landscape from behind the lens of a camera or the window of an automobile without ever entering in."[3]

The first challenge may well be to get people out of their cars. Edward Abbey asked, "What can I tell them? Sealed in their metallic shells like molluscs on wheels, how can I pry the people free? The auto as tin can, the park ranger as opener."[4]

Visitors must be made aware of the possibilities and this orientation can be accomplished in several ways. Many natural and historic sites have a Traveler Information Station (TIS). This is a low-wattage radio station that broadcasts information as cars enter the area. Among other messages, these stations can orient visitors to the place and pry them from their vehicles.

Visitors may also be given information, about what to do, at an entrance station. Usually, visitors are charged an entry fee, provided with a map or brochure, and hustled along. However, the booth attendant should find out how much time the visitors have and what their specific interests are (the first principle), and then make recommendations accordingly. Too often, visitors are left to their own devices and it is no surprise that they wind up following the road to a developed area where there are more cars, a clue that they have arrived at their destination, perhaps a gift shop.

If traffic volume precludes this level of personal interpretation, perhaps groups of visitors could be addressed on the quarter hour at a gathering place near the entrance station or further along at a visitor center. The overall obligation is to give visitors an overview of what they can do that may be rewarding and provoke them to do it.

Those visitors who are motivated to seek experiences on their own (in contrast to interpreter-led services) should be adequately prepared for such adventures. It would be a disservice to send them out without proper knowledge about potential dangers. For example, all visitors to Yellowstone National Park should be provided basic interpretation of park highlights including the history and symbolism of the park, thermal features, current resource issues, and wildlife. Those visitors choosing to venture beyond the parking lots and guided walks should then be provided the following additional information: 1) recommended action in case of confrontation with bears, bison, moose, or other wildlife, 2) hazards present in the geyser basins, and 3) hazards associated with restricted areas (e.g., grizzly closures or unstable cliffs).

Preservation of the Treasure

Based on the interpreter's intimate knowledge, the soul of the setting may be revealed. Why has this place been set aside for past, present and future generations? What is the *genius loci*: the unique and representative values, the distinctive atmosphere, the pervading character of the place? What should everyone *know* about this remarkable setting?

As an interpreter, it may be useful to ask yourself about the most striking aspect of the place you interpret. What did *you* find most enchanting, most enthralling about the place during your first experiences? How has that changed, if at all, as you have matured in your tenure at the site? This firsthand perspective can be fascinating to visitors who will relate to your own initial experiences.

When diplomats and missionaries first arrive in a foreign country they are often encouraged to take photographs because after a short time things become too familiar. The uniqueness of people and places fades. Scenes that were exciting soon enough become mundane. The photographs taken early on provide a record of what was initially inspiring. Similarly, newly-hired interpreters should be encouraged to record their first impressions in words and pictures. Later, such a record could be used to bring the veteran interpreter back to a clearer understanding of visitor perceptions.

It may also be useful to solicit the opinions of visitors as to what they find most resplendent about the place—this could be surprising. These insights could then be used to target and bolster future interpretive programming. Through exposure to the soul of the place, visitors will be inclined to seek further knowledge and experiences.

Among the benefits of solid interpretation is preservation of the area: parks, forests, wildlife preserves, historic homes, battlefields, or other monuments dedicated to our culture. Most visitors are truly concerned and responsive to calls for the preservation of a place of natural beauty or cultural significance.

Furthermore, this type of interpretation may be effective for those who, out of ignorance or selfishness, might do the resource harm. Provocative interpretation speaks to those who may purposefully deface something rare and precious. According to Freeman Tilden, "If you vandalize a beautiful thing, you vandalize yourself. And this is what true interpretation can inject into the consciousness." [5]

As a result of such interpretation, unthinking visitors may be less inclined to vandalize the resource and more motivated to respect it. At best, interpretation should encourage in visitors a sense of self-love, self-respect, and self-worth because it is out of these emotions that responsible behavior originates. [6]

Producing Behavior Change

Most interpreters attempt to affect the visitor's attitudes and behaviors toward the resource. A recent survey of interpreters found that 82% of respondents believed that the role of the interpreter is to challenge the visitors' belief systems. [7]

If interpreters are seeking to change attitudes and behavior, then they must offer experiences that accomplish that objective (see, also, Chapter 12). Recent research provides a validated framework of goals to assist interpreters in producing programs that attempt to affect attitudes and behavior. The following account is a synthesis of more than 100 principles, goals, and objectives of interpretation in conjunction with a review of learning theories related to environmental behavior change.[8] The three levels of program goals are: entry level goals, ownership goals, and empowerment goals.

The entry-level goals are broken down into four components which promote basic site information. These goals, in sum, provide the visitor with 1) overview information (layout, visitor amenities, other pertinent site characteristics) and general awareness of the ecology and cultural history, 2) opportunities to comprehend the ecological and cultural relationships between the resource site and the surrounding area, 3) an awareness of management policies and objectives and the effect these policies have on the resource, and 4) experiences that inspire environmental sensitivity through greater appreciation and enhanced enjoyment of the site.

Ownership goals are separated into two components in which interpretation seeks to 1) foster an awareness of the collective actions of visitors on the quality of the resource site and 2) encourage investigation and evaluation of these resource issues. The skills associated with pursuing the ecological and cultural implications of human impact could also be used to investigate broader environmental issues.

Empowerment goals are structured to encourage visitors to embrace responsible actions. Interpretive programming would promote experiences that develop visitors' abilities to differentiate the types of actions available for solving resource issues and to choose responsible courses of action.

Empowerment goals are consistent with Aldo Leopold's concept of ecological consciousness and the development of a land ethic. "It is inconceivable to me," Leopold wrote, "that an ethical relation to land can exist without love, respect, and admiration." Or more to the point, "A thing is right when it tends to preserve the integrity, stability, and beauty of the biotic community. It is wrong when it tends otherwise."[9]

The most powerful use of the above framework is to offer interpretive experiences that represent all three levels in a sequential order. Herein lie opportunities to stimulate attitude and behavior change in visitors. But, how do interpreters *achieve* empowerment outcomes?

Sharing the Vision

A shared vision becomes a force in people's hearts. At its most basic level, a shared vision is the answer to the question, "What is it that we want to *do*?" A shared vision is one that many visitors commit to because it reflects their own personal vision. In other instances visitors may shift their existing attitudes and behaviors.

The role of the interpreter is to provide meaning and revelation, to generate a context that relates to visitors' lives. By sharing a vision the interpreter can spark a flame that creates a common identity among diverse people.

Interpreters who seek to build shared visions must be willing to share their *personal* visions. They must also be prepared to ask, in essence, "Will you follow my lead?"

To expect enrollment or commitment to a cause from others, the interpreter must be committed. To do otherwise, of course, would be hypocritical. We must also be on the level. The vision must be presented with honesty without inflating the benefits or neglecting the costs. By delineating a vision that is worthy of commitment, we shouldn't have to further convince anyone of anything—the vision should speak for itself.

Two distinct strategies can motivate people—fear and aspiration.[10] The response motivated by fear (*reacting* to change) is at the root of negative visions. The source of energy behind aspiration (*generating* change) drives positive visions. Although petitioning to people's fear may foster changes in the short term, it is only by appealing to aspiration that long term change will occur. A vision comes alive only when people feel they can shape their future. Visitors to our treasures of natural and cultural history will commit to a cause over the long term not because they have to, but because they want to.

To be most effective in sharing a vision we should "know" and relate to the audience. This is the first principle of interpretation, for knowing the audience allows us to make the presentation

interesting and relevant. Undoubtedly, in some interpretive instances this is logistically difficult.

Moreover, the interpreter must *know* the vision. A broad and
deep knowledge of the cause provides the confidence to explain it
and defend it. Not knowing and understanding the vision is a sure
way to lose credibility.

Guy Kawasaki suggested the following elements for effective
presentation of your vision: 1) Foster the tone of the presentation
to be upbeat, optimistic, and bold. 2) Communicate ambitious goals.
Large goals will not scare off those committed to the vision and
even small ones will scare off those who are doubters. 3) High-
light personal benefits. How will what you propose translate into
changes in an individual's life? 4) Reach a peak. As the presentation progresses it should nudge the audience's emotions higher
and higher until it reaches a summit. This approach makes the
presentation vivid and exciting.[11]

The Courage to Look for Trouble

We have moved from relatively safe modes of provoking visitors (inspiration by example, promoting the place, and preserving
the treasure) to a framework for producing behavior change and
the principles for sharing vision. Indeed, there is some overlap in
these various persuasive approaches.

Now, we're going to take it a step further recognizing that
this last level of provocation may not be appropriate in all instances.
It conflicts with many instincts of a bureaucracy and may pose
discomfort for some interpreters. In essence we are presenting
here the concept of going out on a limb, facing conflict head on, in
support of our convictions.

Sigurd Olson noted that courage is a multi-faceted virtue.
There is courage to withstand adversity without complaint, to show
humility in the midst of success, or to stand and be counted for
deep personal convictions.[12]

Conflict is painful, yet it is also educational, and it leads us to
the crux of our environmental problems. According to Bill
McKibben, for example, if someone can acknowledge that grizzly
bear habitat is as important as sheep ranches, then they have taken
a giant step toward realizing that their own way of life or job may

require change in order that the upper atmosphere stay intact. McKibben continues:

> The person closest at hand is least likely to learn the lesson, I fear—stockmen may never be reconciled to grizzlies. But, to use a loaded analogy, Martin Luther King, Jr. and the civil rights movement did not concentrate as much on winning over the rednecks who were burning crosses as they did on converting the great mute majority of Americans to a new way of thinking. They created a series of confrontations that served to educate … those of us who simply had never given the issue enough attention. [13]

Of course, complex environmental issues are not as straightforward as civil rights crusades and stockmen are not Klansmen. But the same kind of shifts in attitude—toward understanding, appreciation, unselfishness, compassion, enlightenment—are as necessary and perhaps as possible. McKibben concluded:

> In any event, those who run our parks should remember that every decision that involves a choice between people on the one hand and trees and animals and rivers on the other is an opportunity for education in humility. It will not be easy … But if your goal is to teach the public about the natural world, your work can't stop with the nature trail and the diorama. [14]

An interpreter who has the "courage to look for trouble" does so in an intelligent way. Focus on what it is about your program that will cause someone to say ten, twenty, thirty years later, "I heard an interpreter say this a long time ago. It made sense to me and I changed. I'll never forget it."

Do everything reasonable to allow your listeners to like you. They will be more open to your message if you appear caring, sensitive, confident, competent, honest, nonjudgmental, and genuinely friendly.

If the audience mostly favors your view on a controversial issue, then the presentation should reinforce existing beliefs and be of a motivational nature. Bring the listeners beyond complacency to a level of firm commitment with specific recommendations for action.

If the audience mostly opposes your position, then guide listeners to basic principles and establish common agreement, even if it is only harmony of opinion that there is a problem to be solved.

Structure the presentation to minimize the differences between the interpreter and the audience by focusing on facts that are irrefutable and basic strands of perception that are common to each view.

If the audience is in the middleground—primarily neutral, or perhaps apathetic—convince them that the subject is truly important and that it affects their lives. The thrust of the presentation may be to help people see the issue more clearly and to eliminate irresponsible solutions to the problem.

If the audience is mixed, then the interpreter will want to use a combination of these approaches. Whatever the makeup of the audience, when the goal is to persuade others on a controversial topic we must phrase our appeal in terms of the higher principles of the listeners. For example, we can show the audience how the issue coincides with such noble motives as empathy, compassion, and justice.

Interpreters are obligated to present the truth. They must acknowledge issues that have not yet been resolved and those with conflicting evidence. Yet when it is clear that, as Leopold admonished, "a thing is right" or "it is wrong," then it must be logically and forcefully presented as such.

As a broad example, consider the importance of protecting the diversity of life on this planet. Edward Wilson demands that the ethical imperative be, first of all, prudence: we should not knowingly allow any species to go extinct. The responsible stewardship of our Earth preserves not only the well-being and freedom of other species, but also the health and spiritual uplift of our own. This is uncontestable; upon any probing something which we should all be able to agree. As Wilson suggested, "Those committed by religion to believe that life was put on earth in one divine stroke will recognize that we are destroying the Creation, and those who perceive biodiversity to be the product of blind evolution will agree."[15]

Interpreters have, at different levels of commitment and approach, a responsibility to broaden horizons and provoke a more sensitive, a more caring attitude toward our cultural and natural resources. To do anything else would be an act of professional irresponsibility.

> *Whatever you can do, or dream you can, begin it.*
> *Boldness has genius, power and magic in it.*

—Johann Wolfgang von Goethe

■ *Chapter Five* ■

HOLISTIC INTERPRETATION

I nterpretation should present a complete theme or thesis and address the whole person.

Wholeness is the sum total ... it is the ephemeral essence, the ultimate that puts one in tune with cosmic values.

—Sigurd Olson

Sigurd Olson suggested that to explain wholeness we must return to the very depths of being, for it entails all that has gone before us. "It is harmony and oneness, the very antithesis of fragmentation, emptiness, and frustration. It means being alive and aware of all about you and all that has ever been. It is being in tune with waters and rocks, with vistas and horizons, with constellations and the infinity of time and space."[1] Two major issues are addressed by this principle: presenting a whole picture and interpreting to the whole person. We will address each separately. In addition, we will consider regional and global interpretation as important factors in interpreting a whole.

Presenting A Whole

It is important not to misconstrue this principle to mean that interpreters should present *the* whole—to not leave anything out. It would be impossible to tell the whole story of any site. Barry

Commoner's First Law of Ecology succinctly stated, "Everything is connected to everything else."[2] If we were to attempt to communicate everything known about a topic, we would find ourselves facing an infinite web of information. But, even if *the* whole story of an event or place could be presented, visitors could not receive the whole message. People are limited by their short-term memories and attention spans. More than 40 years ago, psychologist George Miller found that people can only concentrate on or hold about seven "chunks" of information (plus or minus two) in their short-term memory.[3] For example, when going to the store for more than seven items one usually resorts to making a list rather than relying on memory. By grouping facts into "chunks" we can condense several items that are similar and thereby remember more information. It helps to remember a nine digit social security number by combining the numbers into three chunks. Similarly, nine tree names may be too much for a nature hike participant to remember, but if the interpreter presents them as three oaks, three maples, and three hickories, the visitor might be able to remember them.

Freeman Tilden stated, "A cardinal purpose of interpretation, it seems to me, is to present a whole, rather than a part, no matter how interesting the specific part may be." [4] Whether planning a battlefield tour or a nature trail, interpreters must be selective in deciding which "parts" to present to make a whole. Given the limited capacity of human memory, interpreters should not present more than a few important concepts, eloquently put forth. Yet, it is not unusual to see large amounts of miscellaneous facts presented to the public.

For example, interpreters at battlefields sometimes merely recount the statistics of personnel, weaponry, and casualties. From battlefields where thousands fell, to local sites memorializing those who fought in an almost forgotten skirmish, interpretive media tend to focus on technical descriptions of the weapons and the numbers and affiliation of dead and wounded. The statistics are often presented, and read, like a baseball boxscore.

Self-guiding nature trails often offer an abundance of information with 20+ stops ranging from geology to wildflowers to history to ecology. When the stops offer no linkage or continuity, the information will exceed capabilities for even short-term memory. The information presented may be well-intended, but it won't be effective in that format. As tempting as it may be to include everything, the interpretation should support a focused whole.

Interpretation of Meaningful Themes

The possession of facts is knowledge; the use of them wisdom; the choice of them education.
—Thomas Jefferson

Interpretation toward a whole makes visitors more knowledgeable by communicating facts, it makes visitors wise by attaching meaning to the facts, and it educates them by guiding them through mountains of information, presenting only the most salient and rewarding themes. The key to making this selection lies in theme-based interpretation.

All interpretation, whether written or spoken, should have a theme—a specific message to communicate. Themes are statements (often expressed in one complete sentence) of what the interpreter wants the audience members to understand and take away with them.[5] In the context of this principle, a theme is a "whole."

Thematic interpretation eliminates the tendency to present a collection of unrelated facts. Focusing on a single "whole" directs interpreters only to those facts that must be presented to develop and support the theme. This not only avoids overloading the audience, but it saves time for the interpreter preparing the presentation.

Another important advantage of thematic interpretation is that research has shown people remember themes but forget facts. When people know the theme—at the beginning of the presentation, exhibition, or trail—attention is enhanced and they comprehend and remember more of the information. When no theme is identified, then attention, comprehension and retention is weaker. One study found that when a theme isn't given, comprehension and recall is no better than when an audience is presented with a jumbled story made up of unrelated sentences![6]

Themes are not the same as topics or subject matter. At a historic site such as the Little Bighorn Battlefield National Monument a topic could be broad, such as "the battle" or as narrow as "the Colt Single Action Army model 1873 revolver." Countless facts about the battle or firearm could be presented to the visitor, but presenting these facts would not be thematic. Interpretive planners at the Little Bighorn Battlefield have identified six themes (see Box 1). All interpretation at the Battlefield must address one of these themes, each of which represents a whole.

Box 1
The Interpretive Themes and Selected Sub-themes at Little Bighorn Battlefield National Monument

I.   The battle of the Little Bighorn has a symbolic dimension which far exceeds its military significance.

—   The battlefield name change and the Indian monument create symbols of inclusion, rather than exclusion. It is no longer Custer's or Sitting Bull's battlefield, but the nation's.

—   All of the participants saw themselves as patriots—fighting for their country, land, and way of life.

II.   The Great Sioux War of 1876-77, the climax of the plains Indian wars, was an inevitable conflict similar to the 17th century and 18th century phases.

—   Since colonial times Native Americans were 1) assimilated, 2) segregated, or 3) exterminated.

—   The Northern Great Plains were the most lush and diverse of all. It is not surprising that the demise of the bison and the Indian way of life associated with them should end here.

III. The United States Army was an instrument of government policy, and a buffer between Indians and the dominant society. Government policy was, in turn, an expression of public will.

—   The small size of the U.S.Army was a reflection of the government's and the public's perception that the Indian problems posed no real threat to the republic.

—   From the Indian perspective, imperialism took their land; control and assimilation tried (and sometimes succeeded) to take their spirit.

IV.   Intertribal conflicts and alliances, frequently influenced by the advance of European culture, are evident in the events.

—   The Little Bighorn also was an Indian against Indian conflict.
—   Indians fought Indians for Indian reasons. The association with whites was often only a convenience or a means to drive away enemies.

V.   Command and conduct of the battle were intimately related to terrain and fighting styles of the adversaries.

—   The concept of total war against a population worked for Sheridan and Sherman in the Civil War and was applied here as well.
—   Man for man the Indians were more skilled in fighting than the U.S. troopers.

VI.   The battle of the Little Bighorn was the high water mark in a clash of cultures that had begun on this continent four centuries earlier.

—   Crazy Horse and those of his generation represented the last stage of resistance to white attempts to remove Indians from their land and eradicate their culture.
—   To the victors the battle was both a source of pride and sadness. Pride because the battle was won; sadness because the victory did not preserve the Indian way of life.
—   To most whites the battle is regarded as a historical event, but to the Indians it is still part of recent remembrance.

From Little Bighorn Battlefield National Monument Interpretive Prospectus, unpublished document.

People from all ages and cultures are drawn to certain themes with universal significance. These themes typically involve human conflict: conflict within a person; conflict among people, or conflict between humans and their environment.

At battlefields, meaningful stories abound among the statistics—stories about bravery, cowardice, intelligence, suffering, honor, terror, heroism, and pain. These stories have the power to move and inspire people. The lasting results of warfare can have a meaning to present day visitors, whether it be in the grand concept of freedom or in the name of a local landmark. Abraham Lincoln attached meaning to the statistics at the Gettysburg battlefield and gave his Gettysburg Address, a history-changing interpretation of events.

In selecting themes interpreters should consider the special characteristics of the place. Sometimes interpreters present topics with little relationship to their setting. Interpreters should focus on themes derived from the site's *genius loci*—special meaning—and directed at the visitors' interests. [7]

Thesis-Based Interpretation

A current issue in the profession is whether thematic interpretation goes far enough. Ann Lundberg argued that a thesis (as opposed to a theme) goes beyond subject content to challenging visitor's attitudes or perspectives. A thesis is an expression of an opinion—something that someone might disagree with. "The inclusion of an opposing point of view inherent to a thesis statement adds a dynamic tension to what is being said, an element of suspense which interests the audience in how you will prove your case. Suddenly their own point of view matters; they will have to choose sides."[8]

Lundberg provided two examples of turning a theme into a thesis as follows:

> **Theme:** Native American rock art has been interpreted in many different ways.
>
> **Thesis:** The ways in which prehistoric Native American rock art has been interpreted tells us more about the desires of those who do the interpreting than about what the ancients meant.
>
> **Theme:** Geyser function is dependent upon three variables.
>
> **Thesis:** Changes in the three variables which determine geyser function suggest that Old Faithful may not be faithful for long.[9]

Lundberg concluded that thesis-based interpretation seeks to have an effect in the world: "By disturbing and unsettling an audience, we can wake them from complacency to responsibility and to action."[10]

In the last chapter we discussed a spectrum of interpretive modes to provoke visitors that closed with "the courage to look for trouble." Thesis-based interpretation likewise involves risks to the interpreter because the thesis is a statement with which people may disagree. However, at issue *here* is the notion of themes versus theses and the argument is partly rooted in semantics.

We believe that good theme statements have the potential to provoke an audience. Nonetheless, not all themes argue a single thesis or point of view. This should be acceptable. For example, an interpretive program may be provocative by enlightening people to see something in a new way without introducing an overriding point of view. Or an interpretive program may be provocative by arguing a point of view. Or it may be provocative by presenting *multiple* points of view with an argument for each. Differing circumstances may define which approach is used. Some interpreters are limited in their expression of personal opinions if they don't represent the official position of their agency. Some interpreters, as a matter of style, may prefer less confrontational—but perhaps no less effective—approaches.

Finally, some statements, traditionally classified as themes, may argue a point of view and fall into the thesis category as well. (Refer, again, to Box 1).

Meeting the Needs of the Whole Person

Interpretation must address itself to the whole man rather than any phase.

—Freeman Tilden

As detailed in Chapter One, we must know our audiences to target messages effectively. To apply this principle fully, interpreters must know the needs and motivations of those they address. Psychologist Abraham Maslow developed a theoretical model of motivation based on human needs.[11] He combined Freudianism (which focused only on internal and intrinsic determinants of behavior) and behaviorism (which focused on extrinsic or environmental determinants of behavior) to study the *whole* person. Maslow's model is built upon a hierarchy of motivations from physiological needs, to safety, to social connectedness, to esteem, to self-actualization.

People with unmet physiological needs (e.g., thirst, hunger) still require the higher needs, but their attention is focused on satisfying immediate requirements first. As individuals meet lower level needs, they can then satisfy the higher level needs.

In industrialized countries, Maslow found that few people are motivated by basic physiological needs as these have already been met. Interpreters can expect to encounter people primarily in the mid-levels of the hierarchy. Visitors often are motivated by safety, belonging, and esteem needs. As we assist people to meet lower level needs, they can be lifted to realizing higher needs. Self-actualization, the apex of Maslow's model, consists of moments of highest happiness.

Working upwards in Maslow's hierarchy, interpreters should strive to understand visitors' fears and safety concerns. Once these concerns are identified and understood, then they may be countered to assure that visitors are not preoccupied with them.

Interpreters also encounter people who seek to fulfill belonging needs. We live in a time of increasing mobility and scattered families. Many people don't know their neighbors. People with unmet belonging needs may exhibit feelings of loneliness and alienation. Interpreters have the opportunity to welcome such people and make them feel like they belong to a certain group or the broad "family" of visitors to the site. One particularly effective strategy is to call visitors by their names.

Those visitors motivated by unmet esteem needs may feel a sense of inferiority, of not achieving their potential. Sometimes, due to their own lack of esteem, they will hold others in low regard, too. These people can often be detected by their introverted demeanor or pessimism. We can give such visitors our attention and our respect to enhance their esteem. This has the potential to lift them above their self-consciousness. We might recognize individuals for their special abilities or valuable characteristics.

Presenting a Multi-sensory Whole

What a joy it is to feel the soft, springy earth under my feet once more, to follow grassy roads that lead to ferny brooks where I can bathe my fingers in a cataract of rippling notes, or to clamber over a stone wall into green fields that tumble and roll and climb in riotous gladness.

—Helen Keller

Helen Keller's sense of touch provided her with much information and emotion. Engaging as many of the visitor's senses as possible allows the interpreter to go beyond meeting intellectual needs alone. Touching, seeing, smelling, tasting, and listening all help communicate a whole. Each sense can offer new supporting information. Activating all the senses creates a holistic experience for the visitor.

Underestimating the Intelligence of Visitors

If you do not understand a man's ignorance, you will remain ignorant of his understanding.
—Samuel Taylor Coleridge

Tilden observed that interpreters tend to underestimate the visitor's intelligence and that it is "easy to put the visitor down as a moron."[12] Responding kindly to exasperating questions tests the patience of some interpreters. Yet an impatient or harsh rejoinder will exacerbate the needs visitors have for security, acceptance, or esteem.

Edward Abbey, from his experiences at Arches National Park, concluded that park visitors are, "most of them, really good people and not actually as simple-minded as they . . . encourage me to pretend us all to be."[13]

To meet the needs of the whole visitor we must respect the whole visitor, including weaknesses and ignorance. Yet, we need not only tolerate ignorance, but, at some level, embrace it, because it is interpretation that may shift misunderstanding to understanding and ignorance to knowledge (see Box 2).

Minda Borun, at the Franklin Institute in Philadelphia, found that "naive notions" about science are not only held by children, but are widespread in adults. For example, Borun and her research associates found that regardless of age, most visitors did not fully comprehend the concept of gravity. Correcting misconceptions and changing tightly-held, but naive, beliefs requires a different approach than merely teaching new information. By making application of this insight, Borun and her associates found that a "corrective" interpretive exhibit changed many of the visitors' misconceptions about gravity.[14]

Box 2
A Case of Wildlife Misidentification

When I worked at Denali National Park and Preserve in Alaska, I was surprised at the number of visitors who were confused in their attempts to distinguish between various wildlife species—such as caribou and moose. However, it was one of my colleagues who was confronted with the most astounding case of wildlife misidentification.

At the remote Eilson Visitor Center (near the base of Mt. McKinley) a woman was looking through one of the viewing telescopes. All of a sudden she exclaimed that she saw a grizzly bear. The viewing area was crowded and other visitors quickly surrounded the woman. She reported that the bear had risen on its hind feet and was waving to her!

My colleague was nearby. He broke through the crowd and asked to look through the telescope because he couldn't see the bear with his naked eyes. He wanted to locate the bear both out of safety concerns and so he could orient the visitors and tell them about grizzlies.

As he stepped up to the telescope he realized that it was pointed almost straight down. The woman had focused on an arctic ground squirrel about 15 feet away. In an extreme display of hope and imagination, this person had mistaken a squirrel for a bear.

-L.B.

Interpreting Regional Wholes

Interpreting a whole may mean going beyond park boundaries that were set using economic or political criteria, rather than ecological or historical criteria. For example, interpreting natural history themes may involve an entire watershed. A park's wetland in the upper reaches of a watershed may provide benefits such as flood control, sediment trapping, and groundwater recharge for those who live downstream.

Similarly, at Grand Canyon National Park interpreters address the theme of air quality. That is, air pollution from coal burning power plants hundreds of miles away obscures the view from rim to rim of the canyon.

At historic sites, to present a whole, it may be necessary to give an overview of an entire trail, such as the Oregon Trail of westward expansion. As another example, visitors to a specific "Underground Railroad" hiding place would need to understand the full extent of the "Railroad" to gain the full meaning of the site.

Interpretive sites in the same region sometimes coordinate efforts when interpreting similar broad regional topics. This can prevent undue redundancy among these sites. Planners can collaborate in deciding which themes will be presented at each particular site. For example, at two nearby parks each with a similar restored farmstead, one may interpret 1890s family life emphasizing themes involving the role of the farm wife and what it was like to be a child on the farm, whereas the farm equipment of the period will be interpreted at the other site.

Interpreters within a region can also coordinate state-of-the-art interpretation of the same themes at several related sites. The Great Lakes Lighthouse Keepers Association, in conjunction with interpretation faculty and students at the University of Michigan, Dearborn, developed an innovative interpretive program which uses music, video tapes, cassette tapes, written materials, and youth involvement to interpret and preserve historic lighthouses at locations throughout Michigan. [15]

Interpreting Global Wholes

Each of us must take a greater personal responsibility for this deteriorating global environment; each of us must take a hard look at the habits of mind and action that reflect—and have led to—this grave crisis.

—Al Gore

On a larger scale, cumulative individual and local actions may have global ramifications. Bumper stickers call out for us to "Think Globally—Act Locally." Consider themes involving migratory species, international trade in plants and animals, and issues dealing with the global atmosphere. To what degree should interpreters become involved in issues that may be controversial, that challenge the complacency of the average American?

Michael Frome asked the tough question, "What should interpreters really be interpreting?" Then he answered, "If you ask me, interpretation as a profession and interpreters as individuals are failing in their stewardship responsibility. Of course, there are good interpreters with conscience and courage, but they are the minority." [16]

We face grave environmental problems: species extinction, climate change, disposal of toxic waste, desertification, acid rain, food and water shortages, infectious diseases, human overpopulation. Interpreters, by their training in the natural sciences, generally have an understanding of these complex issues. Or, put differently, interpreters *should* understand these issues. These global environmental concerns permeate various interpretive themes. That being the case, we should be able to weave *pertinent* information into our interpretation of a place. Abraham Lincoln said, "To sin by silence when they should cry out makes cowards out of men." [17]

The dictionary offers the words "healed" and "restored" as synonyms of "whole." Interpretation toward a whole seeks to restore the whole person. By meeting personal needs, interpretation can enhance the visitor's well-being. Furthermore, interpretation can lend itself to the cause of restoring our planet to environmental health. Tilden wrote, "Of all the words in our English language, none is more beautiful and significant than the word 'whole'." [18] By knowing our visitors and our interpretive place (both in its immediate and larger context), we may best interpret a "whole" that will be meaningful and enduring.

■ *Chapter Six* ■

INTERPRETATION THROUGHOUT THE LIFESPAN

Interpretation for children, teenagers, and seniors—when these comprise uniform groups—should follow fundamentally different approaches.

If I had influence with the good fairy who is supposed to preside over the christening of all children I should ask that her gift to each child in the world be a sense of wonder so indestructible that it would last throughout life, as an unfailing antidote against the boredom and disenchantments of later years, the sterile preoccupation with things that are artificial, the alienation from the sources of our strength.

Rachel Carson

Enos Mills devoted considerable attention to interpretation for children. He wrote, "No other school [as Nature] is likely so to inspire children, so to give them vision and fire their imagination."[1] He continued by suggesting that this "unrivaled" outdoor school and playground is always open as a library, a museum, a zoological garden, and as a type of wilderness frontier. Mills allowed that interpreters may enter "a little more intimately" into the experiences of children and that there would logically be "slight re-adjustments" necessary in interpretation to meet their needs.[2] However, he was adamant that children should not be talked down to.

Freeman Tilden's sixth principle of interpretation stated: "Interpretation addressed to children (say, up to the age of twelve) should not be a dilution of the presentation to adults, but should follow a fundamentally different approach. To be at its best it will require a separate program." [3]

We agree with Mills and Tilden but expand the concept to include two other unique age groups—teenagers and seniors. We recognize, too, the tremendous diversity within these groups as well as the commonalities among all people. At some level, we'd like to believe, we are all children. Nevertheless, we propose that each of the aforementioned groups—if uniform in age—can gain from various deviations from, and enhancements to, standard mass-oriented interpretive programs.

According to Gary Machlis and Donald Field, matching an interpretive approach with the appropriate audience is perhaps the most difficult challenge facing interpreters. They suggested, "The bases for assessing differences are numerous . . . Perhaps the most obvious difference among visitors is their age." [4] And they concluded, "Yet an assessment of programs offered reveals a low number of interpretive options specifically designed for either the young or the old." [5]

This chapter will address interpretation which can be thoughtfully designed and presented for uniform groupings of children, teenagers, and seniors. Our emphasis will be on children because, as we shall see, more is at stake. Also, a much broader and deeper literature addresses children's interpretation (primarily in the arena of children and nature). Specifically programmed interpretation for teenagers and seniors is a relatively newer frontier. [6]

Children

Nothing you do for children is ever wasted. They seem not to notice us, hovering, averting our eyes, and they seldom offer thanks, but what we do for them is never wasted.
—Garrison Keillor

Children can be, at the same time, exasperating and the greatest earthly gift imaginable. Part of what is so engaging (and unnerving) about children is their unpredictability. They are also distinguished by their innocence, trust, raw enthusiasm, spontaneity, vitality, and curiosity. As Garrison Keillor related, there is nothing that we do for children that is wasted. This section of the chapter explores the concern that children are not bonding with nature and the reasons why. It then focuses on efforts designed to attract children to nature and to interpret effectively for them once they arrive.

Kids Are Not Bonding With Nature

In a book titled *Childhood's Future*, columnist Richard Louv observed that just as children need meaningful adult contact and a sense of connection to the broader human community, they also need independence, solitude, adventure, and a sense of wonder.[7] These latter needs, in the past, have been met through contact with nature. However, although children have so much to gain from experiences in nature, these opportunities are increasingly limited.

In an extensive review of the literature on children's concern for the natural environment, Louise Chawla concluded that "children care about nature more when they are more familiar with it, at a time when this opportunity is becoming less and less available."[8]

Children in the inner city are not bonding with nature because it is so overwhelmed by human factors. René Dubos warned about "the wholesale and constant exposure of children to noise, ugliness and garbage in the street, thereby conditioning [children] to accept public squalor as the normal state of affairs."[9] Furthermore, although suburban tracts may be less noisy, less ugly, and less filthy, they are often "sterile and restrictive in their own way."[10] In intensely farmed areas, children are also isolated from nature as natural biotic communities have been replaced with expansive monocultures of corn, wheat, cotton, citrus, or other cash crops.

In sum, children are growing up not connecting with nature because nature is not readily available. In addition, children are heavily influenced by mesmerizing sedentary activities—television, videos, and computer games.

Even if natural landscapes were accessible we question whether children would be drawn to them as in the past. Gary Paul Nabhan and Steve Trimble provide evidence that rural kids, in remote areas of Mexico, Alaska, and the American West, learn more about nature from television than from first hand experience.[11]

This is disconcerting at best and frightening at worst. A fourth-grader interviewed by Louv said, "I like to play indoors better 'cause that's where all the electrical outlets are."[12]

The Irony of Educational Nature TV

Scattered among much of the trash that makes up television programming are some excellent nature programs—*The Planet Earth, Nova, National Geographic Specials, Nature, The World of Audubon,* and many offerings by "The Discovery Channel." Yet even these well-respected programs send a wrong message in part. The problem is two-fold. First, even the best programs instruct that nature is something that is learned about inside and "that it is passive, prepackaged, apart from human existence." [13] Second, these programs create false expectations. Kids can watch the development of a baby cub into a full grown grizzly bear in an hour. Anything they might observe firsthand in nature, by comparison, is going to be less spectacular and will require more effort and patience.

Barbara Kingsolver, in *High Tide in Tuscon,* quotes Robert Michael Pyle's pointed question, "If we can watch rhinos mating in our living rooms, who's going to notice the wren in the backyard?" Kingsolver adds, "The real Wild Kingdom is as small and brown as a wren, as tedious as a squirrel turning back the scales of a pine cone, as quiet as a milkweed seed on the wind—the long, slow stillness between takes." [14]

"Nature is Frightening and Disgusting and Uncomfortable"

Not only are there no electrical outlets, but nature for many children is a fearful, dreaded, and alien place.

Some children are familiar with natural landscapes through family excursions, summer camp, or similar experiences. Others, however, without such previous opportunities, may hold negative preconceptions about natural areas. They may be overwhelmed by their lack of familiarity with the sights, smells, and sounds of natural settings. Even when no immediate dangers exist, children may fear the unknown and may exhibit various phobias. These fears stem from misimpressions of natural environments portrayed via movies, videos, television, newscasts, and ill-informed word-of-mouth.

Robert Bixler and his colleagues surveyed interpreters at nature and environmental education centers to determine the anxiety reactions of children. Interpreters were asked to recall and list fears by children on field trips to wildland areas. Major categories of fears and discomforts were ranked and those results follow. [15]

As may well be predicted, the fear of snakes was the most common response (87%). The second ranked response was fear of insects, primarily bees (79%).

The third ranked response, fascinatingly, was fear of nonindigenous animals (73%). It may be speculated that television and zoos contributed to the frequent references to these fears. For example, many children, having no concept of what to expect, expressed fears of being attacked by such predators as lions, tigers, and alligators.

In addition to a litany of other fears (including, but not limited to, poisonous plants, spiders, bats, ticks, worms, and getting lost), Bixler and his colleagues found that children reacted with disgust (as opposed to fear) to various organisms such as slugs, and the odor of decaying plants.

Also of concern to some children in these field settings was their lack of comfort. That is, children were anxious about getting dirty or wet, or becoming too hot or too cold. This may be explained in part by the fact that many urban children have a narrow comfort range due to their dependence on more sterile settings and modern conveniences.

One of the challenges for those who interpret to children is that programs may have to include corrective as well as formative measures. Interpreters may have to provide special assistance to those apprehensive children who carry negative and unpleasant perceptions of nature. This should be accomplished early by explaining any misconceptions, generating a sense of security, and establishing the child's confidence in the interpreter's knowledge and competencies.

Fighting Fire with Fire

One novel suggestion is to fight television with television. "Getting kids back to nature through the visual media is probably the only way we're ever going to turn the tide...We have to take what's been doing the damage and turn it around. And I think we can do that if people get serious about producing some really good, solid materials that are aimed at getting kids back out to nature. I haven't seen anyone concentrate on this."[16]

As appealing as this solution appears to be, and we fully endorse it, it is perhaps unlikely. The television industry is aware that any widespread success in getting kids outdoors would, in the long run, put them out of business. At least in past actions, the TV industry has been reluctant to embrace this level of altruism out of concern for the public good.

The solution to the problem is more likely to arise through proactive measures in the home that get kids outside and in comprehensive environmental education offerings in the schools. Furthermore, the interpretive field contributes by offering programs that introduce babies to nature so that they don't fear it later and in providing stimulating children's programs as the kids get older.

Inoculating Babies with Doses of Nature

Perhaps the best action to assure that children's interpretive programs are successful is to start them early. Through exposure to nature (early inoculation) children can learn to enjoy natural settings before it becomes too late and they come to fear them. Through early experiences in nature, children can learn firsthand that there is little to fear, that the disgusting can alternately be perceived as fascinating, and that getting dirty and exploring with all the senses is *fun*.

At the Austin Nature Center in Texas, interpretive programs were designed and offered specifically for one-and-a-half to two-and-a-half year olds.[17] This "Babies and Beasties" program included basic "instruction" and self-awareness activities. In three different classes, the babies learned about themselves in comparison to other animals. In the mammals class they were exposed to similarities among all mammals. In the birds class they made comparisons between characteristics such as beaks and mouths, arms and wings, and feathers and hair. The reptiles class was the "climax" of the program: "Many people have an aversion to reptiles, but by demonstrating an accepting attitude to these 'slimy' and 'horrible' creatures, perhaps some of this accepting attitude will rub off on the participants, both babies and parents."[18] This observation sums up the importance of such programs. Children who are provided an accurate perception of nature from early firsthand experiences are more likely to be "inoculated" against accepting the inaccurate depictions of nature which are so prevalent in the media or through word-of-mouth myths and misnomers[19] (see Box 1).

Similarly, the Missouri Department of Conservation has developed a nature walk for those up to three years of age (and their parents) titled, "Babes in the Woods."[20] This is a 45-minute guided walk with parents pushing children in strollers. For obvious reasons these programs are offered at times which avoid weather ex-

Box 1
Interpretive Tips for Working
with the Very Young

1.   Limit adults to one per child. This more effectively permits adults and children to focus on the program.

2.   Keep the class size small; a maximum of 10, although fewer would be better. Otherwise, it may become too chaotic for an effective program.

3.   Incorporate an element (or several elements) of surprise.

4.   Keep the program relatively short and moving rapidly to accommodate short attention spans.

5.   Be sure the area is childproof (safe and nontoxic).

6.   See that each child has an opportunity for direct contact with the interpreter.

7.   Encourage vocalization through use of songs, rhymes, and animal noises. It isn't going to be quiet anyway, so make positive use of noise!

8.   Encourage movement. Again, this will occur anyway, so channel it into good learning opportunities.

tremes, as well as avoiding early morning, meal times, and early afternoon nap times. A short trail with a smooth, level surface is best for this type of walk. The intent of the program is to expose babies to nature, in a positive way.

Just as adults can never be too old, children can never be too young to enjoy nature. During the walk, babies are encouraged to imitate their parents in using their senses to explore natural objects. "Even though babies may not converse with their caregivers, they gain just from hearing words, the tone of a voice, and the enthusiasm."[21] The overall goal of the program is to allow the child and adult to become familiar with, and feel comfortable in, their surroundings. As just one example, participants learn experientially about trees. Parents and their babies explore the textures of bark, compare shapes of leaves, smell bark or foliage, and listen to the rustling of leaves in the wind.

Adults learn that such shared nature outings are a rewarding way to spend time with their baby. What the babies learn to enjoy now, they will not fear later.

Providing Quality Interpretation
for Children

From a general and practical perspective, Tilden and Mills agreed that children are capable of rapid learning, delight in the superlative, are generally lacking in inhibitions, desire personal examination of items through all of the senses, relish companionship, and thrive on a sense of adventure. [22]

With these broad insights in mind, the interpreter attempts to answer the question, "How can interpretive programs be designed to be exciting and effective for children?" (see Box 2).

Box 2
The Effective Children's Interpreter Should:

Shed inhibitions!

Be patient!

Be creative!

Tell a story!

Create a sense of adventure!

Be animated and positive!

Show interest in what the kids are interested in!

> Maintain some semblance of order,
> without stifling the kids!
>
> Love kids!
>
> SMILE!!

Gary Machlis and Donald Field explored the concept of "connecting" interpretive programs with children. "Getting connected" requires an understanding of the developmental stages of childhood and in what ways these offer interpretive opportunities or limitations. Note that the phases of childhood are strictly conceptual and a continuum of development gradually occurs, not always exactly on schedule and often in transition. "Connecting" children with interpretation requires consideration of children's social groups.[23] The intent of the group will have a bearing on the message. The role of the interpreter may range from inspirational to educational to recreational.

The group size will also have a bearing on the structure of the program. Small groups are more conducive to learning and inspirational experiences than larger groups.

The group's composition is another important consideration. It is useful to know the age range of the children, as well as social and educational backgrounds. What is of interest to the children? What have they been studying in school? To what degree do they have experiences in natural landscapes? What are their fears? What would they like, or what do they need, to know? Ideally, knowledge of the group's social context can be used as a motivational tool to get the group "connected" to the interpretation. This knowledge can also be useful in providing briefing materials for the group prior to the visit.

The interpretive approach for children, according to Machlis and Field, is derived from three basic modes of human expression: action, fantasy, and instruction.[24] Allowing children to become involved in the interpretation is critical. They learn best through active and appropriate participation. Demonstrations that involve children in an activity are especially effective.

Fantasy can be a "powerful and far reaching mode of inter-pretation" for children.[25] For example, interpreters can effectively combine action with fantasy to engage children in play-acting to replicate past events and to provide a notion of how and why people responded as they did. Although children are so often involved in imaginative pursuits, "this approach is seldom openly used by in-terpretation planners and programmers."[26]

For children, as with adults, the success of instruction is re-lated to its degree of meaningfulness and usefulness (which re-turns us to the first principle). A combination of action, fantasy, and instruction approaches can be orchestrated to educate, moti-vate and inspire any given children's group. This, as with all good interpretation, takes thought, research, planning, and care.

Tilden suggested, in terms of the cost and staffing of children's programs, "there is no preserve so small that it cannot employ some devices [for interpreting to children], if it desires to do interpreta-tion at all."[27] Enos Mills considered the end result as follows, "Chil-dren from Nature's Book and School stand highest in the examina-tions of life and carry life's richest treasures: health, individuality, sincerity, wholesome self-reliance, and efficiency."[28]

Teenagers

When I was a boy of fourteen, my father was so ignorant I could hardly stand to have the old man around. But when I got to be twenty-one, I was astonished at how much he had learned in seven years.

—Mark Twain

As Mark Twain observed, teenagers can be judgmental, harsh, incorrigible, and self-centered. They may be every bit as belliger-ent as two-year-olds, but without so many of the other defining (and redeeming) qualities noted in the previous section. Teenag-ers are seemingly in a world consumed by themselves and their peers. They are often stereotyped as having a general lack of re-sponsibility and quarrelsome nature, but many teenagers contra-dict this stereotype and are fine citizens contributing to their schools and communities. Through an understanding of teenagers, and with careful planning, they can be successfully brought into an interpre-tive program.

Relating to teenagers does not mean interpreters should act like teenagers by adopting their vocabulary and mannerisms. Interpreters should treat teenagers as young adults emphasizing mutual respect and responsibility.

Teenagers tend to prefer being with their peers. They want independence from parents and traditional family groups. They are action-oriented and enjoy physical challenges. They want to *do* something. Teenagers tend to be more focused on their future than their history. Interpretation may be structured with these motivations in mind. For example, historical messages should relate past events to current or future consequences.

It is possible to target interpretive programs specifically for teens. At Burr Oak Woods Conservation Nature Center in Blue Springs, Missouri, programs for teenagers are offered under the umbrella title, "Wild Ones." Specific programs include the following: Sketching Wildflowers (the basics of sketching wildflowers and other natural objects), Back 40 Hike ("a mega-hike through uncharted territory"), Fly Tying (tying three or four fishing flies), Orienteering (using map and compass), Creek Crawl (looking for wildlife signs and picking up trash), and Bonfire (roasting weiners and marshmallows while listening to pioneer tales and ghost stories).[29]

Another approach to attracting teens is to permit them to be totally involved in your program as volunteers (see Box 3).

Box 3
Principles for Working with Teenagers

1. The person working with teens must be genuinely interested in them.

2. Working with teens may be professional and personal. Teens will look to their peers for direction, but will also seek adult's opinions in addition (often preferred) to those of their parents.

3.   Teens need time—working with them requires a lot of physical and emotional time and effort.

4.   Teens are confident (on the outside) and don't feel they need to learn anymore. Get them working on a task together and they are seemingly unstoppable.

5.   At this age teens want to be with their friends. Allow them to work together, but do not allow cliques to form.

6.   Allow for fun times. For example, visit other nature centers, go canoeing or hiking, or eat pizza together.

7.   Provide positive support and motivation. Let the teens know that what they are doing is important.

8.   Give teens as much responsibility as they are competent and comfortable with.

Adapted from Michele Baumer's "Principles for Working with Teenagers"—an unpublished statement requested by the authors.

The Stevens Nature Center at Hemlock Bluffs Nature Preserve in Cary, North Carolina, designed an interpretive program to generate excitement among teens. This is a long-term program, called Hemlock Rangers, in which the goal is to "develop an awareness for the intricacies of the natural world which leads to stewardship for the environment at the local level."[30]

Teenagers are exposed to a "hear it, see it, do it" process that has proved successful. The volunteer teens work along-side preserve staff on a variety of projects from erosion control to wildlife habitat improvement. Sessions begin with a roundtable discussion which allows for an open channel of communication between the staff and teens. Next is a learning phase—an audio-visual presentation detailing why the project is important. Next is the actual work in the preserve. It is this hands-on approach to learning that works so well with teens. As they internalize these activities, "they can form positive ideas about natural resource management that can lead to a feeling of stewardship for the environment." [31]

At Runge Conservation Nature Center in Jefferson City, Missouri, teens are even more integrated into the interpretive program where they take on the responsibility of giving presentations and leading walks. Teens tend to think that they, like Mark Twain at the age of fourteen, know everything. Therefore, when asked to lead a hike or other program "they are not afraid and will give the presentation with zeal and gusto." [32] In an interview with a local newspaper about why it is important to teach others about conservation, one teen volunteer noted, "Earth's natural ecosystem is being altered, and in some cases, destroyed by man. I think that we should learn to conserve earth's resources and encourage others to do so before it is too late." [33] It can be useful in designing experiences for teens to know what motivates them to volunteer (see Box 4).

Box 4
Why Teenagers Volunteer

By understanding the motivation of teens, interpreters may better structure volunteer experiences.

- Young teens volunteer to have something to do, to be with friends, or to be away from home.

- Mature teens volunteer to give back to the community.

- College bound or career-oriented teens volunteer for job experience.

- Some teens volunteer as a part of a civic group (e.g., scouts).

- Some teens have a strong interest in nature.

Adapted from Michele Baumer's "Why Teenagers Volunteer"—an unpublished statement requested by the authors.

Seniors

First you forget names, then you forget faces, then you forget to
pull your zipper up, then you forget to pull your zipper down.
                                                    —Leo Rosenburg

One view of aging suggests that the older years are a period of steady decline as noted, with humor, in the quote above. This perspective focuses on the older years as a time of social useless- ness and personal hopelessness—being senile, lonely, and cranky.

The other view is of the older years as a time of personal growth and accomplishment. This perspective has been advocated in a number of popular books of recent years including *Ageless Body, Timeless Mind* (by Deepak Chopra), *Forever Young* (by Stuart Berger), and *New Passages* (by Gail Sheehy).

We will advocate the view that each year of life provides oc- casions for renewal as well as vitality. Although aging does result in losses, primarily physiological, these are a natural part of the aging process. [34] In addition there are positive aspects associated with aging (see Box 5).

Box 5
Some Positive Characteristics of Older Persons

They are:

Patient and kind.

Wise and knowing.

More dependable.

A powerful political force.

Free to do as they choose.

Peaceful and serene.

Adapted from F. McGuire, R. Boyd and R. Tedrick, 1996, Leisure and Aging.

We are currently experiencing the greying of America. More people 65 and over live in this country than ever before. Furthermore, older individuals are generally more healthy, financially secure, adventuresome, knowledgeable, independent, and vocal than previous generations of seniors.[35] Serving older persons through quality interpretation will be increasingly important in interpretive programming.

Seniors have a strong intrinsic interest in subjects dealing with the past. At historical sites, older persons may have lived through the events or heard tales of those times. They like to reflect on the past. Sometimes interpretation will trigger important memories.

Seniors appreciate depth in interpretive programs. Their knowledge and experience allows them to make connections between concepts. They have a sophisticated grasp of time, so they may relate better to interpretation of complex life cycles and long-term processes such as succession or eutrophication. Sixty-year timber rotations and 100-year-old buildings may mean more to them than to children or teenagers.

Older persons tend to visit interpretive sites more frequently in the off-seasons when they are less crowded. They often stay longer than other visitors and therefore are more likely to understand the resources on a deeper level, and also ask more questions. This interest and attentiveness can make for rewarding interpretation.

Certain physical limitations may impede participation by older persons. These limitations, associated with the aging process, include lack of stamina, vision, hearing, and mobility. However, all of the common ailments of the elderly can be mitigated (e.g., shorter hikes to accommodate those with less stamina, larger print for visual impairment, assisted listening devices for hearing impairment, and paved surfaces with gentle slopes for those with restricted mobility). In an age when older persons run marathons, those who are physically fit should be encouraged to participate in more demanding interpretive activities.

Researchers studied elderly visitors to national parks and concluded that interpreters should consider age-specific programs for seniors.[36] They found that older persons appreciate social interaction with peers. Special programs for seniors allow for a common ground of sharing between participants. These programs also negate the possibility of disruptions by unruly children. (Older persons are not especially tolerant of unruly children, unless they are the grandparents of those children.) Typically seniors prefer day programs rather than evening ones. Overall, eliminating distractions, mitigating age-related impairments, scheduling activities at favorable times, and creating a synergistic and enthusiastic atmosphere between peers, enhances and promotes interest by older persons.

In addition to promoting separate programs, interpreters can target older persons to assist through rewarding volunteer opportunities or to assist the program financially (see Chapter Twelve). People with higher incomes, more education, and professional types of occupations (much of the older adult population) are not only more likely to give money to worthy causes, but more likely to volunteer their time to organizations. [37]

Age is not all decay; it is the ripening, the swelling, of the fresh life within, that withers and bursts the husk.

-George MacDonald

Interpreters can meet the needs of people throughout the lifespan-from the tender stem of young growth, to the budding flower, to the green formative fruit, to the ripe fruit bursting with new life. There has been tremendous growth in segmenting and serving children over the past few decades in interpretive-related ventures. We expect to see similar growth in segmenting and serving teenagers and older persons in the future.

Chapter Seven

BRINGING THE PAST ALIVE

E very place has a history. Interpreters can bring the past alive to make the present more enjoyable and the future more meaningful.

There is no peculiar merit in ancient things, but there is merit in integrity, and integrity entails the keeping together of the parts of any whole, and if those parts are scattered throughout time, then the maintenance of integrity entails a knowledge, a memory, of ancient things.... To think, feel or act as though the past is done with, is equivalent to believing that a railway station through which our train has just passed, only existed for as long as our train was in it.

— Edward Hyams

Presenting interpretive programs which have a historical content relies on relating to the audience, revealing deeper meaning and truth, and inspiring individuals as discussed in previous chapters. Methods that apply to all interpretive efforts are valid in the interpretation of history. In this chapter our focus will be on living history and current dilemmas in historical interpretation.

Living History

In many respects, interpreting historical objects and events is not significantly different from interpreting natural resource themes. The fundamental principles and techniques of effective interpretation do not change with the subject. Heritage interpretation and natural resource interpretation take place in similar settings. Both occur in museums and visitor centers; along trails and roadsides; and at public parks and private tourist attractions. Every natural area has a history to interpret and every historic site is linked to a natural resource base that can be fruitfully interpreted.

History interpreters give talks and lead walks, sometimes in costume, sometimes in uniform. A study of 122 heritage sites found that 95 percent used personal interpretation, with guided tours at 84 percent of the sites.[1]

The most distinctive interpretive approach is living history. Living history has been defined as the recreation of specific periods of the past or specific events using interpreters usually clothed and equipped with the correct tools and accouterments of a depicted era.[2]

When the interpreter is playing the role of a specific character or visitor from the past it is considered "first-person" interpretation. This approach occurs at 38 percent of heritage sites.[3] When the living history interpreter is in costume, but is speaking *about* the historic characters or events, rather than pretending to be an actual person from that time period, then it is considered "third-person" style. This approach was represented at 43 percent of heritage sites.[4] Third-person living history is sometimes referred to as "costumed" interpretation.

Some living history interpreters portray common people carrying out typical activities associated with life in a particular period. Others portray famous individuals or reenact an important event. For years, Lee Stetson has been entertaining and educating audiences at Yosemite National Park with his portrayal of John Muir. Similarly, professional actor Earll Kingston gives a captivating portrayal of John Wesley Powell to evening crowds at Grand Canyon National Park.

In conducting first-person interpretation, the interpreter becomes totally immersed in the identity of the historic person portrayed. This involves more than merely wearing authentic clothes, exhibiting authentic objects or demonstrating certain skills. The best living history interpreters know the subtle mannerisms, perceptions, and attitudes of the people they are portraying. They delve into the mind of the character to fully understand and become that person.

Such visitors from the past feign total ignorance of events that have occurred since their time and act oblivious to modern conveniences and lifestyles. First-person interpreters must think quickly and respond in character when visitors challenge the time period context (e.g., by calling attention to a plane flying overhead) or ask unsolicited questions that would draw the interpreter out of character.

Living history provides tremendous opportunities for visitor involvement and enjoyment. Participants can see, hear, touch, and even, at times, smell the past. With just a little imagination visitors can slip back in time and become immersed in the presentation.

Living history provides opportunities for serious amateurs to demonstrate skills and share their interest in history. Results can be impressive when individuals from specific ethnic groups are given the opportunity to perform an authentic interpretation of their heritage and culture. In short, for both participants and observers, living history presents the closest tactile conception we have of our past.[5]

Jay Anderson, in *Time Machines: The World of Living History*, noted, "Living history is a medium of historical research [such as Thor Heyerdahl's highly publicized imitative South Sea voyages], interpretation, and celebration that is absolutely right for our times."[6] He identified the following three characteristics which insure its significance as an effective way to interpret history:[7]

1. Living history strives for what T.S. Eliot called "felt-truth." It challenges us to think *and* feel. To living historians, empathy is as important as understanding.
2. The medium is presbyterian. Living history lies outside the boundary of established academic and public history. It thrives on independence. Each museum, each project, and each unit makes its own covenant with historical truth and determines the way it will carry on its dialogue with the past.
3. Finally, living history rejects a linear view of the past. It argues that, before you can study a forest, you must become totally familiar with the trees. Living historians point out that the history establishment has often failed to study, interpret, and experience the everyday reality of ordinary people in the past.

Like all interpretive media, living history techniques have some disadvantages and limited applications. David Peterson provided a dissenting opinion to Anderson's enthusiastic treatment of living history in an essay titled, "There is no Living History, There are no Time Machines." Peterson suggested that "living history" is an oxymoron: "Historical re-creations are imperfect interpretations of the past, not the past itself."[8] He acknowledged that good living history "is a popular and effective" interpretive tool, but that it does not fully depict *all* aspects of life. [9]

Living history programs are labor-intensive requiring much advance preparation. Besides the normal planning that would go into any interpretive endeavor, living history requires thorough researching and collecting—or creation—of accurate artifacts, props, sets, and costumes.

Staffing living history programs can also be problematic. It takes special people to carry-out living history, particularly first-person style. The ability to think quickly, some acting talent, and a high level of commitment are necessary to make the performance believable. Rather than using a script, living history interpreters typically have only an outline for direction. This allows the presentation to develop naturally as the interpreter interacts with visitors. Due to a high level of audience involvement and flexibility, living history interpreters must be able to *ad lib*.

Living history interpretation requires an ability to gauge the audiences' comfort level and willingness to participate, because sometimes this medium gets in the way of the message. Costumed interpreters pretending to be living in the past may confuse or intimidate visitors. The sight of men milling around in Revolutionary War uniforms and engaging visitors in conversation may send some visitors scurrying. Although visitor participation is a desirable aspect of living history, some visitors may feel uncomfortable. We need to know how our visitors react to such presentations and then prepare them in advance for unconventional deliveries.

Visitors like to know what they are getting themselves into if they choose to participate in an interpretive activity. In fairness to our visitors we must educate them using signs, brochures, announcements, and other typical media to allow them to make informed decisions about whether to get involved. During this visitor preparation process, we can encourage involvement by revealing the benefits of participation in the program.

Another potential limiting factor of living history is the difficulty of protecting artifacts. Living history environments are usually not as protected as a sealed museum case where environmental factors such as light, humidity, and temperature can be controlled. Because of the nature of living history programs, objects are more likely to come in contact with visitors. This increases the chances of wear and tear, or worse, vandalism. For these reasons, replicas rather than original objects are often used in such situations. And, as will be discussed in detail below, living history has limited application in situations associated with cruelty, suffering, and death.

In spite of these limiting factors, living history has proven to be a valuable interpretive medium. It is widely popular with the public and this popularity continues to grow. Living history speaks powerfully to people today. Clay Jenkinson, a Jeffersonian scholar, conducts living history presentations as Thomas Jefferson. Dressed as President Jefferson, he answers questions about contemporary issues using Jefferson's words.[10] In response to a question about use of U.S. troops in Bosnia, Jenkinson, as Jefferson, says, "I am an isolationist." To a question about the increase in militia groups in the United States, he replies, "Terror is an important tool of liberty. I would never renounce it. But if a militia exists only on the fringe, and the majority does not approve of its ways, then it cannot be considered a militia in any sense of the term." Jenkinson has taken Jefferson's words to prisons, elementary schools, and even the White House. He has spoken to oenophiles about Jefferson's wine cellar and to Mayo Clinic staff about Jefferson's medical theories. People have an interest in what Jefferson has to say to them today. They seek his wisdom and, according to Jenkinson, they want Jefferson's approval. Modern Americans don't want Jefferson to be disappointed in what has become of the United States. [11]

Even Peterson, in his dissenting essay, admitted, "Historical re-creations indeed seem to make the past come alive." [12] Living history allows us to learn about the past in compelling ways and how the past affects the present and the future.

Interpretation Dilemmas:
Debauchery, Disney, and Death

History is a set of lies agreed upon.
> —Napoleon Bonaparte

Interpretation of history is based on interpreting other people's interpretations of events. Thus, interpreters find themselves interpreting *interpretations*. Like geologists, cosmologists, and paleontologists who also find themselves interpreting the past, interpreters of human history are faced with speculative and controversial themes. The difficulty in defining historical truth has been noted by many including Napoleon. The interpreter's task is to sort through the agreed-upon lies for truth.

Interpreting human deeds may be both easier and more difficult than interpreting a rock formation or a grove of trees. It can be easier to identify compelling stories in human actions than to find powerful stories about nonhuman objects or processes. On the other hand, the complexities and mysteriousness of human nature make it sometimes difficult to derive meaning and identify truth.

Debauchery: Filtered Facts

A difficulty with interpreting history is that the values which form the basis of our interpretations of historical events change. The facts about human actions do not change, but historians and society at large assign meanings and motives to historic deeds within their current ethical frameworks. Society judges historical characters by this continually shifting framework and so our assessments of their actions shift. For example, in recent decades, General George Custer and Christopher Columbus have undergone metamorphoses from heroes to villains in the eyes of many people.

John Golda traced variations in Americans' assessment of the Conquistadors and their actions. The following discussion is based on his review and illustrates the challenges of interpreting a shifting, value-laden, historical subject.

"In 1899, renowned historian Hubert H. Bancroft wrote in his book *The New Pacific* that the Spanish in the New World were 'by nature unjust, untruthful, and merciless.' This was an understandably popular view of the Spanish as the Spanish-American War raged on."[13] Soon after the war ended, as Americans became intrigued with the expeditions of other nations into what became the United States, historians portrayed these same men—among them Cabrillo, de Soto, and Coronado—as courageous and noble, living in a world of enchantment. Tales of adventure and romance thrilled us.

During the 1920s and 1930s, historians began to acknowledge the roles of native cultures that pre-dated the explorers. A broader and richer interpretation of events developed as historians considered different cultures in our history.

In the 1960s and 1970s, at the height of the civil rights and environmental movements, Americans became more sensitive to the plight of native peoples and developed an awareness of cultural accountability. Rather than romantic and adventurous, the Conquistadors' actions were seen as debauchery and ruthless destruction of a wondrous landscape.[14]

By the 1990s, the Conquistadors' age of exploration was evaluated as "years of environmental despoliation and waste, of ignorant and destructive transplantation of one culture, and agriculture, heedlessly upon another."[15] A pervasive modern view is that instead of bringing the benefits of Western Civilization to the New World, Conquistadors destroyed what existed and replaced it with something alien.

Golda concluded, "In their actions, one can see the best and worst of human nature. In examining the interpretations of their history, one is given a mirror on the ideals and concerns of generations of Americans. Ultimately, the role of history is to provide the opportunity to examine ourselves and how we have become what we are today."[16]

As heritage interpreters develop themes and theses, their choices should acknowledge our changes in values over time. We should also be aware of, and sensitive to, audience members holding diverse values through which they interpret historical events.

Disney: History Interpretation and Commercial Entertainment

God cannot alter the past, but historians can.
—Samuel Butler

The popularity of living history presentations makes them vulnerable to becoming merely money-making entertainment. The lure of potential profits may corrupt heritage interpretation by determining which themes will be presented and in what ways. Today, Samuel Butler might add script writers, exhibit designers, and theatrical producers to the list of those who can alter history.

Commercial and public sites that generate revenue from fees may want to "jazz up" a historical presentation to make it more entertaining, even if it means drifting from the facts. Some of this may be rationalized as poetic license. Or, it may be shrugged off with the belief that nobody will notice fallacies. Of course, there should be zero tolerance of misleading or false information.

This issue surfaced nationally when the Disney Corporation *proposed* building a historic theme park in Virginia. Disney Chairman Michael Eisner said the theme park would "include reminders of the painful, disturbing, and agonizing chapters in our history, from the introduction of slaves to the struggle in Vietnam."[17] However, the park's general manager said, "The idea is to walk out of 'Disney's America' with a smile on your face. We don't want people to come out with a sour face. It is going to be fun with a capital F."[18] Can "agonizing chapters in our history" be made fun—with a capital F? To be a financial success in a mass tourism market, apparently, history must be fun, even if it means ignoring or modifying the facts. Columnist David Broder noted that "... the more Disney rewrites history into myth and converts America into Fantasyland, the more popular the park may be."[19]

We do not intend to make a villain of the Disney Corporation. Disney wonderfully interprets American history at Epcot's American Pavilion and their service orientation to guests is a model for the way all interpretive sites should treat their visitors. But, in the Magic Kingdom and other historic venues, there may be illicit incentive to have the facts take a back seat to entertainment.

Death: "War Is Hell"

In anticipation of the 50th anniversary of World War II, James Bigley wrote a thoughtful essay titled, "Living History and Battle Reenactment: The Dilemma of Selective Interpretation" in which he contrasts Stud Terkel's portrayal of WWII as "The Good War" with Civil War General William Sherman's notion that "war is hell."[20] Bigley observed that battle reenactments can evoke a wave of nostalgia for selective aspects of WWII—"a unified country, rampant patriotism, Glenn Miller dance bands, Rosie the Riveter and the joyous homecoming of a victorious army."[21]

Likewise, interpreters may selectively interpret relatively safe aspects of war such as the technology used or strategies employed, while ignoring the grim realities of the social impact of war—the pain and sorrow associated with death, devastation, and destruction.

But, how far should an interpreter go in presenting death and destruction? We suggested that interpreters go beyond statistics to interpret a "whole" in Chapter Five. When interpreters go beyond statistics at battlefields, they risk either glorifying or trivializing the "hell" of war and offending people in the process. It is generally considered good technique to make interpretation participatory and enjoyable. How can this be done when the subject is warfare? Is it appropriate to interpret acts of cruelty or war with hands-on exhibits? Is it appropriate to make these exhibits fun? (See Box 1)

Box 1
A "Hands-on" Wartime Exhibit

My first and most memorable childhood interpretive experience occurred on a Sunday afternoon visit to Chicago's Museum of Science and Industry with my grandfather. The Vietnam War was raging. I ran up the long marble steps hurrying to get to the new exhibit – a replica of an Army helicopter complete with gunner's chair. While sitting behind a mounted machine gun visitors could shoot and score hits on Vietnamese villages and people passing below. This hands-on exhibit did a masterfully realistic job of interpreting what it was like being the gunner in a helicopter gunship flying over the forests and rice paddies of Vietnam.

This was decades before video games and color television was still a novelty. Children stood in long lines for the chance to sit behind one of the machine guns and play with this marvelously realistic toy. To the child's mind it was a high-tech shooting gallery. I took my turn.

I remember being confused when I left the museum to find adults carrying signs and passing out literature protesting the very exhibit that had just brought me so much pleasure. As I passed through the protesters—they were local church members—I received a leaflet demanding that the exhibit be closed.

Years later, as I approached draft age, death and destruction became more real and I understood why people protested such a fun exhibit. High-tech simulations where killing becomes the object of participation trivialize war and are not appropriate.

-T.C.

To responsibly interpret war, it is necessary to include the tragic social impacts. However, it is unnecessary to include these in a gruesome, sensationalistic manner that distracts from interpretive objectives or offends audience members.

With the culturally diverse audiences we serve, we are challenged with presenting an objective program. Native Americans at the Little Bighorn Battlefield, Japanese visitors to Pearl Harbor, and southern visitors to Civil War battlefields require sensitive treatment. Interpreters must be thoroughly informed to correct misconceptions and prepared to bring different perspectives together in a balanced manner. In interpreting the "hell" of war, interpreters should reinforce that both sides were dying for what they thought was right and both sides fought for their beliefs.[22]

Reenactments

One genre of living history interpretation, at some sites, is military reenactment. Often hobbyists come by the hundreds from all over the country to reenact wartime events, usually a battle. Realism is normally something to be strived for in interpretation, but for obvious reasons reenactors fall short of total commitment to this concept on the battlefield.

What happens when a private reenactment group wants to use your site to carry out an extravaganza that will attract large crowds and, perhaps, large profits? Using "Tora Tora Tora," the Confederate Air Force's reenactment of the bombing of Pearl Harbor as an example, Bigley investigated the issue of selectively interpreting only impersonal aspects of war (see Box 2).

BOX 2
"TORA TORA TORA!"
Working with Reenactors to Eliminate Selective Interpretation

The Texas-based Confederate Air Force (CAF) is famous for its spectacular, spine-tingling reenactment of the bombing of Pearl Harbor. As Japanese dive bombers streak low over the horizon heading for an airfield lined with American troops and aircraft, a public address announcer shouts "Air raid, Pearl Harbor—This is no drill!" Radio-controlled explosions on the ground appear to coincide with the aircraft dropping their bombs. Unsuspecting ground personnel scatter for their lives. More planes come and more explosions and flames rip across the ground. The whole time an announcer gives a play by play to the crowd of spectators. Above the crowd, dogfights ensue, complete with orange muzzle flashes from the aircraft machine guns and sound recordings of the gunfire. Ground forces wear authentic World War II uniforms, carry authentic gear and weapons, and drive authentic vehicles. The several thousand spectators are totally enthralled, glued to their seats for the 30-minute performance. When the smoke clears, they leave having been fully entertained and having seen, heard, and felt the historic weapons and aircraft. And, in the aftermath of the battle, the sponsoring agency is left with huge financial and public relations gains.

By any measure of entertainment or financial impact the "Tora Tora Tora" reenactment is a resounding success. However, "Tora Tora Tora" and other similar battlefield reenactments raise many questions for living history interpreters. What are the interpretive objectives of such presentations? How far can interpreters go in recreating life and death struggles of people, sometimes the struggles of people who are still alive? How detailed and explicit should interpreters be in recreating the suffering and carnage? Should they ignore the ugly aspects of war?

Specifically, in terms of interpretation, what was accomplished by the "Tora Tora Tora" show? During the "Tora Tora Tora" presentation spectators get a clear, accurate and multi-sensory picture of the equipment used by both sides in the battle. Like artifact exhibitions at many museums, reenactments focus on the technology, thereby presenting an incomplete view of war. People often are more interested in the weapons of war than the social impact of war. They want to see and hear muskets fire, bombs drop, and cannons bombard realistic targets. But, that is not the complete story of the battle. People seem less interested in the rest of the story—the results of that technology on human lives and property. When spectators do consider the human impacts of war, they tend to revel in acts of heroism, family involvement or nationalistic pride. They distinguish the good guys from the bad guys.

It doesn't have to be this way. Reenactments can move away from being merely war games and instead educate the public about both the technology and social impacts of war. The Admiral Nimitz Museum in Fredericksburg, Texas uses many types of media to interpret the social history of the Pacific theater of World War II. Administrators there believe that reenactments provide a "texture" that embraces all the traditional interpretive media by allowing people to experience the sights and sounds of war. They offer annual symposia and special exhibits along with more typical museum exhibits and reference materials. As part of the 50th Anniversary of the Pearl Harbor attack, the Nimitz Museum decided to present the Confederate Air Force's "Tora Tora Tora" reenactment. However, the staff had the foresight and wisdom to act on their concerns about the lack of interpretive content in the commentary and the selective nature of the reenactment. Museum staff had a series of meetings with CAF officials. The result was a revised script, including new elements mentioning casualties, and the attack's impact on the American psyche and future war efforts. Now at the conclusion of many reenactments, medical teams reenact the evacuation of casualties from the battlefield while a commentator explains the grim realities of the battle.

To responsibly interpret war, it is necessary to include the tragic social impacts. However, it is unnecessary to include these in a sensationalistic manner.

Administrators do not necessarily have to forego the profits and goodwill that reenactments bring to their sites. However, it behooves them to keep a tight rein in matters of authenticity and accuracy. They should work with the reenactors to identify, in writing, the interpretive objectives and strategies for achieving those objectives.

Adapted from Bigley, 1991, "Living History and Battle Reenactment—The Dilemma of Selective Interpretation."

Obviously, a reenactment must be consistent with the mission and interpretive objectives for the site. If this is the case, then it is possible to work with these groups ahead of time to ensure that they present an accurate reenactment and that they use appropriate uniforms and equipment. Any time outsiders or volunteers are used in historical interpretation they should receive training on interpretive objectives, appropriate themes, visitor sensitivities, cultural biases, and principles of interpretation. In this way, volunteers can be integrated into the staff in a meaningful way.

Graphic "blood and guts" reenactments and high-tech simulations of suffering and death may be offensive. Seemingly real demonstrations of battlefield bullet extractions or amputations exceed most measures of good taste. These portrayals of pain are not necessary to convince audiences that "war is hell." At best, such reenactments may leave people focusing on special effects rather than on the message. Visitors walk away asking "How did they do that?"

Although a strong supporter of living history, the National Park Service recognizes that violent, private, or repulsive themes should not be reenacted. The NPS has policy prohibiting simulated warfare that involves "firing" at opposing lines or the "taking of casualties." This policy is rooted both in concerns for participant and visitor safety and also a belief that a battle simulation is a travesty with regard to those who actually endured it.[23] The NPS uses oral history accounts, slide shows, exhibits, film footage, books, and brochures to interpret warfare.

A further limitation of living history is that certain events are not appropriate for reenactment, (e.g., the Bataan Death March and Nazi concentration camps).[24] Instead, the Holocaust Memorial Museum in Washington, D.C. offers a powerful interpretation of the persecution and murder of six million Jews and millions of other victims of Nazi tyranny from 1933 to 1945 using a variety of emotionally moving exhibits. The mission of the museum is to inform Americans about this unprecedented tragedy, to remember those who suffered, and to inspire visitors to contemplate the moral implications of their choices and responsibilities as citizens in an interdependent world.[25]

Interpreters must thoughtfully consider their interpretive goals and as they do, remember to interpret not only Terkel's goodness, but also Sherman's hell. Balance is the key. Furthermore, we must avoid choosing themes or theses built around trendy topics. In developing a theme or thesis, we should make sure it is period or site specific—historically correct for its time, not just politically correct for ours.[26]

History fights a stereotype of dark museum hallways, dusty books, and boring lectures. That is not what historical interpretation is about today. Tilden stated that the ideal interpretation implies re-creation of the past and kinship with it.[27] The mission of history interpreters is to re-create the past in such a way as to make the past come alive. As we shall see in the next chapter, history interpreters can use high-tech tools such as interactive computers and sophisticated multi-media technology to carry out this mission. We can be enriched and enthralled by heroic deeds and we can empathize and be inspired by common people who lived their lives in a different time and place.

There is merit in keeping together the parts of any whole, and in maintaining a memory of ancient things. The past is not something we are done with and can forget. A healthy society has a vivid and accurate memory. Interpreters contribute to that memory.

▪ *Chapter Eight* ▪

HIGH-TECH GADGETRY

H igh technology can reveal the world in exciting new ways. However, incorporating this technology into the interpretive program must be done with foresight and care.

The central struggle of men has ever been to understand one another, to join together for the common weal. And it is this very thing that the machine helps them to do! It begins by annihilating time and space.

—Antoine de Saint-Exupéry (1939)

It is unlikely that Enos Mills or Freeman Tilden ever imagined the possibilities associated with using current technologies in interpretation. New tools are available to interpreters as technology races ahead opening the doors to new worlds, both virtual and real. Interpretive sites are making application of everything from holograms and animatronics to computer-based CD-ROMs and satellite distance education. Through high-tech gadgetry, local nature centers and the smallest of museums have expanded their sphere of influence both on-site and to the world beyond.

Computer technology allows us to travel the globe with just a few clicks of the mouse. Museums and parks are locating themselves on the "information super highway" so that people from all over the world can learn about their resources (see Box 1). Professional organizations such as the Museum Computer Network (MCN) have been formed to assist interpreters as they make use of computer technology.

Box 1
Museum Visits Without Walking

This morning I visited the Field Museum of Natural History in Chicago and toured their "Life Over Time" exhibit. I watched videos of *Triceratops* and sabertooth cats, and saw a *Moropus* eat. Then I played some interactive quiz games about dinosaurs. Before leaving the exhibit I got a copy of a Teacher's Guide and took a quick glance at an exhibit of 80 Javanese masks. I next traveled to the Denver Museum of Natural History to see their "Imperial Tombs of China" exhibit. I saw and read about some of the 250 artifacts recovered from the Imperial tombs. Then I returned to Chicago, this time visiting the Chicago Art Institute. There I got a copy of Hopper's "*Nighthawk's*" along with an interpretive commentary about the painting. I accomplished all of this without leaving my office. The possibilities for enrichment via the Internet are seemingly endless.

–T.C.

Mills wrote in a time before television and Tilden's concept of increasing levels of technology was limited to "more automatic projection equipment, more sound installations, more recorders and tapes, more gadgets to be self-operated by visitors, more motion pictures of fidelity and professional skill, and so on." [1]

Still, Tilden correctly predicted that "whether one likes it or not, we are going to have more—and I should hope, better—mechanical devices aimed at multiplying the interpretive effort." [2] Indeed, there are more, and better, devices today. Undoubtedly, there will be more, and better, devices tomorrow.

Throughout their writings, Mills and Tilden honor and revere humanness. Machines cannot express exhilaration or wonder. They cannot respond emotionally and spontaneously to the audience. Looking toward the future, Sydney Harris said, "The real danger is not that computers will begin to think like men, but that men will begin to think like computers."[3] We must be careful in our use and application of technology and maintain a human approach to interpretation.

We offer two observations which are not intended to be contradictory, but rather seed for thoughtful application of technology:

1) Machines by themselves can be impersonal and complex, and therefore counterproductive. It has been said, "Elegance without warmth is arrogance."[4] Likewise, high-tech exhibits that threaten the audience with their complexity or sophistication result in a technological arrogance. Many people, especially adults, are still intimidated by computers and other technological devices. Without friendly interpreters to personally encourage, assist, and guide visitors, the technologically timid will be driven away by the machines.

2) However, modern technology can allow visitors to view things that previously could not be seen, experience environments that could not be experienced, and manipulate and respond to stimuli that previously could not be perceived. These advances expand, rather than stifle, interpretive opportunities. We can open new worlds of meaningful experiences to our visitors.

Three important attributes characterize proper application of high technology. First, the technology should be engaging. Just because a high-tech exhibit is interactive does not mean that it will be effective. An activity must be perceived as something fun and rewarding. It must be challenging enough to be interesting without being so difficult that it frustrates participants. On the other hand, gadgets that are strictly fun, but not educational, have no place in an interpretation setting. Such gadgets distract people from the worthwhile exhibits.

Second, the technology must be dependable. High-tech exhibits must consistently perform well and be quickly serviced when they do not. High-tech gadgets can be expensive to purchase and they require regular maintenance which is also costly. Before a commitment is made to use gadgets, we must consider the costs in terms of what must be given up to acquire and maintain the technology. As Tilden noted, when gadgets are inoperative "they are a source of shame and chagrin, as well as an imposition on the public..."[5] Keeping high-tech machines operating can be time consuming. Frustrated interpreters in facilities with undependable gadgets have echoed Thoreau's lament "Lo! Men have become tools of their tools."[6]

Third, the best high-tech gadgets are those that "reveal" something. The power of many new technologies, whether in the fields of medicine, astrophysics or interpretation, lies in their ability to allow people to go beyond their senses to see things as we have never seen them before. High technology can reveal startling new perceptions about our world. For example, one of the most culturally profound revelations occurred when technology first allowed us to see the earth from space (see Box 2). Interpretive gadgets, whether microscopes, telescopes, satellite images, or computer simulations, should be judged on their power to *reveal*.

Box 2
Technological Revelations

Russell Schweickart reflecting on his Apollo 9 experience in Earth orbit:

Up there you go around every hour and a half, time after time after time. You wake up usually in the mornings. And just the way that the track of your orbits go, you wake up over the Mideast, over North Africa. As you eat breakfast you look out the window as you're going past and there's the Mediterranean area, and Greece, and Rome, and North Africa, and the Sinai, the whole area. And you realize in one glance that what you're seeing is what was the whole history of man for years–the cradle of civilization. And you think of all the history you can imagine looking at that scene.

And you go around down across North Africa and out over the Indian Ocean, and look up at that great sub-continent of India pointed down toward you as you go past it. And Ceylon off to the side, Burma, Southeast Asia, out over the Philippines, and up across that monstrous Pacific Ocean, vast body of water–you've never realized how big that is before. And you finally come up across the coast of California and look for those friendly things: Los Angeles, and Phoenix, and on across El Paso and

there's Houston, there's home, and you look and sure enough
there's the Astrodome. And you identify with that...

And the next thing you recognize in yourself, is you're
identifying with North Africa. You look forward to that, you
anticipate it. And there it is. That whole process begins to shift
what it is you identify with. When you go around it in an hour
and a half you begin to recognize that your identity is with the
whole thing. And that makes a change...

*Reflecting on the experience of an astronaut looking at the
Earth from the surface of the Moon:*

[I]t becomes so small and so fragile, and such a precious little
spot in the universe, that you can block it out with your thumb,
and you realize that on that small spot, that little blue and white
thing is everything that means anything to you. All of history and
music, and poetry and art and war and death and birth and love,
tears, joy, games, all of it is on that little spot out there that you
can cover with your thumb.

*Excerpt from speech by Russell Schweickart, Apollo 9
astronaut, to the Lindisfarne Association, 1974, printed as
"Whose Earth," in The Next Whole Earth Catalog, Stewart Brand
(Ed.), 1980. By permission of publisher and author.*

Video

The television generation, now equipped with seemingly ubiq-
uitous VCRs and camcorders, identifies with and has an affinity for
video format. Video programs are replacing slide shows, films, and
some personal presentations at many facilities. They are relatively
maintenance free, especially on videodisc format. Videodiscs are
superior to videotape because they last longer, have fewer maintenance problems, and offer higher quality resolution. The Smithsonian
and other agencies are copying their slide shows to videodiscs to
avoid the maintenance problems that slides present. Furthermore,
videos can be mass produced for easy distribution off-site and

multilingual versions can be made to serve a wide diversity of visitors.

Use of video in exhibits adds color, motion, and sound. These characteristics attract attention and are engaging. Although most people will watch a video exhibit for only three minutes or less, we can do several things to increase attention at video exhibits. First, we can make people more comfortable by having seating available. Second, we can control sounds that might compete with the audio narration or put in place acoustic barriers. Third, we can direct sound with parabolic speakers which hang from the ceiling and project sound downward, or offer headsets. Fourth, we can provide corresponding text for those who cannot hear well.

Animatronics

Animatronics are robots that are used in exhibits. John James Audubon, Charles Darwin, Abraham Lincoln and other notable individuals have been portrayed using animatronics. These robots typically have moving mouths and are capable of making some limited body movements as they "speak." The moving, speaking figure attracts and holds attention well. The animatronic Charles Darwin at "The Living World," the Saint Louis Zoo's high-tech exhibition center, was the exhibit visitors remembered best.[7]

Private sector robotic shows travel the country, attracting large crowds. Some interpretive programs have "booked" these shows into local malls and museums as a fund-raising venture. One such show is "Backyard Monsters: The World of Insects" ®. This touring exhibit has been viewed by over two million people since 1992. It features giant robotic insects that are anatomically correct down to minute details. These insects are shown in their typical backyard habitat. The exhibit has interactive educational play stations which introduce children to the world of insects and it includes a highly-acclaimed private insect collection in sophisticated easy-to-see showcases.

One potential problem associated with animatronics is that the amount of information learned from a robot monologue may be minimal. Initially, this was the case at "The Living World" Darwin exhibit. Learning was enhanced when staff at "The Living World" decided to reproduce the narrative on a graphic so people could read along. This also helped those with hearing impairments.[8]

Holograms

Holograms are three-dimensional images that project out of two-dimensional surfaces. They are created by reflecting laser light on photographic film. The curiosity of seeing apparently three-dimensional pictures on a flat surface is enough to attract the attention of most visitors.

Holograms can project several images in sequence or an image can appear to move as visitors shift position. Intrigued visitors may walk back and forth several times to replay the movement. "The Living World" has a hologram of a life size *Tyrannosaurus rex* skull and a series of head replicas of prehistoric hominids in order of their appearance in the fossil record.[9]

Although the technology has been available for some 30 years, holograms are still a novelty. Holograms have the advantage of using space efficiently by showing a three-dimensional object without taking up the physical space that the actual object would require. This was a motivating factor for using this technology at "The Living World" exhibit. Moreover, holograms can show motion without moving parts and without breakdowns. The limitations, besides the initial cost, are that holograms require special lighting, and floor plans must allow for these to be viewed from a particular angle and distance.

Interactive Computer Exhibits

Interactive computer exhibits can take three forms. They can be used as a reference device, as a personal tour guide, or they can offer simulation, often in the form of a game.

As a reference device, interactive computer exhibits allow visitors to retrieve information (textual or graphic) about a topic of their choosing. For example, the "Since You Were Born" exhibit at "The Living World" allows visitors to travel across time. Upon entering your date of birth, you receive a printout of environmental changes since then (e.g., acres of rainforest destroyed, population growth). Interactive computers can be used at information kiosks to direct visitors to a particular trail, program, or exhibit to meet their needs, interests, and abilities.

Interactive computers may serve as personal tour guides. Art museums have successfully used on-site computer exhibits to interpret works of art by directing visitors to make comparisons and contrasts, and by interpreting the meanings and significance of each piece of art, just as a museum guide might do. At some parks, visitors can get a guided tour of the park's features via interactive computer.

Simulation exhibits encourage visitors to manipulate variables, observe the effects, and respond to them. Computer "games" reward wise choices with points in a learning process. For example, players can become a certain animal in the food chain of an ecosystem and score points by successfully consuming a sufficient number of calories or by eating the correct prey while avoiding being eaten themselves. Such "games" teach ecological principles and simulate survival in nature. At Mount St. Helens, visitors can play the role of a "pioneer species" using a touch screen computer exhibit to make decisions about survival strategies in the post-eruption landscape. Participants learn about plant succession and how mammals, insects, and other organisms have reestablished themselves since the eruption.

Research has shown that interactive exhibits of any sort are more effective than passive exhibits at attracting and holding attention, and enhancing learning.[10] Interactive computer exhibits are no exception. They have been shown to strongly attract and hold attention and promote learning.[11]

A study at "The Living World" showed that computer interactives are second only to live animals in popularity, have the longest holding power of any exhibit, and are effective in teaching visitors. [12] Visitors who played a "Bat Game" that allowed them to use audio cues to hunt like a bat were far more likely to know that bats used echolocation and ate moths than those who did not play the game.[13]

Even without formal evaluation studies, interpreters at sites with interactive computer exhibits are touting them as their most effective exhibits. Word of mouth endorsements are spreading through the field and are so convincing that facilities which can afford them are switching from traditional displays to interactive computer exhibits.

For example, based on the extraordinary success of their existing computer exhibits, Runge Conservation Nature Center in Missouri is hoping to replace some traditional displays with additional interactive computers.This commitment to computer exhibits is especially noteworthy because the $3.7 million building containing $900,000 worth of displays had only been open for three years.The displays would be replaced based on the belief that the interactive exhibits are more effective, not because the existing exhibits are obsolete.[14]

Computers can make learning fun, and fun is a key ingredient to all interpretive efforts.To today's visitors, particularly younger people, playing an exciting and stimulating educational computer game about predator-prey relationships or the choices pioneers had to make on their travels is preferable to a static display or reading brochures on the same topics.

Interactive computer exhibits have other advantages.Touch screen technology makes them simple to use, even for those with limited dexterity. Computer exhibits can collect information about the visitors in an enjoyable and unobtrusive manner. These data can be stored and analyzed for visitor research and evaluation studies. Most important, by incorporating personal background information, and allowing the participant to choose subjects and levels of difficulty, computers can "individualize" the material.

Interactive computer exhibits can promote non-sequential learning. Unlike an interpretive talk, brochure, slide show or video, where every audience member receives the same introduction, body and conclusion, interactive computer exhibits allow people to select the kinds of information they receive and the level of detail. Instead of a linear process from a specific beginning to a specific conclusion, non-sequential learning can be pictured as an organizational chart with different layers of information. For example, an interactive exhibit about elk could first offer the opportunity to learn about general subjects such as what elk look like, their range, and their preferred habitat. Individuals wanting to learn more specific information could seek it in many directions. Those interested in food habits could access detailed information about elk diets and even link to scientific papers on the subject. Others might have heard an elk bugling and want to know about elk mating behavior. Such individuals could select information on that topic and if interested go on to learn about population dynamics within elk herds. Furthermore, quizzes or simulations can be provided as options, and at the most detailed level, visitors could access data bases from elk research projects. Within non-sequential learning environments participants select the path and the pace. This flexibility circumvents one of the most difficult challenges in interpretation—how to meet the needs of diverse audiences in a single display.

The Internet

Interpreters can now reach the world with information about their interpretive sites over the Internet. Parks or museums can have their own web sites providing sights and sounds as well as printed information. Some interpreters have their own home page with information ranging from favorite nature quotes to the birds they saw on their morning bird walk.

In the early 1990s many interpretive organizations developed Bulletin Board Systems (BBS). For the cost of a phone call, a person with a computer and modem could get up-to-date information about interpretive programs and other opportunities. Most organizations have replaced BBSs with web sites. Web sites allow parks or museums to provide current and accurate information in a cost-effective and environmentally sensitive way. People with Internet access can read on the computer screen or print interpretive brochures, articles, technical documents, program schedules, photographs, and maps. They can get up-to-the-minute weather or campground information, or make reservations for special exhibitions or events. Messages can be "posted" back and forth between users and naturalists or curators. Special subsections can be set up where people can ask questions about specific topics such as birds, astronomy, plants, or current environmental issues. Web sites have the advantages of being on-duty all day, every day of the year and they are relatively inexpensive. Web sites reduce the consumption of printed brochures and information sheets which are often discarded anyway, thereby reducing printing costs and potential litter. Postage and handling of mailings are also saved as the public comes to rely on the web site for information. Park agencies and museums use web sites to disseminate information to tens of thousands of people each year, many of whom would not normally visit the park or museum.

Internet users can travel the "web" to link to other parks, park-related agencies, or even individuals who have recently visited the park and who have posted their photographs or trip journals. When designing web sites, interpreters should apply standard interpretive principles. Color, movement, limited sections of text, the use of personal words and questions, all enhance attention and communication. Moreover, web pages should be designed to encourage repeat visits. This requires designing a dynamic web site with regular updates. Like a visitor center that never changes its displays or programs, static web sites offer little incentive for repeat visits.

News groups dealing with topics of interest to interpreters can be read like a daily newspaper devoted to a specific topic. Or, interpreters can ask questions, share ideas and information, or just chat with other interpreters in these interest groups.

News groups can be a valuable research tool to find current information about an issue. Recent topics on one interpretation-related group included a request for information on state-of-the art self guiding trail designs, a review of an article about exhibit-design research, a discussion of applying interpretive principles to web site design, and a request for information about Automated Visitor Survey systems using touch screens in a kiosk. Feedback came from all around North America and as far away as Australia.

Data bases are also available at some web sites. Sea World in Florida provides a marine science database for teachers and students that includes recent research findings, lesson plans, graphics, and photographs. Currently, more than 36,000 people access this database each month.[15]

The Internet can be both a source of information for interpreters and a means for interpreters to disseminate their information to the world.

CD-ROM and Laser Disc Technology

Compact discs (CD's) and laser discs store large amounts of information. Interpreters can take advantage of CD-ROM technology in interactive exhibits or use them to get a message into peoples' homes and schools.

For example, the Smithsonian Museums distributed a CD titled "Treasures of the Smithsonian" that allows people to use their personal computers to view 150 objects from the 14 Smithsonian museums. The viewer can look at several photos of each object, even manipulating some for closer views. Audio discussion and detailed text accompanies each object. Information about the objects can be accessed alphabetically, by time period, by museum, or as a thematic tour.[16]

Interpreters can also use CD's as a reference for answering questions or preparing programs. CD-ROMs have replaced printed sets of encyclopedias and reference books in many homes, nature centers, and museums. Interpreters can use a bird identification CD to read text on identification tips and life histories of almost 900 species. Or they can listen to bird songs, and see still photographs and video of birds flying. These programs can be interactive exhibits in themselves as most feature "name that bird" or "name that song" quizzes for different levels of expertise.

Interpreters planning astronomy programs can access star charts according to the date, time, and location of the program. These charts, as well as photographs, can be printed from the CD. Interpreters can get information about the location of the planets, time of moon rise and its phase, as well as schedules and flight paths of satellites passing over that evening. Some interpreters have astounded audiences by casually looking at the time and confidently stating that a communications satellite would be going over in two minutes. As it appeared and passed overhead people invariably asked "How did you know that?" Such questions provide openings for teachable moments.

CD's and laser discs can be used for archival purposes. A museum's, park's or agency's entire visuals library can be stored on disc. Tens of thousands of images can be cataloged for easy retrieval or projection in programs or exhibits. Large data bases consisting of nonvisual data such as visitor information, wildlife population data, or other statistical data can also be stored and easily retrieved. History interpreters are recording oral histories and saving them on CD-ROM, along with photographs and video of the persons interviewed.

Much thought must go into designing the structure of CD-ROM programs. If designers are not careful, important messages may get buried in enormous amounts of information stored on a CD. Additionally, users can easily get lost in a program and find themselves in the frustrating position of not being able to find their way out or back to a reference point. The layout needs to consider the learning paths that might occur and provide ways for the user to go forward, backward, or directly to reference points. Key messages related to the theme must be easily found. As with web sites, the same principles of provocative interpretive writing and design must be applied. CD-ROM has a distinct advantage of being able to present the same information in different forms. For example, if a technical word is used, with the click of the button a user might get a written definition, and an animated explanation. The ideal CD-ROM program reveals exciting discoveries on each new page.

Distance Education Systems

Through distance education systems interpreters can expand their sphere of influence nationally and even globally. These systems use satellites to broadcast live interpretive programs to audiences at other locations. Students respond through phone or computer links. Furthermore, these systems can bring data and "real world" science into an interpretive setting.

For example, 38 schools recently linked up simultaneously to receive a live satellite program titled "Raptors Live" produced by The Raptor Project at the University of Minnesota. Students can participate in a field research project involving osprey migration using transmitters placed on ospreys that send signals to orbiting ARGOS satellites. Using the Internet, students track the ospreys and communicate with scientists and with schools in areas where the ospreys are wintering.[17]

Sea World in Florida's SHAMU TV produces and broadcasts programs, such as "All About Manatees," which have the potential to reach 14 million students. During the program, students call a toll-free phone number to ask or answer questions. If students are unable to have their questions answered on the air, they can still get a response because educators staff phone lines every day. Currently, SHAMU TV is receiving about 10,000 phone calls per month.[18]

Project JASON, named for the Greek mythological explorer, allows students and teachers to join scientists at remote research sites all over the world. Through an interactive "telepresence," students explore hydrothermal vents on the bottom of the Mediterranean Sea, rainforests and Mayan ruins in Belize, and warships on the bottom of Lake Ontario, among other fascinating research sites. A recent JASON project at Hawaii Volcanoes National Park resulted in 60 programs. About half a million students and teachers "joined" geologists, biologists, astronomers, and engineers at an active volcano in the park. Teachers used a curriculum produced by the JASON Foundation and attended associated training workshops. Through broadcast on cable television and public television, and through the Internet and other electronic media, 33 million students were reached through this JASON project.[19]

Distance education using satellite communications can also be used to train new interpreters or provide continuing education for veteran interpreters. For example, the Bureau of Land Management (BLM) recently offered a broadcast of a course titled "Introduction to Interpretation: Making it Happen Interpretively." The two-and-a-half day course was available free to all who wanted to participate. Workbooks for the course were available on the BLM web page.

Geographic Information Systems (GIS) and Remote Sensing

Aerial photographs and satellite data imagery allow people to see their world from an entirely new perspective—from above. Birds-eye views of familiar areas fascinate people. Evidence of this fascination can be found by perusing bookstores' travel sections. Invariably, they will have coffee table books consisting of aerial photographs of major cities and some natural areas (e.g., Chicago From the Air, Paris from the Air, Yosemite From the Air). Patterns impossible to discern from the ground can be seen clearly from above. Spatial relationships can be striking when viewed from this perspective.

Geologic and archaeological features are often best identified from the air. These views can be used effectively to interpret land use changes, landscape ecology, or scores of other environmental and cultural themes.

At Grand Teton National Park, interpreters used satellite imagery to make computer generated panoramic photographs for interpretive wayside exhibits. This technology allowed interpreters to change the angle of view to show important features not always visible from the specific wayside exhibit. For example, visitors could see the mountains before them *and* "see" lakes hidden at the base of the mountains.[20]

Geographic Information Systems (GIS) uses images and data points collected on the ground to create maps that reveal information. At Black Canyon of the Gunnison National Monument and other sites, students from local schools are using GIS and hand-held Global Positioning System instruments to create full color digitized maps on which schools, homes, roads, habitat types, recreation areas, hydrography, and other physical and social features are precisely located.[21] Interpreters can use such activities to teach environmental science concepts and a variety of mathematical and technical skills. People enjoy applying practical, hands-on technology to issues in their home communities.

    Tilden concluded, "Gadgets do not supplant the personal contact; we accept them as valuable alternatives and supplements."[22] We agree. Modern devices now allow us to see and experience our world differently. Although there will always be a place for personal contact and performance, computers and other high tech gadgets can be useful supplementary tools in the hands of thoughtful interpreters.

    When Diaghilev commissioned Stravinsky to write the ballet score for "The Rite of Spring" Stravinsky asked what sort of music he should compose. Diaghilev answered, "Itonnez-moi!" (Astonish me!). We have heard the wonderful result. Today, visitors come to our museums and parks with the same request, "Itonnez-moi!" High technology can be used effectively by interpreters to do exactly that—astonish and inspire people.

▪ *Chapter Nine* ▪

Enough is Enough

I nterpreters must concern themselves with the quantity and quality (selection and accuracy) of information presented. Focused, well-researched interpretation will be more powerful than a longer discourse.

> To gild refined gold, to paint the lily,
> To throw a perfume on the violet,
> To smooth the ice, or add another hue
> Unto the rainbow, or with taper-light
> To seek the beauteous eye of heaven to garnish,
> Is wasteful and ridiculous excess?
>
> —Shakespeare, King John, IV, 2

This chapter addresses the *quantity* and *quality* of information presented to the public. The quantity issue speaks to the tendency of interpreters to offer too much information or display too many objects. An excessive amount of information or number of artifacts overwhelms the audience's ability or motivation to process the information. The quality issue refers to the accuracy of information that is presented. In the case of misinformation or overstatement, Freeman Tilden likens some interpretive efforts to the "florid exponent of chamber of commerce literature."[1] Discerning people dismiss overstatements and interpreters lose credibility.

Excess

Good interpreters become excited about the resources they are interpreting. Many museum and nature center storage areas burst with slide collections, rocks, pressed plants, assorted skins, skulls, fossils, invertebrate collections, and other good "stuff." The combination of abundant enthusiasm and available treasures render many interpreters impotent against the temptation to use everything at their disposal.

Examples of excess abound in museums, nature centers, and parks. Talks exceed time limits, extraneous slides sneak into carousels, and crowded artifacts push the limits of space and attention spans.

An expert carpenter once advised that to avoid splitting wooden shingles, do not give the nail the last tap. Tilden observed, "There are so many instances where, injuriously and to the detriment of an otherwise fine presentation, the nail has been given 'the last tap.'"[2]

Talks

We have all witnessed talks that have gone on too long. Our charge as interpreters is to keep our talks focused and interesting. Once talks go beyond what an audience can endure they have progressively less value. Listeners who were previously inspired may leave, instead, tired. Successful provocation of audiences depends on not going overboard.

Success may breed excess. Gratifying and flattering feedback tempts interpreters to do more. However, interpreters must be vigilant against giving the public too much of a good thing. An old showbiz adage says to "leave the audience wanting to come back for more." This is sage advice for interpreters.

A good (and often well-intended) example of excess is the seemingly obligatory question, at the end of programs, "Are there any questions?" Interpreters should welcome the opportunity to answer people's questions. But, it should not be at the expense of the entire audience. As bold individuals begin to ask questions, the others in the audience wonder, "Can we leave now?"

Interpreters should make it clear that they are anxious to answer questions on a personal basis after the program. Those who have a true interest will stay. Those who were too shy or intimidated to ask a question in front of the group now have nothing to fear. This one-on-one interaction after the audience has been dismissed provides us with some of the richest and most productive interpretive opportunities we will experience.

Exhibits

Museums have their roots in building collections. Often, it is the curator's job to build a "type" or reference collection, requiring the collecting of many examples of the same "class" (category) of artifacts for future research or preservation. Whether it be china plates or cannons, the collection curator's goal is to accumulate as many variations as possible, with storage space being the primary limiting factor at most sites. Dedication to this important museum function has manifested itself in a tendency for zealous curators to carry this "more is better" philosophy into the exhibit halls.

Military museums are notorious for cases filled with scores of rifles, swords, or medals, all looking superficially identical to the untrained eye. Musket balls and arrowheads are among the most over-displayed artifacts. A significant battle could be waged with all the musket balls and arrowheads on display at some museums. Tilden noted that seeing too many of a class of object leads to a diffusion of interest which, in turn, leads to a numbness:"You have seen nothing because you have seen everything."[3]

Both the collections curator and interpreter need to be sensitive to their respective goals and needs. The mission of the curator is to collect, catalog and store large numbers of objects. The interpreter's responsibility is to display only those objects that are consistent with a well-thought-out interpretive theme and then only in numbers which do not exceed the visitor's attention span.

Our obligation is to determine how many examples are necessary to accomplish the interpretive objectives. Then we must discipline ourselves to display only that number. When several examples of the same thing—whether rifles, rocking chairs, bowls, or bullets—are displayed together, the interpretive challenge is to show the differences and explain the significance of those differences. If we do not do this, our exhibits will be excessive for most visitors.

Research Findings

Research generally supports the notion that excess leads to a loss of attention.[4] The classic study by George Miller (see Chapter Five) described our limited short-term memory as being able to handle only seven pieces of information (plus or minus two) at one time.[5]

Researchers have since documented satiation (also called museum fatigue) at sites ranging from zoo reptile houses to prestigious art galleries.[6] Regardless of the setting, the most attention is given to the first exhibits encountered and visitors spend decreasing amounts of time viewing exhibits or paintings as the number encountered increases.

"Information overload" is another problem related to excessive material.[7] Overload occurs when the audience fails to process information because they receive too many simultaneous stimuli. Like children tearing through a pile of gifts that compete for their attention on Christmas morning, eager visitors may flit from exhibit to exhibit always being distracted by the next one.

Authors of one study speculated that first-time museum visitors perceive a museum differently than repeat visitors in part because of information overload.[8] Interpreters must be aware that their exhibits or programs may compete with each other. Likewise, elements within an exhibit may compete with other elements of the same exhibit.

Research has been less helpful in precisely prescribing how much is too much. Most studies assessing how much information is enough have focused on visitor attention as measured by the percentage of people stopping at an exhibit ("attracting power") and the amount of time visitors spend once they stop ("holding power").

A quantitative experiment comparing signs that were identical except for differing lengths of text was conducted at the Birmingham (Alabama) Zoo. Signs about predators used text of 30, 60, 120 and 240 words in 30 word blocks. As text length was increased, fewer people read the signs, with 15.2 percent, 14.9 percent, 11.3 percent, and 9.7 percent of the visitors reading as text length increased.[9] In a study of an Egyptian mummy exhibit, a 150 word label was divided into three 50 word segments, with readership increasing from 12.3 percent to 28.4 percent.[10]

Other variables such as audience characteristics, comfort, the topic's intrinsic interest, the exhibit's physical characteristics, time constraints, competing stimuli, and a host of other factors influence how much is too much. Furthermore, time standing in front of a display does not necessarily mean individuals are processing the information. While conducting an evaluation of exhibits at the Birmingham Zoo Predator House researchers noted that visitors spent more time viewing an empty exhibit than they did viewing a small mammal exhibit with animals present. Undoubtedly the visitors were searching in vain for animals in an empty enclosure.[11]

A study at Chicago's Field Museum of Natural History found that about three-quarters of the visitors stopped at less than 40 percent of the exhibit cases in the animal halls and visitors spent an average of less than 12 seconds at each case. Nevertheless, the researchers state (in their provocatively titled paper "*Stuffed Birds on Sticks*"—from one visitor's description of the museum's animal halls), that exhibit planners should not concern themselves with trying to answer the questions, "What percent of the cases should a visitor look at?" or "How much time should a visitor spend looking at an exhibit case?" Instead, they suggest that "it doesn't matter, because we assume that visitors can and will and should look at whatever appeals to them in the manner they wish. We are not attempting to control their patterns of looking, which are highly influenced by such difficult to quantify factors as fatigue, number and mood of children, personal experience, prior knowledge, weather, parking meters, and time since last meal, etc."[12]

These researchers shift the focus from exhibit *quantity* to *quality*. They direct planners to create ways to entice visitors to stay longer, to get them to say: "Yes, this exhibit was designed with me and my interests in mind, and I want to come back again and look at more of these cases." They concluded, "We do not expect or predict that many visitors will want to or be able to see it all. Rather, the *quality* [italics added] of their experiences, however and wherever they choose to spend their time, will be improved."[13]

Clearly, the perception of what is excessive is related to the quality of the display. A common approach to thinking about displays uses a cost-benefit model. The expected benefits from interacting with an exhibit must exceed the perceived cost in time or effort, otherwise the "consumer" will not "purchase" the experience by expending time and energy. Excessive text lowers the expected reward by appearing boring and difficult *and* it requires greater effort to read.

Rules of Thumb

In the absence of empirical data, experienced interpreters have formulated widely-communicated "rules of thumb" for avoiding excess. These recommendations are grounded more in anecdotal information and professional intuition than in quantitative research. For example, it is often stated that slide shows should be no more than 20 minutes. For exhibit text, many recommend that no segment of text be more than 50 words and that no more than 150 words be on any one panel. Self-guiding nature trails should *generally* be limited to a half to three-fourths of a mile.

Note that these are only "rules of thumb" and other possibilities may be quite effective depending on specific circumstances. We encourage interpreters to use good professional judgment and to be bold—to experiment and adjust. Evaluation of attendance and audience attention will detect excessiveness.

Other Excesses

Facilities, themselves, can be excessive, although tight budgets seldom allow extravagant interpretive facilities. Yet, occasionally an agency or a private organization experiences a political windfall that is devoted to "bricks and mortar." Structures are excessive when they detract from the interpretive messages. Just as people engrossed with a cathedral's beauty or interesting architecture may miss the more important spiritual message, visitors to a museum or visitor center may be so taken with the architecture or technology that they ignore interpretive messages.

Painting the Lily, Adorning the Rose

"A mouse is a miracle enough to stagger sextillion of infidels," wrote Walt Whitman.[14] Everything in nature is a miracle and no living thing needs embellishment.

The tendency for interpreters to exaggerate is not born out of deceit. Sometimes it is a matter of ignorance—interpreters parroting erroneous information they have heard or read. Often, misinformation is a manifestation of the love interpreters have for the resource. This affinity may feed a propensity to accept and disseminate interesting and favorable information about a subject without questioning it. Like proud parents touting their offspring, good interpreters love to sing the praises of their site's resources.

Occasionally over-zealous interpreters misinform audiences concerning natural history information. A widespread example of this is the myth that purple martins eat mosquitos. Tens of thousands of people, as well as nature centers and municipalities, have purchased martin houses to help eradicate mosquitos. Yet research has shown that martins generally do not eat mosquitos, but rather eat dragonflies, which do eat mosquitos.[15] Purple martins are certainly worthy of appreciation and protection. By assigning martins attributes they do not possess, interpreters are "adorning the rose."

Historic Myths

Many historical figures deserve appreciation, honor, and reverence, but some interpreters assign false characteristics and actions to them. Some historical sites and individuals have bodies of myth that seem to exceed bodies of knowledge. George Washington, Betsy Ross, Abraham Lincoln, and Davy Crockett are among the most fictionalized characters. Historic sites such as the Little Bighorn Battlefield National Monument and the Alamo have been "misinterpreted" for decades.

The National Park Service has made a special effort to eliminate myths surrounding Custer and events at the Little Bighorn Battlefield. (See Chapter Five for interpretive themes at the site.) They have adjusted interpretive content to put both the person and the battle in historically proper perspective. But, it is not easy in light of competing misinformation.[16]

For example, films and popular paintings may launch and perpetuate misinterpretations. Since the first Custer film in 1908, many Hollywood movies have been made, each giving a different version of history. "They Died With Their Boots On" made in 1941 and starring Errol Flynn, portrayed Custer as a heroic martyr, while fueling the sale of War Bonds. In 1970, at the height of the Vietnam War an anti-war film, "Little Big Man," portrayed Custer and the 7th Cavalry as villains. Some even equated the Plains Indians with the North Vietnamese.

Paintings also perpetuate myths. "Custer's Last Fight" painted by Otto Becker in the 1890s, is the most popular and famous painting of the battle. The initial printing was of 150,000 copies and the total number hanging in saloons and family dens now numbers in the millions. What's wrong with the painting? Just about everything but the landscape! The painting shows Custer with long hair (he had short hair at the time), carrying a decorative saber (sabers were not taken into battle), and wearing buckskin (he took it off before the battle). It shows the Indians mounted on horseback (this was a dismounted battle by both sides), carrying shields (not used by Plain's Indians), and wearing Iroquoian headdresses (worn by woodland tribes from the eastern United States).

Challenging the folklore surrounding cultural icons takes courage because the truth is sometimes difficult for the public to accept. Historians sometimes become the targets of ridicule and charges of false motives. Box 1 describes the controversy associated with interpretation at the Alamo.

Our job is to integrate these various truths into the whole truth, which should be our only loyalty.

—Abraham Maslow

Box 1
Remember the Alamo!

The battle for the Alamo still rages in the hearts of many people. At issue is the authenticity of the site and the account of how the battle ended. Interpreters have the difficult task of interpreting a site that has undergone massive changes since the historic battle and a site that is buried in emotional baggage and folklore. Now surrounded by skyscrapers and busy city streets, none of the perimeter walls are original and the reconstructed buildings do not even resemble the originals. The most recognizable feature, the "Taco Bell"™ roof line, was not added until years later. Only the bottom level of the mission building is original.

A private group called the Daughters of the Texas Revolution (DTR) purchased the site and has been responsible for managing it for the State of Texas since 1903. They do a fine job of raising money to fund the operations and interpretation at the site and they have fended off efforts of local businesses to impact the site further (e.g., building an atrium enclosing the site and connecting it to a downtown hotel). But, leaders of this group have sometimes had their own version of history and have found it difficult to accept other, more credible, accounts.

Much of the controversy surrounds the fate of the legendary Davy Crockett. The journals and testimony of at least seven eyewitnesses independently and consistently relate the story of how Crockett and several comrades were brutally killed at the end of the battle.

A review of historical accounts of the battle show, according to historian Dan Kilgore, that "Crockett's herosim seemed to expand in direct proportion to the distance news about him had to travel." Some of these accounts written shortly after the battle claimed he was found dead with a shattered rifle, surrounded with piles of 20 or 30 dead Mexicans that he took with him.

Journal entries from eyewitness accounts of the torture and killing of Crockett and the others reported that they died honorably, *"without complaining and without humiliating themselves before their torturers."* Crockett's death apparently was not honorable enough to suit the regional and nationalistic pride of many people. They continue to "gild refined gold and throw perfume on the violet." The DTR refuses to believe that the "King of the Wild Frontier" died in a demeaning and inglorious way. They claim he was taken prisoner. Some believe reports that he was seen again after having escaped captivity. The DTR even banned their bookstore's best-selling book, Davy Crockett's autobiography, because the Introduction spoke of Davy's death in a way that was "unacceptable." It has recently been restocked and this seems to be a sign of changes for the better at the Alamo.

Screenwriters also took liberties with history in the 1960 blockbuster movie, starring John Wayne, by having Davy Crockett and others blow themselves up with the ammunition depot rather than surrendering. This popular movie added to the confusion in the minds of the public about the final moments of the battle.

The battle for the Alamo continues as a vitriolic war of words. Some historians refer to the DTR as a tea club running a historic site. Some Hispanic Americans object to the way Mexicans are portrayed. Some Texans don't like outsiders (non-Texans) interpreting Texas history. Even the *patriotism* of some historians has been questioned.

The Alamo is an American icon. It is one of the world's most recognizable visual images. Seeking and interpreting truth without excess at such a highly modified site and at a site with such deep meaning and strong emotional ties is an arduous task.

Based on Kilgore, 1978, How Did Davy Die? *and personal communication with Andrew Paul Hutton, University of New Mexico, July 1996.*

The Myth of Chief Seattle

A commentary titled, "Are We Ministers of Misinformation?" identified common fallacies propagated by some interpreters, including the debunked "Web of Life" speech by Chief Seattle. This "speech" is well-known to many interpreters. It includes the following: "How can you buy or sell the sky, the warmth of the land? The idea is strange to us . . . This we know: The earth does not belong to man; man belongs to the earth. This we know. All things are connected like the blood which unites one family. All things are connected."[17]

As it turns out, the speech was written by Ted Perry, a screenwriter for the 1972 film documentary, *Home,* which was produced by the Southern Baptist Convention. Perry did not intend to be deceptive; the producers of the film simply neglected to credit him for his script. This oversight has fueled the dissemination of a fallacy that has been referred to as "The Gospel of Chief Seattle." Indeed, it continues to be evoked around campfires and other interpretive venues across the country despite several exposés.[18]

What To Do?

The following recommendations may be offered to ensure accurate interpretation: 1) We must work even more diligently to ensure personal competency, and 2) The interpretive profession must evolve as an institution that provides an environment for responsible, considerate, professional criticism.[19]

Costa Dillon encourages interpreters to take a proactive approach when confronted with myths. He presented seven principles summarized as follows: [20]

1) *Know the myths.* Interpreters should make a point of reading novels and seeing television shows and movies about the subjects they interpret. Then we are in a position to reveal deeper meaning and truth. We can maintain a list of misconceptions and myths for reference and training of new interpreters.

2) *Don't have a superior attitude.* Those who believe myths are not necessarily unteachable. Knowing a myth in itself is often an indication that a person has an interest in the subject. We should take advantage of that interest.

3) *Use the myth as an entry point.* We can acknowledge the popular misconception and then use it to reveal facts and show how the myth relates to the truth. For example, many believe the Gettysburg Address was written on the back of an envelope. Lincoln, in fact, wrote many drafts knowing that it was a tremendously important speech. The myth can be a springboard into the discussion of why it was such an important speech and the care Lincoln took in preparing it.

4) *Address the reasons and origins of the misconception.* The reasons behind the Parson Weems fables about George Washington (e.g., chopping down a cherry tree) tells us something about the formation of American culture. Likewise, the Betsy Ross myth (that she sewed the first U.S. flag) tells us something about the flag as a symbol and the feelings of Americans during the country's Centennial when the story first circulated.

5) *Know credible sources and apply good research techniques.* We must critically evaluate sources and be prepared to give references when challenged.

6) *Make the interpretation as good as the myth.* People remember myths because they are good stories. Interpreters must research, formulate, and tell memorable stories.

7) *The interpreter's job is not to bust myths or deflate legends.* Our charge is to "make the reality available, accurate and believable."[21] An overt attempt to knock a hero off a pedestal or deflate an image of patriotism will lead to bad feelings and conflict. As Dillon noted, "If someone leaves your site secure in their long-held misconception, then so be it."[22]

Myths are important in all cultures. They help us define and understand our world and ourselves. Interpreters should eagerly take myths and use them as *tools* to bring people to the truth.[23]

Ensuring personal competency is more difficult than ever. The amount of information about our world is growing at unprecedented rates as previously noted in Chapter Two. Researchers constantly are discovering new information which necessitates new interpretations of past events and natural history. Keeping up with the literature in the diverse fields related to a site's cultural and natural resources is a daunting, but critical task.

In Chapter One we quoted Anatole France who cautioned against, "satisfying our vanity by teaching a great many things..." To avoid excess, interpreters must teach a few great things well.

Reining ourselves in a bit and making sure we speak the truth need not put a damper on our interpretive efforts. It will certainly not limit our effectiveness. As we gain and maintain credibility we will be more effective because our audiences will sense our authority and take our messages more seriously. Furthermore, having confidence we are speaking the truth makes interpreting it more personally satisfying.

• *Chapter Ten* •

TECHNIQUE BEFORE ART

Before applying the arts in interpretation, the interpreter must be familiar with basic communication techniques. Quality interpretation depends on the interpreter's knowledge and skills which should be developed continually.

Interpretation is a voyage of discovery in the field of human emotions and intellectual growth, and it is hard to foresee that time when the interpreter can confidently say, "Now we are wholly adequate to our task."

–Freeman Tilden

This principle relates to the third principle which indicated that interpretation is an art. Applying art in interpretation is surely a worthy aspiration. However, basic elements of public speaking— such as body language, voice control, and presentation structure— must be developed before an interpreter proceeds to artistry. Furthermore, we all continue to grow in knowledge and expertise and there are specific ways to promote this growth.

The Basics

It takes practice to be a good interpreter. We must learn those methods that contribute to quality interpretation and then we must practice them. Some of the learning that is done may seem tedious or extraneous. Many of us have struggled through difficult or seemingly irrelevant courses. Furthermore, we all must go through the "gut-wrenching" process of our first talks in front of an audience. The learning and practice is not much different than that required in other artistic endeavors.

Take, for example, the techniques that must be built before musicians create personal styles. It is necessary, first, to master a knowledge of notes and scales. This is repetitious and laborious, but it must be done. Only after a musician has command over notes and scales can we expect virtuoso performance.

To a certain degree, the interpreter goes through a similar process learning the basics of communication. Once the basics are mastered, we become "artisans" of the craft—in a sense "painting" a program by interjecting our own personal styles. We can inspire the confidence of our listeners by paying attention to basic communication strategies and then going on to hone personal nuances.

An intimate knowledge of the subject matter—its depth and breadth—is essential. So, too, is an ability to convey the material. It is often assumed that people can give a talk on a subject they know about, regardless of whether they have been trained in effective speaking techniques. Yet, there is plenty of evidence to the contrary. Indeed, a disorganized, rambling, monotone speech can do more harm than good. The following discussion offers basic direction on how to speak effectively.[1]

The Fear Factor

Even the most experienced speakers will feel apprehension. This is normal. To avoid being *overcome* by fear, several useful strategies may be employed.

Most important, for the sake of the audience and the interpreter's degree of confidence, is that the presentation is impeccably prepared. The wise interpreter uses apprehension as a motivating force for researching and organizing an excellent presentation. Some of us choose to write out the entire story while others choose to make an outline. However the presentation is constructed, remember to *speak,* not read.

After assembling the structure of an inspiring talk, the conscientious interpreter will want to rehearse it. You may isolate yourself and practice, try your story on someone you know (and trust), or record the presentation and listen carefully for areas of improvement.

As a check on attention to detail, you might also answer the following question: "What are the indicators that my story was adequately and carefully prepared?"

Interpreters should not anticipate being afraid of the audience. Rather, use any nervous energy to project excitement. Rehearse with the confidence that the presentation will be well-received. Arriving early and talking with visitors builds rapport and can have a settling effect.

Under no circumstances should the interpreter apologize for apprehension. A little quavering in the voice or other signs of nervousness may not be noticed and will soon go away. However, if you announce your apprehension, then the audience will be even more attuned to it.

In most instances it is best to stick with the game plan—what has been prepared—even if supposedly better ideas occur just before the presentation. Of course, there can be extemporaneous elements of the talk, although it is well-advised that you stick with the prepared opening and closing lines. When a speaker panics and attempts to reconstruct a presentation on the spot, it inevitably shows.

While speaking, make eye contact with members of the audience. Seek out those who have "friendly eyes" and are obviously interested in what is being said. This positive reinforcement will build confidence. Try not to focus on those who are not paying attention; they may have distractions in their personal lives that have no bearing on the quality of your talk.

Speaking Ability

Developing the ability to speak in public situations comes with practice. Especially early on it is important to get constructive feedback. A supervisor or colleague can offer insights that, as the speaker, you may not be aware of. The following speaking skills are essential so that the message is clearly received because voice is the key link between the interpreter and the audience.

A good speaking voice is one that is conversational and natural. Seek to speak in a friendly tone and be certain that you clearly articulate your words and avoid verbal crutches (such as "uh").

An effective speaking voice should be balanced between extremes of volume, pitch, and rate. Obviously, speak at a volume that is pleasant and can be heard by everyone. Vary the loudness or softness of your voice to add emphasis or provide an element of drama.

Likewise, speak with a different pitch to your voice to convey emotion and conviction. Change voice inflections so that you are not speaking in a monotone.

Finally, speak at a rate that is neither too fast nor too slow. Speakers who move along too quickly will lose their listeners and those who speak too slowly will put them to sleep. However, it is beneficial to vary your speaking pace to emphasize points or to indicate mood changes. Silence is also a powerful tool. A confident speaker is aware of the potency of a silent pause.

Overall, strive to speak with vitality, providing the impression of confidence and conviction. This keeps the audience alert to your message.

Body Language

Body language is likewise a critical component of effective speaking. Hand gestures and facial expressions work in tandem with the interpreter's vocal skills to bring sight and sound into harmony.

As you launch the presentation be certain that you are standing upright, although not rigid. Your hands, when you are not gesturing, should be at your sides. Be careful not to cross your arms in front of your chest for this signals self-consciousness, a symbolic barrier between you and the audience.

Because you are speaking on a topic that you truly believe in, express your sincerity by putting your entire self into the talk. Facial expressions that reflect the various moods of your presentation should come naturally, although these may not be visible to the whole audience if you are speaking in front of a large group. The most visually expressive part of body language, therefore, is the use of hands and arms to illustrate your words and show what you mean. For example, gestures may reflect size, shape, direction, or importance. However, be careful not to allow gestures to take over the presentation, where flailing arms pose a distraction from your message.

As in many aspects of learning about effective speaking, it is worthwhile to observe how polished speakers use gestures that appear smooth, natural, and spontaneous. The interpreter may also rehearse body language in front of a mirror or videotape the presentation to evaluate progress.

Organize The Presentation

To ensure that the presentation is effective and makes sense to the audience it is critical that the material be sequenced properly—in the form of a story. Accomplished speakers know exactly where they are going to begin and end. Even a well-intended and sincere speech, making use of the best material, will be ineffective if it is not organized carefully (see Box 1).

Box 1
Barry Lopez on Storytelling

Barry Lopez explains that the storyteller's responsibility is not to be wise; "a storyteller is the person who creates an atmosphere in which wisdom can reveal itself." When Lopez writes a piece of nonfiction he makes a bow of respect toward the material and a bow of respect to the reader. The interpreter, similarly, pays tribute to the subject matter and to the visitor.

Lopez sums up his respect toward the material in the following way: "Listen. Pay attention. Do your research. Try to learn. Don't presume. And always imagine that there's more there than you could possibly understand or sense." The interpreter owes this same level of deference to the subject matter, be it a natural landscape or historical event.

In paying respects to the reader, Lopez says, "I have assembled this material. I have tried to bring order to these disparate elements. I have tried to use the language elegantly. I have sought, everywhere I could, illumination, clarity. I have tried to organize things with a proper sense of the drama of human life, I have tried to think hard about all these things. I have tried to get rid of all that is unnecessary for you to understand the story." Again, the interpreter owes this same degree of attention to the listener of interpretive presentations. This standard requires substantial effort.

Adapted from L. Beck, 1989, "Conversations with Barry Lopez: Musings on Interpretation."

If the presentation is to make sense and generate results, the story must flow in a logical way. It also must be presented from the point of view of the audience as noted in Chapter One. We should strive to arrange our presentations so that they satisfy what the audience wants. Do not ask "What do I want to say?" but rather "What does the audience seek to hear?" That is, "What will be useful and meaningful to the listeners?"

The best speakers spend a considerable amount of time planning how to maintain the attention of the audience. These experienced speakers know that the telltale way to determine whether a talk is making an impact is to watch the audience throughout the presentation. If listeners are focused on the interpreter's words and watching the interpreter with interest, then the talk is working.

The basic structure of most formal talks includes the introduction, the body, and the conclusion.

In the introduction the interpreter arouses interest for the topic. The opening lines should capture the attention of the audience and express the theme or thesis. The introduction may include an overview of the presentation, a challenging statement, a quotation, or appropriate personal story. It may also include humor. However, stay away from anything that is not central to your theme or thesis.

The body of the talk is where we elaborate on the subject. Any number of illustrative devices can be used throughout: facts, examples, analogies, anecdotes, or references to related news events (see Chapter Three). Again, be sure to include only that information that is pertinent. In the body you continue a step-by-step progression toward the conclusion. This logical sequence will help to hold the listeners' interest, just as a rambling discourse will surely scatter their attention.

The conclusion is the destination of the talk. At this point the interpreter may tie comments back to the introduction, provide a summary of the points that have been made in the body, convey an illustrative message or quotation, or make a clearcut appeal for action. The end of the presentation should be forceful and conclusive. There should be no need to confirm "that's all there is." That point should be made obvious.

Your audience will be able to sense whether or not you are prepared and they will be thankful for every hour you put into researching, organizing, and rehearsing the program. However, the audience does not care to be told about the time and effort you spent. That will be evident. To paraphrase a comment Annie Dillard made about writers, is it pertinent, is it courteous, for us to hear what it cost the speaker personally?[2]

Know Your Site and Be Available to the Audience

The interpreter should strive to know intimately the location and physical layout of where the presentation takes place. This familiarity will generate increased comfort and confidence.

Early arrival allows the interpreter to check the lighting, sound, and equipment if any. Once everything is set up you may interact with those who have arrived early. This mingling with the audience has several benefits summarized by William Lewis as follows:

1.   It establishes a friendly, more intimate atmosphere.
2   It helps weld the audience into a responsive whole.
3.   You may assess the general mood of the audience.
4.   It provides you with information you can use in your presentation.
5.   You may visualize the audience as a collection of individuals rather than a mass of humanity.
6.   It removes nervous tension as you make the transition from talking with smaller groups of people to the entire audience.[3]

Likewise, it is important to make yourself available *after* the presentation. This should be announced in your introduction so as not to distract from a powerful conclusion. Afterward, you may talk casually with those who were inspired by your story or perhaps provide further information for those seeking additional knowledge or experiences.

Building on the Basics

It is only after we master the basics of communication—using nervousness to advantage, learning speaking skills and expressive body language, orchestrating the flow of information—that we can effectively move on to incorporating the various arts. To attempt the art of storytelling or interpretive drama without know-ing about voice projection, the importance of eye contact, or basic organizing and attention-holding principles would certainly be worse than a bad speech, although neither are desirable.

As basic techniques are mastered, and this progresses over time, we continue to grow in our knowledge and expertise. Many channels promote our growth.

We believe that it is essential that interpreters continue to read widely. This helps us to be well-versed in our subjects and assists in our program preparation as we consider how written material is put together and organized for optimal effectiveness. Computer technology allows additional options (from visiting websites to interacting in news groups) for staying current.

We must also keep abreast of news events. It is important to be aware of what is going on in the rest of the world—regionally, nationally, and internationally—otherwise we run the danger of be-coming short-sighted and narrowly focused. As wondrous as our interpretive site is, there is still a whole world out there and both our site and visitors are connected to it.

Continued professional growth is essential to the quality of the interpreter's work. It is important that we are members of professional organizations, and, better yet, active participants. In the United States, the National Association for Interpretation has been the foremost national organization devoted to "inspiring lead-ership and excellence to advance natural and cultural interpreta-tion as a profession."[4] The diversity of this organization is repre-sented by the following sections: African-American Experience, Council for American Indian Interpretation, Environmental Educa-tion, Nature Center Directors and Administrators, Resource Inter-pretation and Heritage Tourism, Cultural Interpretation and Living History, Visual Communications, and Zoos, Wildlife Parks and Aquaria.[5] Other national and international organizations include Interpretation Canada and Heritage Interpretation International.

Attendance at regional, national, and international conferences promotes our growth through listening to experts in the field, net-working and meeting new friends who may face similar challenges, being exposed to new resources and program ideas, and coming away inspired to even better serve our clientele. Furthermore, this association with other professionals enhances our commitment to our life work; provides a sense of belonging to a larger group with similar interests, goals, and aspirations; and affirms the validity and mission of the profession.[6]

In addition to active reading and seeking knowledge, and participation in professional organizations, we grow professionally by attending seminars and pursuing additional coursework. For many of us it is useful to learn other languages or new technologies to better serve our visitors.

Competencies and Certification

Gail Vander Stoep has studied the issues of professionalism and certification for many years. Some of the problems associated with not having universally accepted professional standards are low pay, lack of career paths, limited training opportunities, acceptance of unqualified candidates, and confusion by employing agencies and the general public about the nature of the profession.[7]

The development of a certification system for interpreters is a controversial issue. On the one hand there is strong support for increasing professionalism. On the other hand there is widespread disagreement on how that might be accomplished.

For example, some type of degree, which is the generic basis for "professional certification" in any field, should be required. However, in the interpretive profession many different degrees are appropriate from biology to history to recreation. Furthermore, some express reservations about even having a degree requirement. They recognize that people can learn in ways other than a formal education.

Many intangible qualities are important for an effective interpreter: enthusiasm, sincerity, creativity, patience, maturity, being a team player, having a passion for the resource and working with people. Although these are important qualities, they would be extremely difficult to factor into a certification process. Instead, these attributes should be assessed by those who conduct hiring.[8]

The following is a summary statement of one national workshop process: "Yes, we would like the option (not a mandatory system) of becoming certified, or in some way meeting credentialing standards, but the program must be flexible and allow alternatives to meeting the criteria."[9]

Interpreters, we believe, must have a fundamental grasp of basic communication techniques. These must be understood and practiced, just as a musician practices notes and scales. In addition, we must continue to grow in our knowledge and talent. Otherwise, we risk ineffectiveness or burn-out.

Many avenues contribute to our professional growth. As we continue to work at a particular site we grow in our knowledge of the place, we grow in our experiences there, and we grow to love the place. Our enthusiasm inspires our visitors. We apply our artistic creativity. We fine tune existing programs and try new ones.

How does one pursue interpretation? Ultimately, it is a personal endeavor—a journey. As students we determine how best to prepare ourselves for entering the profession by selecting appropriate coursework, relevant fieldwork and internship experiences and meaningful volunteer opportunities. We build a foundation.

As practitioners we deliberate on how to structure our time to meet our own expectations for excellence. We learn from our colleagues, supervisors, and visitors. We continue to seek out information; to read widely. We collaborate, take on progressively more challenging tasks, contribute our expertise to professional organizations, write for various publications, and share our experience with entry-level interpreters. This constant learning, and assistance we provide to others, keeps us fresh.

As managers of interpretive programs we keep current in all aspects of interpretation as well as create supportive environments for our interpretive employees and volunteers to excel. Our work ethic, our passion for the resource, our concern for the welfare of visitors, our investment in continual growth serves as a model for our employees.

We are on a journey and our success, our contribution, will depend on the foundation we establish and what we make of opportunities to further our growth along the way.

> *I'll interpret the rocks, learn the language of flood, storm, and avalanche. I'll acquaint myself with the glaciers and wild gardens, and get as near the heart of the world as I can.*
>
> —John Muir

▪ *Chapter Eleven* ▪

Interpretive Composition

I nterpretive writing should address what readers would
like to know, with the authority of wisdom and the humility and care that comes with it.

*Write as if you were dying. At the same time, assume you
write for an audience consisting solely of terminal patients.
That is, after all, the case.*

—Annie Dillard

Our purpose is not to teach the reader specific writing techniques, but rather to present general principles that contribute to
good writing. Although Enos Mills was an accomplished writer, he
did not write about interpretive composition so much as interpretive "guiding." However, Freeman Tilden did consider the mission,
and complexities, of interpretive writing. He acknowledged that
although applying certain strategies may improve it, writing is an
endeavor for which "no one person will ever be its complete master." [1]

Tilden said little about brochures, newsletters, feature articles,
or correspondence that make up so much of interpreters' writing
efforts today. Tilden's focus was on writing "inscriptions"— meaning the text of signs and labels. He claimed that adequate inscription is the result of 90% thinking and 10% composition.[2] Perfect
composition, without sound thought, will be fatally flawed, whereas
a well-thought-out piece that contains composition flaws, may still
communicate something meaningful. However, both thinking and
composition are necessary to create a well-written piece.

Thinking

Content

According to Tilden, writers often make the mistake of *only* asking "What is it I wish to say?"[3] A further consideration, and the more important one, is determining what the prospective reader wishes to read.

Tilden also suggested that writers ask themselves if they can write something that is concise, focused, inspirational, and engaging.[4] Some topics do not lend themselves to these criteria. Imagine trying to write a short piece that would thoroughly explain photosynthesis. Moreover, some topics may be beyond the scope of our knowledge. We may not know enough about a topic to go beyond merely presenting facts. The goal of interpretive composition is to *interpret* information in such a way that it reveals meanings and deeper truth, as covered in Chapter Two.

In deciding what to write, author Barbara Kingsolver advised writers that, "it's emotion, not event, that creates a dynamic response in the mind of the reader. The artist's job is to sink a taproot in the reader's brain that will grow downward and find a path into the reader's soul and experience, so that some new emotional inflorescence will grow out of it."[5] The prerequisites for successfully selecting the subject and sinking this taproot, according to Tilden, are that you "must be in love with your material and in tune with your fellow man."[6]

Interpreters must also ask themselves about the keynote of the place being interpreted. Identifying, and then interpreting, the site's *genius loci* is the hallmark of good interpretation. Written interpretive materials should communicate the essence of the place and the reason for its existence. We cheat visitors when we distract them with writing having nothing to do with the site. Although this may seem like common sense, common sense is not always common. The authors have witnessed a poster exhibit about polar bears on display in a prairie park and antique automobiles interpreted at a Civil War battlefield. Unfortunately, similar misguided interpretive efforts are widespread.

Sometimes interpreters are assigned topics or themes to write about. An important function of modern interpretation is its use as a management tool. In these instances, interpreters communicate messages consistent with the goals of park or museum administration. Recognizing that interpretation is the communication link between the interpretive site and the visitor, and recognizing that interpreters should be expert communicators, it is not surprising that administrators call on interpreters to effectively communicate management messages to the clientele.

Inspiration

Many aspiring writers are stymied as they wait for some magical moment of inspiration. Some interpreters passively wait their entire careers. Inspiration is difficult to predict and control, but writers can do things to encourage it (e.g., carefully observing our surroundings and listening to other voices–the voices of nature as well as human voices).

Perhaps the best source of inspiration is reading good writing. Reading provides ideas, information, illustrations—all which make inspiration more likely. Samuel Johnson reportedly once criticized another writer by saying, "He wrote more than he read." [7] Reading well-written pieces has the bonus of exposing us to models of good writing.

Most professional writers consider time spent reading part of their "writing time." Annie Dillard observed, "The writer studies literature, not the world. He lives in the world; he cannot miss it ... He is careful of what he reads, for that is what he will write. He is careful of what he learns, because that is what he will know." [8]

Box 1 presents a highly subjective and eclectic list of recommended readings. These books are profound and eloquently penned. Emulating any of these authors should enhance the quality of one's interpretive writing. Note, too, that each of the authors is a master at revealing meaning and deeper truth.

Interpreters attain inspiration only through effort—observing, listening, reading, and writing. While waiting for inspiration to strike —WRITE. Thomas Edison said "Genius is 1 percent inspiration and 99 percent perspiration." [9] Tilden agreed, stating, "inspiration is usually the mirrored reflection of hard work." [10] Inspired writing is hard, often painfully difficult work. As a West African proverb says, "The pen is heavier than the machete."

Box 1
A Short List of Highly Recommended Natural History Writing

Each of these authors is widely published and we recommend their other books as well. This is a very subjective listing and we have many other favorites.

Edward Abbey, *Desert Solitaire*
Diane Ackerman, *A Natural History of the Senses*
Rachel Carson, *The Sense of Wonder*
Annie Dillard, *Pilgrim at Tinker Creek*
Ralph Waldo Emerson, *Nature*
William Least Heat-Moon, *PrairyErth*   917.81 HEA
Aldo Leopold, *A Sand County Almanac*
Barry Lopez, *Arctic Dreams*
Peter Matthiessen, *The Snow Leopard*
John McPhee, *The Survival of the Bark Canoe*
John Muir, *Our National Parks*
Sigurd Olson, *Reflections from the North Country*
David Quammen, *Natural Acts*
Henry David Thoreau, *Walden*
Charles Wilkinson, *The Eagle Bird*
Terry Tempest Williams, *Refuge*
Edward Wilson, *The Diversity of Life*

Composition

Brevity is a critical component of good composition.[11] It enhances clarity and readability. Avoiding tedious detail and saying only what is necessary preserves the reader's interest. The paradox of brevity is that concise writing takes more effort and time.

Mark Twain noted this paradox when he reportedly wrote to a friend that he would have written a shorter letter, but didn't have time.

As with most everything, moderation is called for. Messages may be so brief that they are incomplete. In striving for brevity, writers may omit important subject matter. Similarly, authors may leave out a necessary explanation of a concept or policy, leaving the reader confused. No specific rule or word count formula exists to determine if something is too brief or too long. Writers must use discernment to not say less than the occasion demands and not say more.

In some cases there should be no written interpretation at all. Tilden noted that some signs "accost" visitors.[12] Sometimes less is more. Like Mozart, who said his rests were more important than his notes, interpreters should be sensitive to circumstances where a sign or label would detract from the desired experience.

Other factors contribute to good composition. Mark Twain said, "The difference between the right word and the almost right word is the difference between lightning and the lightning bug."[13] But, choosing the right word is difficult because its identity may be a moving target. The best word must precisely convey the meaning and feelings of the writer, but because audiences may be diverse or changing, the best word may change with the characteristics of the readers. Reading levels and vocabularies change with age, education, and culture. The word "community" has different connotations to an inner city youth, a suburban business person, or an African villager. Writers must consider their audience's characteristics when choosing words.

Putting the words together in a correct way is critical for credibility. Not only does correct grammar enhance clarity, but if the writing is bad, readers may assume the information is suspect. Furthermore, if the writing appears careless, the reader may think the agency is careless in carrying out its mission.

Style, tone, and many other technical ingredients go into making a well-written piece. Grammar texts and writing manuals, both popular and academic, abound to help writers with the nuts and bolts of good writing. Among many possibilities is the classic slender volume by William Strunk Jr. and E.B. White, *The Elements of Style*.

Quotes

Conflicting views exist among experts about quotes. Emerson said, "Don't recite other people's opinions. I hate quotations. Tell me what you know."[14] Others disagree. Clifton Fadimn said, "I think we must quote whenever we feel that the allusion is interesting or helpful or amusing."[15] Montaigne said "I quote others only the better to express myself."[16] Tilden acknowledged that "sometimes a quotation will be found more effective than anything we can currently invent."[17] We encourage interpreters to use quotes to create a mood, stimulate reflection on the origin of the words, or stop readers in their tracks with a profound idea that came from someone else.

Humor

Humorous writing can delight or, in some instances, enrage. Humor usually depends on creating mental incongruities or contradictions that produce a surprise. William Zinsser calls humor "the secret weapon of the nonfiction writer."[18] He goes on to say that "... few writers realize that humor is often their best tool—their only tool—for making an important point."[19]

Tilden, on the other hand, evaluated humor as "one of the touchiest qualities of inscriptional writing."[20] Humor can be unwieldy and dangerous because it is so subjective. What is humorous to some doesn't work for others. Yet, when it works, it is, as Zinsser says, "the best tool."

Tilden tolerated only a "light touch." He believed that written interpretation should never be funny. His example of a "light touch" was the inscription on a monument in Quebec honoring both Montcalm and Wolfe, leaders of opposing armies who fought and died at the site: "Valor gave them a common death, history a common fame, and posterity a common monument."[21]

Tilden's timid and restrictive view toward using humor in interpretive writing may be because he focused on writing inscriptions. However, contemporary interpreters have found humor to be effective in all types of interpretive writing. The key to using humor effectively and appropriately is to recognize that all humor is not the same. Different kinds of humor exist and being aware of the different types and their utility can make the difference between driving home a message or driving people away. The following discussion, although focused on written interpretation, is valid for oral interpretation as well.

In general, puns are the safest form of humor. Carefully selected jokes, riddles, and witticisms can also be safe and effective. Obviously, jokes directed at any one individual, gender, or ethnic group are offensive and have no place in interpretation.

Burlesque, parody, and satire pack powerful punches but are dangerous because they intend to ridicule. Using these forms of humor is risky and mostly inappropriate in interpretive writing. Sarcasm is always intended to hurt. Even when it is aimed at an enemy of the interpreter's cause, it comes across as unprofessional and mean-spirited. Furthermore, not every reader may agree that the target is deserving of such an attack.

As with all aspects of good writing, interpreters must know their audience to use humor effectively. Jokes that are too sophisticated or require a higher level of reasoning than readers possess will "go over their heads." On the other hand, if jokes are too simple or silly the writer looks foolish.

Using humor with children is especially challenging and rewarding. Children's perceptions of humor are dependent upon their reasoning abilities. Robert Bixler recommends using Piaget's stages of cognitive development to identify the appropriate types of humor to use with young audiences.[22]

If interpreters write for an audience of both children and adults, it is important that when humor is directed at children, the interpreter subtly indicates as much to adults. That is, interpreters must write with a wink toward the adult reader. Sometimes, interpreters can write for situations (e.g., exhibits) where parents or grandparents will be present at the reading of the material. In such cases, the adults will enjoy the reaction of the children and not be irritated at the childish humor.

In addition to knowing how to use humor, it is important to consider how much humor to use. Because humor is based on surprise, it cannot be used continually. Humorist S.J. Perelman gave this advice to a writing class, "When you endeavor to be funny in every line you place an intolerable burden not only on yourself but on the reader. You have to allow the reader to breathe."[23]

In all humorous interpretive presentations, whether written or spoken, it is important that the audience knows the intent of the interpreter is playful, not hurtful. And, like all interpretation efforts, it is critical that the important points being communicated come through.

Humor can enhance the effectiveness of written interpretation. It holds the reader's attention, it makes the reading more enjoyable, and when linked to specific information it may help the reader retain that information. Like any tool, it works wonders if used well, and is equally disastrous if misused.[24]

Technological and Cultural Changes

How has writing changed since Tilden wrote *Interpreting Our Heritage*? We have already mentioned that interpreters are responsible for more than inscriptions and are called upon to be active players in writing management-related messages. Two other overall changes in writing have occurred—one technological and one cultural.

Word Processing

The technology of writing has been completely revolutionized by computers. Word processors have replaced typewriters and the implications for writers are enormous. The attractiveness of word processing is that it allows for efficient changes. Word processors allow writers to consider what they wrote without the burden of thinking about how difficult it will be to go back and change it. Word processors free writers from the dread and energy-draining psychological hurdles of retyping page after page of revisions and cutting and pasting passages of a manuscript. Writers are more willing and able to revise and therefore produce better writing. Zinsser called word processors "God's gift" to good writing because "the essence of writing is rewriting."[25]

Word processors also allow writers to work more efficiently and correctly by offering an electronic spelling checker, an electronic dictionary, and an electronic thesaurus. Most word processing packages also offer a writing assessment program that checks grammar and makes recommendations on style.

Computer technology allows interpreters to become more efficient in their writing. This does not, however, eliminate the importance of dedicated thinking and inspired composition.

Inclusiveness Issues

During the lifetimes of Mills and Tilden gender neutral writing and appropriate terms for ethnic groups and job titles were not issues. Mills and Tilden did not write about such things nor does their writing reflect a sensitivity to these issues. However, their clear commitment to serve the needs of all people through interpretation indicates that if they were alive today they would likely be at the forefront of efforts promoting inclusive writing.

We support inclusive writing. However, when we quote others we always use their precise language (including that of Annie Dillard, an award-winning writer, who has a tendency to use masculine pronouns).

Interpretive audiences are more diverse than in the times of Mills and Tilden. Women and ethnic groups have called attention to inappropriate and sometimes exclusive terminology. Interpreters must write with sensitivity.

The written word can be a powerful means of communication. As John Steinbeck noted, "Great writing has been a staff to lean on, a mother to consult, a wisdom to pick up stumbling folly, a strength in weakness and a courage to support sick cowardice."[26]

Written interpretation has certain advantages over other interpretive media. Written materials can be read at the reader's own pace. Printed materials can be saved and read at the reader's convenience. These can be read off-site and they can be read repeatedly. Furthermore, they can last for generations, for as the old adage says, the strongest mind is weaker than the palest ink. All of these factors make the well-written word a powerful interpretive medium. Tilden concluded, "Whatever is written without enthusiasm will be read without interest."[27] This timeless truth applies whether you are writing with crayons or computers.

When love and skill work together, expect a masterpiece.
—John Ruskin

▪ *Chapter Twelve* ▪

ATTRACTING SUPPORT AND MAKING FRIENDS

The overall interpretive program must be capable of attracting support—financial, volunteer, political, administrative—whatever support is needed for the program to flourish.

He who has a thousand friends has not a friend to spare,
And he who has one enemy shall meet him everywhere.

—Ralph Waldo Emerson (who attributed it to Omar Khyyám)

The first law of economics states that there is no such thing as a free lunch. This law seems to have universal appeal and application. The story of the derivation of this "law" tells of a newly wealthy ruler who seeks to apply the wisdom of economists to managing his riches. Under the threat of death, his economists prepared volumes containing all the economic theories. The ruler is impatient and requires the advisors to condense these theories into a single volume and ultimately to reduce all the volumes of economics wisdom to a single sentence. The free lunch law is what presumably saved the advisors' lives. It has application in economics, ecology and interpretation.

For many years interpreters operated under the premise that interpretation was "free" of economic concerns. But, we've come to understand clearly that there is no such thing as a free interpretation program. In times of limited and shrinking budgets the costs of interpretation become an important issue for decision-makers. Interpreters face the challenge of convincing the public and their administrators that interpretation is not a luxury, but instead an essential service providing multiple benefits to society and sponsoring organizations.

Financial Support:
Opportunities for Friends to Give

Interpretation in the commercial sector has always had to make a profit to survive. In response to taxpayer revolts and a general trend of government budget reductions, many public sector interpretive programs must also generate revenue or face elimination. Revenue can be collected through entrance fees, program fees, or a variety of fund-raising strategies.

Fee or Free

Traditionally, interpretation services were offered free as a public service. Tax dollars supported the programs and as "public servants" interpreters believed they owed these services to taxpayers. As tax dollars dwindled and costs of providing services increased, many organizations eliminated services. Others adapted by changing to fee-based programming.

For example, the Johnson County (Kansas) Parks and Recreation Department serves the citizens of one of the most affluent counties in the U.S. The Park Board has mandated that the interpretation programs be fee supported. Visitors do not pay park entrance fees, but a fee is charged for *every* interpretive program. In 1996, $193,000 were collected from programs and a small nature center gift shop. Although tax dollars subsidize utilities, maintenance, and parts of some salaries, fees support 100 percent of the direct programming costs. More than 80 percent of the entire interpretation budget is covered by fees collected at programs.[1]

Interpreters must think of interpretation programs as a business—a business of manufacturing and selling interpretive experiences. We need to recognize that we have competitors producing substitute experiences. Like any manufacturing process, interpreters must consider the quality and quantity of the experiences being produced. At Johnson County, a budget is developed before any interpretive program is offered. The cost of brochures, advertising, supplies, staff salary, equipment and administrative costs are calculated and a pricing scheme is set based on estimates of minimum and maximum attendance. Administrators recognize that some programs such as a wildflower walk or bird walk cannot be sold at fair market value and still break even. Yet, they are considered part of the interpretive mission so revenues generated from highly profitable interpretive hay rides and summer camps subsidize the interpretation of wildflowers and songbirds.

Decisions about which programs (i.e., products) to produce are market-based. At Johnson County, every program is evaluated to get customer feedback on the program's quality and to assess future demand. Surveys are regularly conducted of both visitors and nonvisitors to determine their needs and desires. Planners use professional contacts and written sources to identify relevant leisure trends. For stability and planning purposes interpreters must have "base programs" that can be counted on for revenue each year (e.g., contractual arrangements with local schools to provide a set number of programs). Once such a base is established, it is possible to slowly add programs based on the market research.

Charging fees has advantages and disadvantages. The disadvantages are that some old-timers resist change saying, "You've never charged before." Others will challenge the change claiming that is what their tax dollars are for and that, philosophically, public programs should be available to everyone. At Johnson County, people have become used to paying and they willingly pay for quality programs. As for the issue of fees eliminating participation by certain individuals or groups, a voucher system or scholarships can be offered to disadvantaged people. If other revenue-generating strategies are used along with fees, then fees can be kept low to minimize economic barriers.

Collecting fees offers several advantages. No-shows are reduced because fee payers who register for a program have made a commitment to participate and are unlikely to forfeit their fees. Interpreters have a greater incentive to provide a high quality program, because the expectations of the audience will be greater if they paid for the experience and because a better product will generate more financial resources. Successful fee programs can subsidize other worthwhile programs that would otherwise not be financially viable.

Grants and Gifts

The success rate in approaching foundations, corporations and philanthropic individuals is commonly believed to be about five percent. But, interpreters can do much better than this by developing symbiotic relationships with donors. We must understand why people give and then help them achieve their goals. Both the receiver and giver must benefit from the gift transaction.

People give for one or more of the following reasons: tax benefits, gratitude for services, belief in a program's mission, recognition or visibility, general altruism, or to "achieve" immortality. If interpreters know which of these motivate a donor, they can strategically target the donor's interests to particular projects. If their interest is in increasing visibility they may want to sponsor a weekend festival. If their interest is immortality they may want to help with a building project.

Seeking donations should be perceived as giving people an opportunity to become part of an important and successful venture. Personal solicitation of gifts from individuals is the most effective way of raising funds. Almost 90 percent of philanthropic dollars comes from individuals.[2]

Special Events

Special events raise money through entrance fees and sales. They attract people from the community that otherwise would not visit the site. Like a supermarket food sample, this approach encourages people to experience a product and decide if they like it. Tim Merriman, currently the Executive Director of the National Association for Interpretation, is legendary for his creative special events that pulled The Greenway and Nature Center of Pueblo (Colorado) from the brink of bankruptcy. These included casino nights, art fairs, rummage sales, dances, raft races, and field trips. Existing trails were adapted seasonally to become Halloween Spook Trails and Easter Egg Trails. Merriman also established a restaurant, a plant store, and gift shop. Through hard work and ingenuity he generated the financial support necessary to allow this private interpretive site to thrive.[3]

Partnerships and Sponsorships

As park and museum budgets shrink, interpreters have to find ways of doing more with less. One way to stretch dollars is to develop partnerships. For example, many nature centers are forming partnerships with local school districts. Schools are looking for new ways to teach science and environmental education. Since many states have specific goals for science in each grade, nature centers can easily identify those that they can help the schools meet. Joining with schools brings strong support from parents, local business, civic and service groups, and the general public.

Branded sponsors can be used to raise funds for interpretive sites, especially when a special event is planned. Branded sponsors are given exclusive rights to sell their products at specified events. In exchange for these rights sponsors pay cash, give discounts on products, or assist in advertising and marketing. Advertising is sometimes the most valuable compensation. Firms provide advertising space on billboards, trucks, and packaging, as well as offering coupons to encourage attendance and participation.

In exchange for advertising, or for altruistic reasons, companies will sponsor certain specific interpretive programs, trails, or other facilities. The newest frontier for sponsorship is web sites on the Internet. Ameritech, a telephone provider to several midwestern states, sponsors "At Home in the Heartland" at the Illinois State Museum's Web Site. Ameritech, in conjunction with the Illinois State Board of Education, provides an opportunity for students to make simulated decisions that the settlers made based on available goods and services. Classes take virtual field trips to the museum and through "At Home in the Heartland" receive information integrating the state curricular objectives for grade levels 3-12 for social studies and language arts. All of this would be beyond the budgets of either the museum or individual school districts.

Teaming Up

Interpreters at both public and private sites are finding it useful to team with other sites when seeking support. In the Kansas City area, an Interpretative Site Coalition (ISC) was formed by bringing together personnel from 13 sites to form a unified cooperative effort. ISC has pooled and shared resources to produce workshops, share volunteers and staff, to generate free publicity, and to conduct an annual city-wide interpretation event called "The Passport to Adventure Hunt." This activity promotes all the cooperating groups by enhancing awareness of interpretation opportunities as participants get their passports stamped at each cooperating site. ISC was able to gain sponsors, donations, and publicity that would not have been possible if acting independently.[4]

In Cincinnati, 10 museums formed a non-profit group called "Historic Homes and Sites of Greater Cincinnati." At least six benefits have been realized by the members of the group: increased visibility and identification, shared technical assistance, shared educational programming, cooperative grant funding, companionship and camaraderie, and a new leadership role in the community.[5]

Much ingenuity with a little money is vastly more profitable and amusing than much money without ingenuity.
—Arnold Bennett

Volunteers: Putting Friends to Work

Volunteers have become an important force in providing interpretive services, particularly in recent years as budget cuts have reduced professional staffs. For example, the National Park Service benefits from tens of thousands of volunteers, receiving $32 worth of work for every dollar spent on recruitment and training.[6]

Some interpretive sites use hundreds of volunteers. More than 300 volunteers donate more than 20,000 hours annually at the Louisiana Nature and Science Center—equivalent to 10 full-time staff positions.[7]

At the Raptor Center at the University of Minnesota, a private, non-profit organization, 150 volunteers donate more than 10,000 hours annually. What makes this program unique is that *volunteers* organize and manage the volunteer program. That is, volunteers formed a Volunteer Board which acts as a liaison between staff and volunteers.[8]

Volunteers have allowed agencies to respond to increasing demand for interpretation. At Año Nuevo State Reserve in California, docents take visitors from around the world on tours to see elephant seals on the beach. This volunteer program was initiated in response to a crisis. After the media publicized the site, thousands of visitors unexpectedly descended on the park, far exceeding the number that the staff could handle. The tranquil elephant seals were threatened by the unmanaged crowds. A reservation ticket system was set up through Ticketron for volunteer-led tours to solve the problem.[9]

Some volunteers coalesce to form "Friends" groups. These groups enter into formal partnerships with the park or museum. They assist by conducting fund raising that would not be allowed within the agency. Friends groups can organize to receive tax deductible donations resulting in a much more competitive position when competing for financial gifts. Friends groups may also operate book stores and gifts shops, and assist with maintenance, cleanups, and publicity campaigns. They can become important advocates when political support is needed.

Finding Volunteers

Volunteers are not made, but asked. Only about 25 percent of volunteers enlist on their own and only 6 to 7 percent respond to newspaper, radio or television appeals. Almost 70 percent of those who volunteer respond to personal invitations.[10] Invitations can be extended individually or take the form of presentations to civic groups, scouts, church groups, or other targeted audiences.

Teenagers are among the best and least tapped populations for recruitment of volunteers. They have the ability, interest, and energy to make outstanding contributions to interpretive programs and facilities. Teen volunteer hours increased 17 percent in the United States between 1992 and 1996. Even if these teens were only paid minimum wage for their volunteer time, it would amount to almost $8 billion. As one writer noted, "that's a pretty nice gift to America."[11] Two out of three high school students favor making volunteer community service a requirement for graduation. But, like adults, teenagers must be asked to volunteer. When asked by an adult to volunteer about 90 percent accept the invitation.[12]

The trend in increasing volunteerism in teens has been noted at many interpretive sites. At the Lindsay Wildlife Museum in Walnut Creek, California, teen volunteers increased 300 percent between 1992 and 1996 and that site now turns away more than they can accept.[13]

Recall from Chapter Six we identified principles for working with teens and reasons why they volunteer. Like adults, teens want volunteer programs to be fun and rewarding. They want responsibility and recognition for accomplishments. They want to learn by doing rather than being bystanders.[14]

Keeping Your Volunteers

Volunteers, regardless of age, should be shown respect and appreciation. They should be treated like paid staff as much as possible. This begins even before they become volunteers. Potential volunteers should be interviewed to determine their interests, motives, and needs, just as prospective employees would be interviewed. Job descriptions, policies, and time commitments should be presented and discussed before the volunteer is accepted. Like employees, volunteers should be evaluated to provide feedback on their performance.

Once selected, volunteers need training. The teenagers with the Missouri Department of Conservation attend seven two-hour training sessions dealing with plant and animal identification and how to lead hikes and give programs.

On the job, volunteers should be provided with their own work space, uniforms or identification badges. They should be made to feel like an important part of the interpretation team. This means keeping them informed of all relevant agency communications and listening closely to what they have to say about policies and practices.

Volunteers must feel needed and appreciated. They should be regularly thanked, privately and publicly, and formally shown appreciation for their contributions.

The Privilege of Service

Volunteers do not "work for nothing." Volunteers benefit richly from the experience. In fact, if the experience is not rewarding, volunteers will look for opportunities to serve elsewhere. The volunteer's motives may be pragmatic such as gaining experience to adorn a resume, or trying out a potential employer or career path. Volunteers may be acting on a commitment to an ideology or purely altruistic motives of helping people. Some volunteers just want to feel useful, taking to heart Dickens's observation that, "No one is useless in this world who lightens the burdens of another."

Many volunteers find profound pleasure in sharing their energy and interests with others. Interpreting cultural and natural resources can be tremendously rewarding personally (see Chapter 14).

By incorporating volunteers into the interpretive program, we not only contribute to the experience of visitors and relieve the burden on professional staff, but we offer the volunteers an opportunity to find personal fulfillment. Moreover, the park or museum receives an important side benefit because volunteers model enthusiasm and appropriate behavior. This enthusiasm is contagious and may positively affect visitor behavior at the site.[15]

The strongest friendships are symbiotic where each party meets the needs of the other. Interpreters must find ways to meet the needs not only of visitors, but of volunteers, gift-givers, and other partners as well.

Political Support

To a large extent, political support is a function of public support. Most politicians and policy-makers will support a consensus of their constituents, particularly if they are well-organized and vocal. Gaining and maintaining public support for interpretation is a matter of both quantity and quality.

Expanding the interpretation program's sphere of influence through publications, mass media interpretation, and off-site programs broadens the base of public support. Another way of expanding the base of support is through family ties. Children's programs have powerful political impacts. If you captivate the children, you've captured the support of their parents. Likewise, programs at nursing homes and assisted living centers enhance the quality of life of seniors, thereby garnering the support of their families and the staff.[16] Having the privilege of presenting programs to the aged enriches the interpreters' lives too.

Politically, it is critical to have advocates and allies in the form of other organizations or agencies. Linkages to schools and health care facilities are especially valuable because health and education lend themselves to strong community support.

The best insurance against unfavorable political decisions is providing a high-quality product—one that the customers would hate to lose and would fight to keep. Interpretation programs must become as customer-oriented as any business. In recent years, business principles and practices have been presented regularly in the interpretation literature and at interpretation workshops.[17] Many interpretation organizations are using such business concepts as Total Quality Management (TQM). Although there are many variations in implementation, TQM is characterized by total dedication to customers to meet their needs and exceed their expectations.[18]

For example, TQM has been used to improve interpretive services at Bonneville Lock and Dam. Dramatic improvements to personal customer service and improved brochures, displays, signs, and safety access for the disabled all have been attributed to implementation of TQM at this site.[19] Satisfied customers, willing to influence policy-makers, are a strong defense against political setbacks.

Friends in High Places: Administrative Support

Sometimes the lack of support for interpretation is not from the outside, but from within the organization. Park administrators, curators, law enforcement rangers, maintenance personnel, and others can be skeptical of interpretation's value. Although interpretation has been used as a management tool since the early days of the National Park Service, conflicts have existed between interpreters and administrators who do not recognize the benefits of interpretation. Grant Sharpe speculated that this may be because managers rarely rise through the interpretation ranks and interpreters do not fully communicate with managers. Interpreters should ask themselves: How do we fit into the organization? How do we become team members? How can we assist management in achieving management goals? Do we even know what management goals are?[20] To thrive interpreters must win their administrators' support and be respected members of the overall team.

Prior to the late 1970s, with few exceptions, evidence for interpretation's effectiveness as a management tool was circumstantial and anecdotal.[21] Interpreters hung on to the oft-quoted intuitive slogan, "Through interpretation, understanding; through understanding, appreciation; through appreciation, protection." The interpreter's "management" task was to have people love their natural and cultural resources. In challenging interpreters to apply better science to documenting the affects of interpretation one respected writer referred to the alleged benefits as the "folklore of environmental education."[22]

The late 1970s and 1980s brought empirical studies that quantified the benefits of interpretation in reducing vandalism, littering and other visitor impacts, and in redistributing visitor use.[23] The 1980s also brought application of social psychology theories to understanding and evaluating interpretation.[24] Application of persuasive communication theory results in attitude and behavior change.[25] With firm theoretical frameworks, interpreters can claim the ability to serve agency administrators and managers by affecting the way the public thinks and behaves. Researchers continue to apply theories, testing and revising them, ultimately to formulate different approaches to enhance the persuasiveness of interpretation.[26]

Many government agencies, including the National Park Service and Corps of Engineers, state that as a matter of policy interpretation will address resource management issues to gain public support and cooperation in protecting those resources. Interpreting such policy issues places interpreters in the political arena, whether or not they choose to be there. Referencing Mark Twain's description of politics as "the devil's work," Gary Machlis wrote a provocative essay titled, "The Devil's Work in God's Country—Politics and Interpretation in the 1990s." Machlis stated:

> Perhaps he [Tilden] hoped it [interpretation] would be aseptic, dignified and humane, provoking and delighting citizens to learn more about Nature and History. But, in contemporary America, interpretation is a political act ... Interpreters have both the potential and responsibility to play a critical role in the functioning of park ecosystems. But, to do so will require new skills and a willingness to grapple with difficult issues. To be effective in the 1990s, I feel (perhaps fear) that interpreters will have to do the devil's work in God's country.[27]

Michael Frome goes a step farther. He takes to task frightened and intimidated interpreters and encourages them to courageously speak out on environmental issues, even if it jeopardizes their jobs.[28] Indeed, some interpreters have quit choice jobs in protest or have been fired for speaking out about an issue. We must weigh the costs and benefits of such choices within our own ethical frameworks. The bottom line is that interpretation can be powerfully persuasive. As more administrators become convinced of that, they will increase the political use, or misuse, of interpretation.

Despite these controversies in application, perhaps it is in this arena of using and understanding interpretation as a management tool that the field of interpretation has exhibited the most professional growth and maturity. The profession has gone from intuition and folklore, to informal field application, to theory, to field applications of theory. In the 1996 inaugural issue of the *Journal of Interpretation Research*, each article had a strong base in social psychological theory and theoretical models of human behavior. Yet, the task remains to motivate field interpreters to apply this theory and to demonstrate to their administrators the power of interpretation.

Grant Sharpe, in a 1993 interview, stated that, "Too many interpreters still think of themselves as interpreters only, often making little or no attempt to work with management in solving or reducing management problems...Interpreters should make themselves so valuable in problem solving that they become indispensable."[29] (See Boxes 1 and 2)

Box 1
Solving Bear Problems and Saving Lives with Interpretation

Interpretation Solves an "Unbearable" Problem

Problem: Managers at Prairie Creek Redwoods State Park were experiencing bear problems. During 1989, 52 bears were seen in the campground, 35 cars were broken into by bears, and two bears had to be killed. In 1990, 136 bear sightings were reported, bears broke into 45 cars, and two more bears had to be euthanized. Park rangers decided that there weren't really bear problems, only uninformed camper problems. Unknowingly, campers were habituating bears to human food.

Interpretive Treatment: Colorful interpretive posters and signs were placed along the road and in the campground. Culvert traps used to catch bears were put on display to explain their function in bear management when they weren't being used. All visitors were given a "Don't Invite Trouble" handout and the annual visitor's guide contained articles and updates on the bear situation. Entrance station operators talked to each visitor about proper food storage, bear habits, and bear avoidance techniques. Campfire programs provided bear information each night during the "warm-up." Bear-damaged ice chests and soda cans were displayed and the audience was invited to share bear stories. One campfire program each week was devoted to bear ecology. Audiences were sometimes quizzed about bear knowledge so that interpreters could customize their talk to correct misconceptions and tailor it to the audience's level.

*Results:*The year after this program started (1991) there were over 200 bear sightings, but only one car was damaged and no bears had to be killed.

Interpretation Saves Lives

Problem: For five consecutive years at least one person had drowned in the Columbia River near the Bonneville Lock and Dam. Each of these drownings resulted from improper anchoring. When the anchor rope is too short in the deep, fast moving water, the short anchor line tightens and pulls the bow under the water. Anglers using boats to get to popular sturgeon fishing sites were drowning while attempting to anchor. J. Patrick Barry, an interpreter with the Corps of Engineers, recalled, "One of the most frustrating feelings I've ever experienced was the sense of defeat I felt while searching in vain for survivors from a capsized boat ..." Agency personnel were struck with the realization that such deaths should be preventable.

Interpretive Treatment: Interpreters improved the safe anchoring posters and passed out reduced versions to anglers so they could keep them for reference. Large signs were put up at boat ramps to advertise that improper anchoring had caused fatalities. Interpreters were stationed at water safety booths at sporting shows and county fairs and used brochures, demonstrations, and an interactive video to convince boaters of the dangers facing them. Boat shops, bait shops, and sporting supply stores were supplied with safe anchoring information. Individual contacts were also made to communicate proper boating safety.

Results: In the five years following the "Safe Anchoring in Current" interpretive effort not a single person has drowned.

Adapted from M. Stalder and B. Cahill, 1992, "Bears, Bears and More Bears" and J.P. Barry, 1993, "Anchoring Safely in Current."

Box 2
Interpretation Making Dollars and Sense

Jay Miller is an administrator with the Arkansas Department of Parks and Tourism. He has seen first-hand the financial benefits of having interpretation in Arkansas State Parks.

Old Davidsonville State Park is a small historic site in northern Arkansas. Old Davidsonville has river access, a small fishing lake, 25 campsites, a visitor center with exhibits about the history of the site, and a shop with a few items for sale. Davidsonville had been home to Arkansas' first post office, first two-story court house, and first land office. Located along the famed Southwest Trail, the town welcomed travelers from St. Louis and points east who were on their way to Mexico. The town was abandoned by 1830. The State Park was almost as abandoned and forgotten as Old Davidsonville itself. That is, until 1995 when Wes Field, a dedicated and talented interpreter, was assigned to become the first full-time interpreter at the park. Through special events, consistent programming, living history, working with local schools, and courting the media, Wes made Old Davidsonville the place to be. Specifically, in one year, the following was accomplished: programs increased from 22 to 109, visitor contacts increased from 1,524 to 10,410, park attendance increased from 28,342 to 79,119, and revenue increased from $7,407 to $23,522!

Jay concluded, "Why doesn't every park across the country have an interpretive staff? Beats me. I find it hard to believe that any park system which wants to be successful doesn't put interpreters in every park as soon as they open the doors to the public."

From personal communication with Jay Miller.

Friendly Fire

The subject of changing attitudes and behavior is always controversial. Research shows that interpreters clearly want to change visitors' attitudes.[30] Are there more efficient ways of regulating behavior and gaining compliance or support? Is it appropriate to change attitudes?

Dan Dustin and Leo McAvoy have made a strong case on both theoretical and practical grounds for using direct regulation of behavior rather than the indirect approach of using education to affect behavior change.[31] Especially when resource protection and visitor safety are critical concerns, strict enforcement of regulations would be most appropriate. Interpretation's role would be one of helping visitors understand and internalize the rationale for the regulations.

These same two observers have a dissenting view of interpretation as a management tool.[32] They fear that preoccupation with the idea will subvert the art of interpretation. If the emphasis becomes accountability in terms of management benefits, interpretation will redirect its focus on only those tasks that produce measurable results. And, as with any art form, many important outcomes of interpretation do not lend themselves to quantification.

The art of interpretation will be lost if we reduce interpretation to teaching facts and then measuring learning or behavior change. In doing so, we violate both the third principle, that interpretation is an art, and the second principle, that interpretation is more than information. When these principles are violated the activity is no longer true interpretation.

Others question whether tax dollars should be spent to change the taxpayers' attitudes. They claim public servants should do things for people, not to people.[33] In a similar vein, some resent interpretation as elitist. They see interpretation as imposing the agency's or interpreter's values on visitors. Gary Machlis quoted a park visitor after enduring "several political diatribes masquerading as interpretative walks" as saying, "I wanted to learn about the park. After the second lecture, I just quit going to the visitor centers or listening to the bastards."[34]

Tilden's response to the perception that interpreters are trying to impose their values on others is that, "We shall not teach morals as such. We use our vast natural and cultural resources to show what true morals are. We do not tell people what they must do, but what they can do; not what they must be, but what they can be ..."[35]

Interpreting Controversial Issues

Efforts to change attitudes about controversial issues can be especially volatile. Controversies abound in interpretation: Creation vs. evolution, timber cutting (and jobs) vs. preserving old-growth forests, conflicts between the perspectives of European settlers and Native Americans. People are easily offended when their core beliefs are challenged. Site managers often are willing to forego the benefits of interpreting controversial issues because they are afraid of generating even more controversy.

The difference between alienating people *over* an issue, educating people *about* an issue or inspiring people *by* an issue is in the interpreter's approach. When presenting a controversial issue interpreters would be wise to do the following:

1. Demonstrate warmth and sincere interest in the audience. People are more likely to consider seriously the words of a new friend. We can exhibit tolerance for other views without compromising our own.
2. Do everything possible to maximize credibility. This includes being particularly well-organized, having a polished professional appearance, using solid data as evidence, carefully distinguishing opinion from fact, demonstrating humility by admitting when you don't know something, and allowing for ambiguity on complex issues.
3. Intensively apply the first principle of interpretation—know your visitors and relate to them. Be able to interpret the issue from alternative perspectives. Understand and communicate to visitors why this issue is important to them personally.
4. Be aware of your biases and emotions regarding the issue. Keep both in check.

National Park Service interpretation administrators presented the Visitor's Bill of Rights at the 1996 meeting of the National Association for Interpretation. Visitors have the right: 1) to privacy, 2) to retain and express their own values, 3) to receive courtesy and consideration, and 4) to receive accurate and well-balanced information.[36] These NPS officials noted that interpretation is not something we "inflict" on people.

If we proselytize to audiences, we will alienate them. Alienating neighbors will result in a loss of public and political support thereby diminishing the interpretation program's influence or eliminating it entirely. Instead, we need to be lights brightening the lives of our audiences. Interpreters are in the business of persuading people to think differently about their world and act differently based on those revelations. But, the persuasion should be gentle, uplifting and civilized. Without exception, to gain the support of superiors and to maintain the support of the public, interpreters must be seen as ladies and gentlemen, interpreting to ladies and gentlemen.

In attracting support and making friends good motives are mandatory. An unfortunate extreme would be exploiting visitors for free labor, making money off them, and brainwashing them into supporting our policies and philosophies. Interpreters should inspire, not indoctrinate. We should call attention to, as Shakespeare wrote, "tongues in trees, books in running brooks, sermons in stones and good in everything." Our goal should be to make friends and then touch them. A gentle touch can have deep effects.

Granger, a character in Ray Bradbury's classic *Fahrenheit 451* said it well regarding the touch of his grandfather:

"Grandfather's been dead for all these years, but if you lifted my skull, by God, in the convolutions of my brain you'd find the big ridges of his thumbprint. He touched me."

Our mission should be merely to leave our thumbprint on our visitors, volunteers, administrators, policy-makers, and other friends. If we do this we will garner all the support we need and leave a legacy worthy of future support.

▪ *Chapter Thirteen* ▪

INTERPRETING BEAUTY

I nterpretation should instill in people the ability, and the desire, to sense the beauty in their surroundings—to provide spiritual uplift and to encourage resource preservation.

Dostoyevsky once wrote, 'Beauty will save the world.'
But who will save beauty?

—Yevgeny Yevtushenko

Beauty defies definition. For centuries the subject has attracted the attention of the world's greatest writers and artists. Yet, the most articulate among them has struggled to capture the full character and meaning of beauty (see Box 1). Beauty is too personal, and therefore too subjective, to lend itself to definition by someone else. One person experiencing something as beautiful does not necessarily make it so for everyone. Interpreters must heed this warning. Freeman Tilden believed that a broad generalization about the beauty of the area contributed to establishing an appropriate mood, while leaving individuals free to make their own judgements about the beauty of any particular objects.[1]

It is among the roles of the interpreter to prepare visitors to be receptive to beauty and "do all that discreetly may be done to establish a mood, or sympathetic atmosphere." [2]

Enos Mills noted, "One of the best lessons gained from the wholesome atmosphere of the Parks is the duty of preserving natural beauties."[3]

Box 1
John Muir's Interpretation of Beauty

When John Muir was in his late twenties he worked in a carriage factory. He stayed late one night to adjust a conveyor belt. A sharp file he was working with slipped from his hands and pierced his right eye; the aqueous humor dropped into his cupped hand. His other eye also became blind from sympathetic nervous shock. For a month Muir was confined to a bed in a dark room. Terrified by his loss of sight he bemoaned his fate: "Closed forever on all God's beauty!"

Seeing only glimpses of light at first, Muir slowly regained his vision. For the rest of his life Muir equated light with God. He bestowed upon his precious Yosemite and Sierra the highest honor: "the range of light." Muir concluded, "No synonym for God is so perfect as Beauty."

Compiled from L.M. Wolfe, 1973, *Son of the Wilderness: The Life of John Muir*.

Classifying Nature's Beauty

The notion of beauty is difficult to articulate, as much of what is beautiful is revealed beyond the senses to the soul; an uplift of one's spirits, a rejoicing in the presence of symmetry, elegance, harmony, grace. Yet wild nature and beautiful human artifacts have powerful appeals, some of which may be captured.

Robert Marshall compared Nature's beauty to that of great works of human art. When asked how many wilderness areas this country needed, he replied, "How many Brahms symphonies do we need?" [4] Marshall meant that beauty, in whatever form, should not be destroyed, that we could never have too much. According to Marshall, natural beauty is comparable in its magnetism and appeal to human art, yet is distinctive for several reasons.

First, there is a timelessness about nature's beauty that is not found in the art of the painter, the poet, the sculptor, the musician, or the architect. Even the paintings of the Renaissance are anchored in time. John Muir understood this when he sang about Nature's beauty:"This grand show is eternal . . . Eternal sunrise, eternal sunset, eternal dawn and gloaming, on sea and continents and islands, each in its turn, as the round earth rolls."[5]

Second, the immensity of natural landscapes has a special esthetic power. We are humbled by the sheer size of Nature as we gaze from the lip of the Grand Canyon or from a lofty mountain summit. We feel like a speck in the universe and are exalted at the same time. Barry Lopez wrote,"To the explorer the land becomes large, alive like an animal; it humbles him in a way he cannot pronounce. It is not that the land is simply beautiful but that it is powerful. Its power derives from the tension between its obvious beauty and its capacity to take life."[6]

Third, in natural settings we are immersed by Nature's artwork. As Marshall suggested,"One looks from outside at works of art and architecture, listens from outside to music or poetry. But when one looks at and listens to the wilderness he is encompassed by his experiences of beauty."[7]

Fourth, natural beauty is dynamic; it changes through the seasons and the years—autumn leaves, the snow of winter, spring wildflowers, verdant summer meadows. According to Marshall, a Beethoven symphony, a Shakespearean drama, a landscape by Corot, or a Gothic cathedral, once they are finished, become virtually static.[8] In contrast, the landscape is in constant flux. Sigurd Olson wrote, "I never watch a sunset without feeling the scene before me is more beautiful than any painting could possibly be, for it has the additional advantage of constant change, is never the same from one instant to the next."[9]

A fifth distinctive quality of Nature's beauty is that it encompasses all of our senses. The smell of the forest after rain. The breath of a cool alpine breeze. The song of a meadowlark or trembling aspen leaves. The sweet taste of a mountain stream. The colorful flash of a monarch or tiger swallowtail on the wing. Or the unfurling leaves of a black oak in spring—the ineffable colors of a ripe peach. Diane Ackerman observed,"Much of our experience in twentieth-century America is an effort to get away from those textures [of the senses], to fade into a stark, simple, solemn, puritanical, all-business routine that doesn't have anything so unseemly as sensuous zest."[10] Nature stimulates and quickens all of our senses.

Finally, Marshall pointed out that Nature offers the best opportunity for "pure esthetic enjoyment." Marshall wrote, "This requires that beauty be observed as a unity, and that for the brief duration of any pure esthetic experience the cognition of the observed object must completely fill the spectator's cosmos."[11] This deep and powerful response to beauty is consistent with Abraham Maslow's concept of peak experiences which he explained as moments of highest happiness.

All of Nature is Beautiful

People are drawn to the deepest canyons, the highest mountains, the spectacular coastlines, and the tallest trees. Alfred Runte refers to this inclination toward nature's spectacles as monumentalism.[12] The "jewel" scenic parks inspire, uplift, and overwhelm us. But are they more meaningful? Are they really more beautiful?

The great naturalists of this country agree that landscape beauty can be subtle as well as monumental. John Muir, although moved by the glaciers and spires of alpine scenery, appreciated foothill landscapes as well. Barry Lopez noted that "unheralded landscapes are still part of the face of God."[13] Agreement can be found in the writings of Aldo Leopold, Edward Abbey, Sigurd Olson, and others.

Tilden suggested that there can be nothing ugly in nature. Nothing. "The seeming exceptions are simply facets of beauty we have not yet grasped."[14] And Ralph Waldo Emerson found that the "inevitable mark of wisdom is to see the miraculous in the common."[15]

Consider the unheralded landscape of the tallgrass prairie. This grassland was celebrated in William Least Heat-Moon's bestseller, *PrairyErth*, a book specifically about Chase County, Kansas, an antidote to one commentator who suggested living in Kansas is a contradiction[16] (see Box 2).

Walt Whitman made the following observation: "As to the scenery (giving my own thought and feeling), while I know the standard claim is that Yosemite, Niagara Falls, the Upper Yellowstone, and the like afford the greatest natural shows, I am not so sure but the prairies and plains, while less stunning at first sight, last longer, fill the esthetic sense fuller, precede all the rest, and make North America's characteristic landscape."[17]

Box 2
The Beauty of an "Ordinary" Place:
A Cultural and Natural History of The Tallgrass Prairie

For years, outsiders have considered this prairie place barren, desolate, monotonous, a land of more nothing than almost any other place you might name, but I know I'm not here to explore vacuousness at the heart of America. I'm only in search of what is here, here in the middle of the Flint Hills of Kansas. I'm in quest of the land and what informs it . . .

These hills are largely limestones and shales distilled from the Permian seas that covered most of middle America off and on for fifty million years in the days when—had human beings and cities been around—a man could have paddled from Pittsburgh to Denver.

I'm walking down into an old marine world: in their journals, early white travelers wrote of the prairie, using a single metaphor as if it were the only one possible—*the ocean of grass*—and no wonder, since this land is *like* the sea and it is *of* the sea.

The four horsemen of the prairie are tornado, locust, drought, and fire, and the greatest of these is fire, a rider with two faces because for everything taken it makes a return in equal measure. The aboriginal peoples received the gift and made it part of their harmony here and used it as a white man would a plow to bring forth sweet and nutritious new grasses, or as a scythe to open a route over the prairie, or as a horse to dislodge deer or drive bison for harvesting, or as a cake of salt to draw the beasts within arrow range, or as a telegraph to send a message with smoking grasses.

More than all other things here, the grasses are the offspring of the wind, the power that helps evaporation equal precipitation to the detriment of trees, the power that breaks off leaves and branches, shakes crowns and rigid trunks to tear roots and disrupt transpiration, respiration, nutrient assimilation. But grasses before the wind bend and straighten and bend ...

Unlike a forest, a grassland lets sound carry, and I can count distant prairie voices: a harrier, a meadowlark, an upland plover. Each calls in plaintive phrases as if it admitted the prairie solitude into its notes. When the air does move, it pulls from the bending grass around me a soft outrush like a deep breath slowly vented, the wind giving voice to the grass, and it lending a face to the wind.

The survival of mammals on a grassland where cover is scarce depends upon at least one, commonly two, and sometimes three facilities: herding, burrowing, running.

Yet the fact remains: limestone is a rock not unlike bone; the fact remains: the chemical nature of the old seawater produced a stony land that produces good grasses that produce good, hoofed protein digestible to man. Flint Hills beef is a 250-million-year-old gift, yet the sense of history here goes back only to 1850 or sometimes a little further to the time of lithic weapons, and then it ceases. Even the three most noted buildings—the courthouse, the Z Bar Ranch home, and the Fox Creek School—made as they are from the primeval, thickened Kansas sea cut and laid up into walls, even these buildings do not carry the people's connections beyond the nineteenth century.

Only the ruins of the [federal] agency building and a few cabins remain in this valley where the people [Kansa] who gave their name to the state watched a ten-thousand-year-old way of life disappear, and with it their hopes for continuance.

The American disease—and I'm quoting someone I can't recall—is forgetfulness. A person or people who cannot recollect their past have little point beyond mere animal existence: it is memory that makes things matter.

I was coming to see that facts carry a traveler only so far: at last he must penetrate the land by a different means, for to know a place in any real and lasting way is sooner or later to dream it. That's how we come to belong to it in the deepest sense.

People may prefer the obvious beauty of mountains and sea-coasts, but we are bipedal because of savannah; we are human because of tallgrass.

Excerpts from William Least Heat-Moon, 1991, PrairyErth. By permission.

Interpreting Beauty in Practice

Establishing a mood conducive to perception and appreciation of a beautiful scene or object means freeing visitors from distractions so they can focus on the beauty. It also means having the audience in the proper frame of mind to maximize the impact of the beauty. An audience that is still laughing at the interpreter's last joke or still buzzing about the last trail stop will not be fully receptive to something beautiful. A quiet, understated exposure to the beauty will enhance the effect on the people viewing it.

Creating a sympathetic atmosphere is more than merely keeping the audience focused and minimizing distractions. It also entails cultivating the ability in people to perceive beauty. As discussed above, some glorious scenes in nature are universally appreciated, such as the Grand Canyon. But what about dank cypress swamps? We are intrigued by eagles and grizzlies; wolves and deer. But how many visitors understand the beauty of a bat? How do we create a sympathetic atmosphere for things that, on the surface, are not as spectacular and may even be perceived as revolting or disgusting?

Aldo Leopold explained these differing levels of appreciation as follows: "Our ability to perceive quality in nature begins, as in art, with the pretty. It expands through successive stages of the beautiful to values as yet uncaptured by language."[18]

We may use the analogies of art and music to make the point. Ask the average person on the street to name their favorite painter and many answer with artists such as Rockwell or Remington, whose fine paintings are easy to understand and appreciate. Few say Dali or Picasso. Their paintings are not as accessible in terms of being "pretty" and their meanings are not necessarily as obvious. Ask people to identify their favorite classical music pieces and, if they can name any at all, many will choose the 1812 Overture, Handel's Messiah, or the Pachelbel Canon in D. Some musicologists have been known to refer to these popular pieces as musical "shlock."

It is similar with appreciation of nature's beauty, as noted above, and the same may hold true in historical settings. Beautiful craftsmanship, say of a chair, or architecture, of a building, is not always immediately discernible to the untrained eye. The public may appreciate the beautiful stained glass of a cathedral, but may be oblivious to the handiwork in the pews.

Instead of condemning people, our role is to assist people, to guide them, to point beyond finding beauty only in obvious grandeur. This returns us to the second principle in which we strive to reveal meaning—the beauty of subtle landscapes, unusual organisms, or complex objects.

Like a master teaching a music or art appreciation course, interpreters can help people see, hear, or feel the beauty that is not readily apparent. It takes time, effort, and exposure to develop one's capabilities. We have all started at the beginning and we can make reference to and apply our own journey toward understanding more subtle beauty, to assist others. We can sensitize and motivate visitors to put forth the effort to appreciate successive stages of the beautiful.

> *Genius is recognizing the uniqueness in the unimpressive. It is looking at a homely caterpillar, an ordinary egg, and a selfish infant and seeing a butterfly, an eagle, and a saint.*
> —Anonymous

Landscapes of Nature and the Mind

Yi-Fu Tuan advanced the idea that beauty is essential in our individual lives and is, collectively, the driving force and ultimate goal of culture. The pervasive role of the esthetic is reflected by its root meaning of "feeling" and is suggested even more by its opposite, anesthetic, "lack of feeling." Tuan reminded us, "The more attuned we are to the beauties of the world, the more we come to life and take joy in it." [19]

Barry Lopez distinguished between the exterior and interior landscape. The exterior landscape is the one we see and experience. Eventually, with time and with practice, we learn not only the identities of those organisms in the environment, but we are able to perceive the relationships in it— "like that between the sparrow and the twig."[20] The interior landscape is that within the self (our thoughts, our moods), yet it is a projection of the exterior landscape. That is, the interior landscape responds to the attributes of the exterior landscape.

Tilden wrote that "the finest uses of national parks, or indeed any of the preserves that come within the range of interpretive work, lie ultimately in spiritual uplift."[21] Mills had observed earlier that in these same places "the geological wonders, the forests, the wild bloom, the folk in fur and feathers are protected for their higher values, for uses in education, for enjoyment, for giving relaxation and universal sympathy, for inspiring visions, and for enriching the imagination." [22]

Beauty, then, brings with it joy and inspiration and spiritual uplift. Yet when the "exterior landscape" is compromised or destroyed it brings revulsion, anger, and aggression.

Destruction of Beauty

Wallace Stegner observed that we need to listen to the land. He wrote: "Instead of easing air-pollution controls in order to postpone the education of the automobile industry; instead of opening our forests to greatly increased timber cutting; instead of running our national parks to please and profit the concessionaires; instead of violating our wilderness areas by allowing oil and mineral exploration with rigs and roads and seismic detonations, we might bear in mind what those precious places are: playgrounds, schoolrooms, laboratories, yes, but above all shrines, in which we can learn to know both the natural world and ourselves, and be at least half reconciled to what we see."[23]

Natural landscapes are "playgrounds" and offer opportunities for the primitive arts of wilderness travel. We paddle lakes, walk trails, ski cross country, lead packstock, climb summits, and run whitewater. These places are also "schoolrooms." Here we learn about cultural and natural history firsthand. This may involve reenactment of explorer lifestyles: retracing the route of Lewis and Clark, following the meanders of the Colorado River through the Grand Canyon in the wake of John Wesley Powell, or following the canoe routes of the voyagers in the Quetico-Superior lake region at the boundary of the United States and Canada. It is within cultural and natural "schoolrooms" that our heritage may be *interpreted* to us. Moreover, the learning process continues as research is conducted in these cultural and natural "laboratories" to expand the knowledge base.

But above all these places are "shrines" and they should be treated accordingly. What Stegner implies, we believe, is that places that commemorate our cultural and natural legacy are sacred, inviolate. They are places where, if we listen to the land, the intangible values of the heart, soul, and spirit take precedence; where we rise to a new plane of understanding, responsible action, and integrity.

In 1972, a vandal entered the Vatican and attacked Michelangelo's Pieta with a hammer, breaking off the nose and eyelid from the face of Mary and breaking her right arm off at the elbow. Although artists were able to restore the nearly 500-year-old sculpture (the only one signed by Michelangelo), this brazenly criminal act outraged people around the world. The most passionately furious called for the death penalty. The vandal ended up being sentenced to nine years in prison. Should there not be similar public reaction when a work of creation, whether it be a plant or animal species or an entire ecosystem, is destroyed?

Charles Little suggested that despoliation of the natural and cultural "shrines" that define us offends our esthetic sensibilities. When outrage follows we should allow it to flourish, since it fuels a defense against cultural or natural wreckage. "Instead of cool analysis," Little recommended, "we should embrace a politics of outrage, fury, indignation, wrath, deep umbrage, resentment, exasperation, rancor, and passion that wells up, if we let it, when we see the landscape destroyed."[24]

The Spiritual Dimensions of Beauty

Perhaps no other writer has so eloquently pursued the fleeting and ineffable nature of beauty as John Muir. He struggled, "Everything is so inseparably united. As soon as one begins to describe a flower or a tree or a storm ... up jumps the whole heavens and earth and God Himself in one inseparable glory!" [25]

Muir believed that God's glory was written over all His works. Furthermore, exposure to nature's beauty transforms a person. Overwhelmed by beauty Muir exulted, "You bathe in these spirit-beams, turning round and round, as if warming at a camp-fire. Presently you lose consciousness of your separate existence: you blend with the landscape, and become part and parcel of nature."[26] In this rapturous state, Muir believed that one might experience the fullest human integrity, the fundamental truths of existence, an understanding of the harmony of nature, the spiritual dimensions of beauty.

In the presence of beauty we feel oneness with the universe. We sense the order and perfection of nature. We rejoice in the moment amidst the harmony of the timeless whole. We feel peace and joy. The experience rings with truth. In beauty we reflect wonder and compassion.

Interpreters can carry out the profound act of interpreting beauty only if they first perceive it themselves. We cannot instill the desire and ability in others to perceive beauty if we do not portray that passion ourselves. It cannot be faked.

The appreciation of beauty is deeply personal. It is not, as the cliche suggests, so much in the *eye* of the beholder. It is in the *heart* of the beholder. Excellent interpretation prepares people's hearts to perceive beauty. Antoine de Saint Exupéry, in his classic *The Little Prince*, wrote, "It is only with the heart that one can see rightly: what is essential is invisible to the eye." [27] This is the mystery of beauty.

▪Chapter Fourteen▪

PROMOTING OPTIMAL EXPERIENCES

I nterpreters can promote optimal experiences through intentional and thoughtful program and facility design.

The conscious desire is to achieve a state, even momentarily,
that, like light, is unbounded, nurturing,
suffused with wisdom.

—Barry Lopez

Aristotle came to the conclusion, some 2300 years ago, that more than anything else people seek happiness. What defines happiness and what contributes to happiness? A leading scholar on optimal experiences, Mihalyi Csikszentmihalyi, has discovered that happiness is not contingent upon money or power or fame. It is not the result of random chance. It doesn't depend on outside events, but rather on how we interpret (perceive) them. Happiness comes as a consequence of being totally involved in our living.[1]

Optimal experience, according to Csikszentmihalyi, is when we feel a sense of exhilaration, a deep sense of enjoyment, that comes when our bodies and minds are "stretched to [their] limits in a voluntary effort to accomplish something difficult and worthwhile."[2] Csikszentmihalyi labelled these moments of peak awareness and learning "flow."

Settings that are effective in advancing learning and promoting optimal experiences are characterized by the absence of anything that might induce anxiety or stress. An attractive element of parks, museums, zoos, aquaria, historic sites and other interpretive areas is that these are informal places generally free of stress, and of an inspirational quality. Within these informal settings, we can design situations in which flow is likely to occur.

Characteristics of Flow

Csikszentmihalyi compiled eight characteristics which define optimal experiences. These have subsequently been reordered and renamed by Alan Hedge to form the acronym PACIFICS: purpose, attention, challenge, involvement, feedback, immersion, control, and sense of time.[3] To assist readers, we have followed this format although Csikszentmihalyi's original phrases are provided in parentheses in the titles.

Purpose (Clear Goals)

The purpose of any given activity must be clear to promote optimal experiences. When we are unaware of why we are doing something, we are less able to properly fulfill the goals. Therefore, purpose and expectations must be well-articulated before we can be fully goal-oriented.

Attention
(Concentration on the Task at Hand)

When we are in flow our attention is completely focused on the task at hand. This high level of concentration, when we are operating in the "here and now," is necessary to fulfill the conditions of a flow experience. It is only possible when the challenge is equivalent to our skill.

Challenge (A Challenging Activity That Requires Skill)

If the challenge facing us is too demanding then we quickly lose interest or become anxious. This is why, for example, we don't ask third graders to read William Faulkner.

If the challenge, however, is too simple then we tend to lose interest through boredom. This is why we don't ask university students to recite the letters of the alphabet. The challenge of the task must be equivalent to one's knowledge or level of skill if there is to be full involvement in the activity. Otherwise, we become anxious or bored and our attention is not focused on the task.

Involvement (The Merging of Action and Awareness)

When we are in flow we are not consumed with other less pleasant aspects of life. We are not worried about past events or concerned about the future. Csikszentmihalyi referred to this dimension of flow as the merging of action and awareness—a person is completely absorbed in the experience.[4] What we are doing is inseparable from what we are thinking about.

Feedback (Provides Immediate Feedback)

Linked with the importance of clear goals is feedback, as appropriate, for those striving to reach the goals. Feedback allows those who are involved in an activity to track their progress. Feedback can also be a motivating factor that encourages people toward further learning or skill development.

Immersion (The Loss of Self-Consciousness)

We noted above that when a mental or physical challenge is equivalent to one's aptitude or skill, then one is immersed in the activity and there is no regression into consideration of past or future concerns. According to Csikszentmihalyi, "One item that disappears from awareness deserves special mention, because in normal life we spend so much time thinking about it: our own self."[5] Being able to move, temporarily, beyond preoccupation with ourselves tends to be both healthy and enjoyable. It allows us, in the long run, to expand the concept of who we are. In flow, we are enriched by new attainments of knowledge and skill. Such achievements occur when we lose our self-consciousness, yet the self (as would be expected) emerges stronger after the experience, because we have grown.

Control (The Paradox of Control)

Optimal experiences occur when people sense that they have some degree of control over their environments.

Csikszentmihalyi revealed that the paradox of control is that a person can become consumed with the ability to direct an enjoyable activity to the exclusion of being able to function in other aspects of life. This extreme (addiction) is not generally pertinent to our discussion, but does illustrate the complexity of optimal experience theory.

Sense of Time
(The Transformation of Time)

The last defining quality of optimal experience is that when we are engaged in a challenging task our perception of time is altered. This characteristic of flow may be expressed in two ways: 1) time seems to accelerate (hours seem to pass like minutes) or 2) the opposite occurs (seconds seem to pass like minutes). Most often, in flow, time seems to pass quickly: time flies when we are having fun. Either way, our sense of time is quite different from the actual passage of time as measured by the clock. Although this is not necessarily a prerequisite for enjoyment, it is one of the most common descriptions associated with optimal experiences. [6]

Visitors in Flow

Interpretive professionals are in the business of creating and managing opportunities for enjoyment. They do not, however, produce that enjoyment. Only the visitor can do that. [7] However, interpretive sites *are* conducive to the attainment of optimal experiences, as noted above. Furthermore, interpreters can promote states of optimality through intentional and thoughtful program and facility design.

People come to places of cultural and natural significance during their leisure, although leisure means different things to different people—from relaxation to pushing oneself to the limits. The interpreter must understand that *not everyone* is seeking an optimal experience.

At one end of the spectrum, many people simply need directions. Perhaps they will achieve an optimal experience once they reach their destination. Others are seeking a pleasurable and relaxing time, but nothing too demanding. Perhaps it is this moment of rest that will serve as a foundation for subsequent growth.

Then there are those who want to push themselves, even though they may not be consciously thinking in those terms. This concept of leisure is consistent with the Greek ideal of leisure (or "schole") which was realized when individuals used their freedom to explore the limits of their potential. The value of leisure was not that it offered relaxation; on the contrary, it required effort to expand the range of one's physical, mental, or spiritual capacities.[8]

Although some dimensions of flow experience are beyond the realm of influence by interpreters, other characteristics may be purposefully encouraged. Furthermore, anything that is done to promote optimal experiences can also be useful and meaningful to those who do not achieve such states.

Promoting Purpose

Without purpose we tend to lose focus and motivation, both of which are essential to achieving states of optimality. Interpreters should provide clear goals to their participants. Facilities should be designed so that the purpose of exhibits, self-guiding trails and other *nonpersonal* interpretation is evident. In *personal* interpretation, a stated purpose must capture the visitors' curiosity and attention, and engage sustained interest, so that visitors can become fully involved in their experiences.

Promoting Challenge

Different visitors require different interpretive accommodations—that, in essence, the challenges meet the skills of those participating. Enjoyment appears at the boundary between boredom and anxiety, when the challenges are just balanced with the person's knowledge or physical ability.[9]

To meet the needs of a wide diversity of visitors, parks often offer a wide spectrum of trails that differ according to their length, type of terrain, and overall difficulty. Likewise, programs may be designed, as discussed in Chapter Six, specifically for children, teen-agers, or seniors to meet the level of their interests and abilities.

Application of this characteristic of flow could also be made at the level of visitor center or museum design. For example, infor-mation can be organized to reveal progressively more complex con-cepts. Perhaps the most simple information, presented via colorful illustrations and simple diagrams, would be at the height of chil-dren while more complex information and graphics would be pre-sented at a higher level. (Of course, this approach would have to be structured with sensitivity and with accessibility of the informa-tion to all visitors including those in wheelchairs.) Another possi-bility would be to design zones of information in increasing levels of complexity (that is, having different areas of a museum or visitor center set aside at different levels of interest and knowledge). Fi-nally, computer technology offers almost limitless possibilities for offering varying degrees of complexity to meet the knowledge and skills visitors possess. Modern technology allows the skill levels to be self-selected and the learning to be non-sequential as discussed in Chapter Eight.

As a person's knowledge and skills increase, he or she tends to seek greater challenges. An internal mechanism urges the indi-vidual onward with respect to seeking out novel and increasingly complex challenges.[10] Interpreters must ask: "Are there provisions for developing skills at gradually increasing levels of competence?"[11] Interpreters should provide progressive levels of challenges to pro-mote optimal experiences.

Promoting Feedback

Interpreters should provide feedback so that visitors know that they are progressing or have completed the endeavor. Interac-tive computer-based exhibits can give immediate feedback acknowl-edging success. Quiz boards and many less sophisticated displays can also give immediate feedback. Sometimes goals may be far-reaching (over a long span of time) and feedback may be possible only over return visits to the site. In any case, it is important to provide feedback and this may be accomplished by verbally acknowledging progress and perhaps giving participants inexpensive but memorable items (such as certificates) for successful completion of the goal. Note, and again this is among the complexities of optimal experience theory, that under certain circumstances external rewards tend to undermine intrinsic motivation because one becomes focused on gaining the reward, rather than on the activity at hand. [12]

Promoting Control

Allowing visitors control over their experience can be promoted by interpreters who encourage some degree of choice or input in their programs. Although on the one hand it is important to establish purpose, it is also important to allow individuals to express themselves within the context of the overall goals for a program. Settings that facilitate optimal experiences support personal autonomy and responsibility.

A sense of control can also be facilitated through nonpersonal interpretation. In active visitor center exhibits (with multimedia technologies) control can be offered by allowing visitors to select the nature, pace, and outcome of information presented.[13]

Interpreters in Flow

Yet another way to pursue the application of optimal experience theory, as it relates to interpretation, is to focus on flow experiences of the interpreter. Indeed, several professions involve work that is conducive to achieving a flow state. Csikszentmihalyi's research revealed that surgeons, music composers, basketball players, and modern dancers experience flow according to the eight dimensions set forth above.[14] Enos Mills commented, "Daily association with inspiring and ever-varying nature and the companionship of thoughtful people mean pleasure and steady development." The interpretive guide, Mills continued, "makes good by growing."[15]

Interpreters must understand the *purpose* and ramifications of what they are doing. To assist interpreters in understanding both their privileges and obligations is the intent of this book. Without a sense of professional purpose we lose direction. We also lose motivation.

Clear goals must be set at several levels. First, the agency must have a clear purpose as stated in a mission statement. What is it that the agency wants to create, to offer, to contribute? Second, the interpretive supervisor must have a clear sense of direction. His or her sense of purpose will infiltrate through the ranks of field interpreters. Third, interpreters themselves must have a clear sense of what they are striving to do. Interpreters are autonomous and self-sufficient and most of what we do is self-directed. Therefore, we are responsible for developing and continually examining our own goals for meeting the needs of visitors.

As interpreters, ideally, we devote full *attention* to what we are doing in our work. We should be able to concentrate on the task at hand. This means that we should be able to have work spaces that are free of distractions. Furthermore, those areas where we perform our interpretation should be conducive to bringing forth our best efforts. Site managers are responsible for seeing that work conditions are such that interpreters can concentrate without undue disruptions.

Just as visitors react to varying levels of *challenges*, according to their skills, interpreters respond to various levels of work complexity. For example, it would be asking too much to require first-time seasonal interpreters to make a presentation in front of an audience of 250 people, or to interpret a controversial topic, in their first week of employment. Yet it is precisely this level of challenge that inspires the veteran interpreter. Without increasing levels of complexity we become bored with what we are doing. Yet if the challenge is beyond our capabilities we become anxious.

The National Park Service has developed a list of competencies that correspond to increasing skill development as follows:

Entry level: prepare and present an effective interpretive talk; demonstrate effective informal interpretation; identify and describe visitor needs and characteristics.

Developmental level: exhibit effective interpretive writing; design and perform conducted activities; develop and present effective education programs; create demonstrations and other illustrated programs.

Full-performance level: develop interpretive media; involvement in interpretive planning; involvement in partners in interpretation; supervisory responsibility for interpretive coaching and peer counseling. [16]

In the National Park Service model, the competencies are made up of an increasing range of knowledge, skill, and ability. The interpreter must *demonstrate* competency at each level before moving upward to the next level. This framework is consistent with matching challenges to skills to promote optimal experiences. As Csikszentmihalyi noted, "One needs to grow, to develop new skills, to take on new challenges to maintain a self-concept as a fully functioning human being." [17] The competent interpreter is motivated to become even more so.

The most successful work output is that which fully *involves* us. We are most effective and most productive when we are totally engaged with the task at hand. Our work experiences should be structured so that we may be completely invested in our interpretive efforts. Once circumstances are set so that there are no distractions (as noted above) then the interpreter can be absorbed in his or her work. Much of the success in this realm of optimal experience is dependent on the interpreter's ability to keep the mind from wandering, although this prospect is lessened if the activity is challenging and engaging. (Note the interconnectedness of the dimensions of optimal experience.)

To operate at the peak of our potential we must be attuned to the *feedback* we receive. One aspect of feedback comes from our supervisors. Supervisors should be able to assist us in meeting the needs of visitors, and in developing and presenting effective interpretation of the place. As suggested under "full-performance level" interpretation in the National Park Service model, supervisors should also be available for peer counseling. If the interpreter faces problems in the workplace, the supervisor should be able to help resolve them. Otherwise, the interpreter will be compromised in his or her pursuit of realizing full potential. Interpreters also receive audience feedback. Interpreters who are in a flow state when they perform in front of others are effective and enthusiastic communicators.

Interpreters may, potentially, become fully *immersed* in their work. It is mentally beneficial and enjoyable to move temporarily beyond preoccupation with our selves. We are fortunate to be in a profession in which the work is sufficiently stimulating that this full immersion occurs. Yet, as we shall see in the concluding chapter, it is what we have *to offer* that is most rewarding to us.

Total immersion in our work may proceed in several areas of our responsibility. For example, we may lose our self-consciousness through immersion in our research and study. Or we may become fully consumed in our creative organization of materials in the composition of our interpretation. Or we may become totally engaged in interpretive planning processes with our colleagues. Or we may be wholly invested in the presentation of an interpretive program. When we lose our self-consciousness is, undoubtedly, when we "perform" at our best.

As with others who achieve optimal experiences, interpreters must have some sense of *control* over their work environment. First, we must feel as if we are trusted; that there is flexibility to exercise independent judgment. Second, we must be assured that responsible risk-taking is encouraged and rewarded in our efforts to achieve excellence. Failures should be considered acceptable learning experiences. Third, we must be allowed sufficient time to foster creativity and innovation. This reflective time should be incorporated into our schedules so that we have time to think in imaginative ways. Fourth, supervisory roles should be structured to emphasize guiding, educating, advising, and encouraging, rather than regulating and controlling.[18]

Interpreters should be given the fullest responsibility consistent with their capabilities. This empowerment, through controlling one's own contribution to the workplace, allows interpreters to continue growing to their fullest potential.

Interpreters fully engaged in their work will lose track of *time*. We often wish we had more time in a day. Time distortion may occur as we immerse ourselves in our study of the place. Or when we create a mix of our experience and knowledge that becomes our interpretation of a subject. It may occur when we are on stage. Our sense of time becomes distorted when we are doing something for the love of the task.

With an understanding of optimal experience theory we are better equipped to serve our visitors. When visitors are engaged in optimal experiences, in our places of cultural and natural wonder, they will be inclined to seek out further enjoyment, learning, and inspiration.

With an understanding of optimal experience theory interpreters can maximize enjoyment, productivity, and effectiveness at work. If we are joyful and enthusiastic in our work, visitors will sense this positive energy and it will be contagious, paving the way to powerful and enriching experiences.

■ *Chapter Fifteen* ■

PASSION

P assion is the essential ingredient for powerful and effective interpretation–passion for the resource and for those people who come to be inspired by the same.

There is a single magic, a single power, a single salvation, and a single happiness, and that is called loving.

—Hermann Hesse

Carl Sharsmith loved Yosemite National Park. He also loved interacting with visitors to the park over a career that spanned some 50 years. As a seasonal interpretive naturalist his enthusiasm for Yosemite and for those to whom he interpreted its beauty was undiminished. He influenced thousands of visitors and the affinity he shared was reciprocal. As children who attended Sharsmith's interpretive programs grew up, they brought their own children to go on interpretive hikes with him. Sharsmith interacted with seemingly countless visitors who wished to experience and understand Yosemite's grandeur.

In the latter part of his career Sharsmith was approached by a woman with a limited itinerary and the age old questions. She asked, "I've only got an hour to spend at Yosemite. What should I do? Where should I go?"

In a slow, deliberate voice the elderly interpreter replied, "Ah lady. Only an hour. I suppose if I had only one hour to spend at Yosemite, I'd just walk over there by the river and sit down and cry." [1]

Carl Sharsmith, and interpreters like him, embody a noble passion for the resource they interpret and those who have come to be inspired by it. Tilden suggested that the "priceless ingredient" for effective interpretation is love.[2]

The Interpreter's Passion for the Resource

One does not generally speak about love, in modern culture, except in the most trivial sense of the word. Those who call upon others to practice brotherly and sisterly love are as likely to be ridiculed as to be taken seriously.[3] But as the "priceless ingredient" of interpretation it has a precise meaning. Interpreters can and do love the forests, the deserts, the canyons, the coasts—the various landscapes—as well as the cultural sites at which they work. This passion for the resource, this intimacy, grows over time.

As with human love for one another, this expression takes meaning as we renew constantly our capacity for the complexity and wonder of the place we interpret. Eventually, a reciprocal relationship with the land becomes established in which we become aware that the landscape is aware of us. What can be achieved through this "erotic" bond is a spiritual connection with the place that brings peace, joy, astonishment, and fulfillment.[4]

In some countries interpreters demonstrate their love for the resource by making the ultimate sacrifice in protecting it. In the West African country of Cote d' Ivoire, two or three park rangers (functioning as guides and interpreters) are killed each year by poachers. At Comoe National Park, Lobi tribesmen hunt and kill both game and rangers with poison arrows. Empowered by the village fetishers, the poachers gain psychological if not spiritual advantage over the rangers. The ill-equipped rangers are often less familiar with the terrain than poachers and may lack proper shoes, functioning guns, binoculars, radios, or other equipment. They are no match for the poachers.

Those who do not die protecting the parks also pay a severe price. Park rangers are social outcasts and are subject to all manner of ridicule. They may also work for months without paychecks. Why? These African rangers conduct their work because they love the landscape and want to protect their vanishing forests and wild-life.

The Interpreter's Passion for People

Interpreters also enthusiastically share their passion for the resource with others. This does not mean that the interpreter loves audience members in a romantic sense, but rather has a passion for educating, enlightening, and inspiring them. We feel a sense of obligation, out of respect for the resource and those who have come to enjoy it, to craft a worthy interpretation of the place. That is to say that interpreters love their work.

Many people do not have the luxury of enjoying their work—of having a career that becomes an intricate part of their lifestyle. Barry Lopez wrote, "Such a life speaks to a need many of us have but few can attend to—long-lived intimacy with a place, being able to speak of it knowledgeably to others." [5]

Consider that throngs of the employed battle traffic and suffer long hours indoors, often in mundane chores, in contrast to work enjoyed by interpreters in places of natural or cultural beauty. And that is precisely what Tilden suggested we remember when we are dealing with less than courteous visitors: "the pestiferous, the unmanageable, the ineducable, and some whose apparent reason for existence is to provide the hangman with work." [6] The interpreter's role is to understand these people, to be patient, to enlist visitor's higher capacities to appreciate where they are at the moment. This is not romantic love, but rather empathetic love.

Interpreters must treat their clientele with respect. Although we may know more about a certain segment of history, or the ecology of a place, we may not have the medical, mechanical, musical, or management expertise of those who are with us. So we may assume, for the essential sake of our own humility, that some in the audience may be at least as accomplished as we are.

There is yet another dimension of our relationship to the visiting public. In our quest to satisfy the visitor we must not lose our integrity. The purpose of the interpreter is not to fill a void for the visitor who has come expecting to be entertained. [7] Furthermore, if a visitor becomes abusive—disturbs other people or harms the resource—then, and only then, but at that point decisively, the interpreter must notify the unwelcome guest that he or she has come to the wrong place.

Of course, self-absorbed interpreters and self-indulgent visitors are the exceptions to the rule. If we treat others with respect and trust, we may expect the same in return.

Some interpreters have a passion for working in areas where both the human and natural resources may need restoration. An urban park or other setting may be used as a vehicle to *help* people. Some interpreters' love for people is so great that they take personal risks to interpret to them. Interpreter Robin White, herself a former gang member, for years led Gary, Indiana gang members into the Indiana Dunes National Lakeshore on day and overnight field trips. Debbie Chavez and her USDA Forest Service staff work with Los Angeles gang members by taking them to the nearby Angeles National Forest.

In addition to federal agencies, many private organizations introduce people to nature who would not otherwise experience it and can benefit greatly from that exposure. The Student Conservation Association, Outward Bound, the Environmental Career Organization, and the North American Association for Environmental Education all have programs targeting inner-city youth.

Rather than taking people to distant natural areas, some programs interpret the resources that surround people in their neighborhoods. In Los Angeles, a program called WOW! (Wonderful Outdoor World) uses city parks and playgrounds as camping and nature study sites. WOW is a partnership program with public agencies including the Bureau of Land Management, USDA Forest Service, National Park Service, California State Parks, California Fish and Game, Los Angeles City Parks, California State University-Long Beach and private organizations such as the National Outdoor Leadership School and the Walt Disney Corporation. This program offers children the opportunity to camp in a Los Angeles city park. During the outing, environmental education activities teach ecological concepts to the children and they learn map reading, fishing, and camping skills.

Interpreters with these programs care about people first, regardless of the quality of the surrounding natural resource base. When they cannot take people to natural areas, they love interpreting the magic of nature found in vacant lots, school yards, and city parks. They conserve lives, not just resources.

The Role of Passion in Inspiring Others

Passion plays a role in influencing visitors. It gives the interpreter a certain charm and credibility. Visitors are more likely to listen to someone who brims with enthusiasm, who is passionate about the place visitors have arrived to, who is fired up about his or her work.

Why is it that some people are passionate and others are not? We don't pretend to know the full answer, but we are compelled to delve deeper into this subject for no other reason than this world would be a better place if there were less deceit, less pessimism, less apathy—and more truth, more optimism, and more passion.

How can we, as interpreters, express the best in human nature? Although this question is ultimately reduced to the level of the individual, we offer some generic thoughts. Through our passion for the resources we interpret we may bring out a similar passion in those we interpret to. To draw visitors into a full appreciation of the interpretive setting, the interpreter displays an affinity for the resource and a respect for humanity. We introduce to visitors something we love, not something we own.

Interpreters may also convey their passion by hinting that what we do isn't a job or occupation, but rather a way of life. According to Barry Lopez, this way of life is a high calling that many in our society don't recognize.[8]

We can promote our work by serving as role models to the public. We have the opportunity to reveal our quality of life as a result of staying close to, and continuing to learn from, the landscape. This relationship with our world, marked by learning that turns to wisdom, and the sense of awe, appreciation, and joy it brings—this relationship is something that visitors will observe. And perhaps they will ask themselves what they might learn from an interpreter's connection to his or her place and consequent passion for life. For many interpreters this passion comes seemingly naturally. Others have to work harder at it. What can we suggest?

A Practical Guide to Passion

Barry Lopez once told one of the authors that it is "terrifically difficult to be a decent human being." With full concurrence with Lopez's observation we offer the following discussion as much for our own good, as for anyone else's.

Carpe diem: Seize the day. With every sunrise comes new opportunities to experience the world, to enjoy others and to serve them. It is essential to recognize that we are responsible for choosing and defining our lives. We must be open to growth and change— to pursue learning—from books, other people, introspection, our experiences. We should strive toward being proactive; to look at our options and choose wisely. As Leo Buscaglia insisted:

> *We're afraid of living life, therefore we don't experience, we don't see. We don't feel. We don't risk. We don't care! And therefore we don't live—because life means being actively involved. Life means getting your hands dirty. Life means jumping in the middle of it all. Life means falling flat on your face. Life means going beyond yourself—into the stars.*[9]

Nothing can change our lives more rapidly, or entail more real or imagined risk, than the consistent outflow of love and passion for life. Everything in our lives—career, friends, lifestyle, contributions to the community—can be transformed through love. Loving all aspects of life, regardless of challenges we may be facing, opens doors and brings forth energy and joy.[10] When we choose to live an inspiring life, we make a difference in the lives of everyone else we interact with.

One of the greatest challenges facing the individual, and the world, finds its roots in a lack of love, a lack of a sense of interdependence. Regardless of the situations, or the people we may feel inclined to dislike, we must resist the temptation. Ernest Holmes wrote, "In some way we have to find something of value in them, no matter how big or little it may be. *Find something to like.*"[11] This approach is not altogether selfless. Our health, both physical and emotional, is related to the amount of love or hate in our thought.

Enos Mills wrote, "In Nature's ennobling and boundless scenes the hateful boundary lines and the forts and flags and prejudices . . . are forgotten. Nature is universal. She hoists no flag of hatred. The supreme triumph of parks is humanity."[12]

The Interpreter's Creed

We believe that educators have a special responsibility to serve as good role models. Because of the nature of their work, and their influence on learners—from kindergarten to college—they should be professional, caring, and truthful. We believe that interpreters are similarly responsible because of the impact and importance of their work (see Box 1).

What I fear and desire most in this world is passion. I fear it because it promises to be spontaneous, out of my control, unnamed, beyond my reasonable self. I desire it because passion has color, like the landscape before me. It is not pale. It is not neutral. It reveals the backside of the heart.

—Terry Tempest Williams

Box 1
The Interpreter's Creed

As A Practicing Interpreter I Shall:

- Seek to *serve* visitors; to be an ambassador for the place I work; to instill in visitors the ability and desire to sense beauty in their surroundings.

- Seek to respect *all* the visitors I come in contact with and welcome them as I would welcome guests in my home; and to share equally my knowledge and passion regardless of the visitor's age, gender, interests, physical abilities, or cultural differences.

- Seek to be agreeable, look good, have a polished presence, speak in a well-modulated voice, and be genuinely friendly.

- Seek to see the good, or the humor, in any situation and answer repetitious questions with enthusiasm, as if they were asked for the first time.

- Seek to convey only well-documented, accurate information.

- Seek to be an exemplary role model for environmentally responsible behavior by word and example.

- Seek to structure interpretive design and programming in such a way as to minimize the impact on cultural and environmental resources.

- Seek to improve my mind, continue learning about the resource, and expand my learning about the principles and processes of interpretation which will ultimately benefit visitors to the site.

- Seek to help other interpreters achieve their interpretive goals, particularly assisting new interpreters to develop confidence and abilities.

- Believe in myself; give my best to the world and expect that the world will give its best to me.

Conclusion

THE GIFT

You give but little when you give of your possessions. It is when you give of yourself that you truly give.

—Kahlil Gibran

We began this book with a celebration of the contributions of Enos Mills and Freeman Tilden to an ever-evolving philosophy of interpretation. Their work has permeated, in varying degrees, the principles set forth in the balance of the book. We now come full circle and return to them in our conclusion.

Mills (in *Adventures of a Nature Guide and Essays in Interpretation*) and Tilden (in *Interpreting Our Heritage*) agreed that the work of the interpreter is like that of an artist. Mills wrote, simply, "A nature guide is an artist."[1]

Quality interpretation demands background preparation and the learning of technique, just as in the traditional arts. And like poetry, music, sculpture, theater, and painting, there is a certain creative element (personal, individualized) associated with interpretation of cultural and natural history.

Lewis Hyde, in *The Gift*, suggests that a work of art is a gift and not a commodity.[2] If interpretation is an art, and a work of art is a gift, then it follows that interpretation must be a gift. The interpreter, like the artist, bears a gift. Furthermore, the work of the interpreter, like that of the artist, is often misunderstood.

The Interpreter's Plight

W. B. Yeats, in the first stanza of a poem titled "Adam's Curse," seems to capture the plight of interpreters, like artists, who labor out of love in a profession that is not always recognized or understood by the public. The work that is done is considered idleness by much of the world, yet the commitment and perseverance to create inspiring art is far more difficult than the most demanding physical labor. Yeats wrote:

> We sat together at one summer's end,
> That beautiful mild woman, your close friend,
> And you and I, and talked of poetry.
> I said: 'A line will take us hours maybe;
> Yet if it does not seem a moment's thought,
> Our stitching and unstitching has been naught.
> Better go down upon your marrow-bones
> And scrub a kitchen pavement, or break stones
> Like an old pauper, in all kinds of weather;
> For to articulate sweet sounds together
> Is to work harder than all these, and yet
> Be thought an idler by the noisy set . . .' [3]

The work of interpreters is sometimes scorned. At the far end of the spectrum are those who dismiss or despise interpreters' "work" as either meaningless or counterproductive. Environmental interpreters have been labelled with such derogatory terms as "fern feelers," "tree huggers," "environmental extremists," or, more recently, "environmental wackos."

The first two terms suggest that interpreters engage in worthless, childish, superfluous endeavors. According to this perspective, interpretation is insignificant. In many instances the public does not understand the commitment, devotion, dedication, and difficulty required "to articulate sweet sounds together."

In 1995 the wire services reported that tax dollars were being spent to send federal employees (with the National Park Service, U.S. Forest Service, and Bureau of Land Management) to a conference of the National Association for Interpretation in Orlando, Florida. The articles were slanted to emphasize the close proximity of Disney World and other attractions rather than the professional growth opportunities offered at the workshop. Note the language of the Associated Press account: "More than 200 federal workers whirled off to Disney World—at taxpayer expense—for a week of training to be better tour guides."[4]

The last two terms ("environmental extremists" and "environmental wackos") suggest that interpreters' concern for our cultural and natural legacy is counterproductive in that it interferes with private enterprise, development, growth, and profit-making. To answer these charges we must look at the *motivation* of interpreters. Is the motivation to interpret our cultural and natural inheritance selfish—to make lots of money, to become famous, to have power, to impress others, to "retire" on the job? No, this is clearly not the case; the motivation is more honorable than self-indulgence. Interpreters interpret because they love their work and want to share a gift. The gift is the place itself—a place of cultural significance or natural wonder—and the interpreter's creative rendition of the place, as we shall further explore in a moment.

Whereas the interpreter generally operates out of selfless motives, those who seek to destroy our heritage operate out of selfish ones and in the process are willing to ruin the very resources the interpreter seeks to protect. John Muir did not mince words when he considered this prospect: "These temple destroyers, devotees of ravaging commercialism, seem to have a perfect contempt for Nature, and instead of lifting their eyes to the God of the Mountains, lift them to the Almighty Dollar."[5]

Tolerating disregard and resisting those who would destroy the nation's cultural and natural resources takes a heavy toll. Edward Abbey offers sage counsel in his "one final paragraph of advice:"

Do not burn yourselves out...It is not enough to fight for the land; it is even more important to enjoy it. While you can. While it's still here... [S]it quietly for a while and contemplate the precious stillness, that lovely, mysterious and awesome space. Enjoy yourselves... and I promise you this much: I promise you this one sweet victory over our enemies, over those deskbound people with their hearts in a safe deposit box and their eyes hypnotized by desk calculators. I promise you this: you will outlive [them].[6]

The Gift of the Place

Before we consider the interpretation of place as a gift, we will look at the place itself as a gift. Those settings that define our cultural and natural legacy are gifts to us now and for future generations. These gifts celebrate our national identity. It is inconceivable that we might exist without these documentaries of our heritage and we are indebted to the visionary men and women who understood the essential need to preserve such national treasures. Too, we must remember that we are responsible for adding to this system those important areas that are currently unprotected.[7]

Here is a sampling of 15 gifts, of a cultural slant, administered by the U.S. National Park Service: Chaco Culture National Historic Park, New Mexico; Thomas Jefferson Memorial, Washington, D.C.; Little Bighorn Battlefield National Monument, Montana; Vanderbilt Mansion National Historic Site, New York; George Washington Birthplace National Monument, Virginia; Abraham Lincoln Birthplace National Historic Site, Kentucky; Antietam National Battlefield, Maryland; Wright Brothers National Memorial, South Carolina; George Washington Carver National Monument, Missouri; Booker T. Washington National Monument, Virginia; John Muir National Historic Site, California; Clara Barton National Historic Site, Maryland; Eleanor Roosevelt National Historic Site, New York; Martin Luther King, Jr. National Historic Site, Georgia; and Manzanar National Historic Site, California.[8] These are just a few key pieces of a much larger puzzle that help us to celebrate, understand, and be moved by our cultural inheritance.

Here too is a sampling of 15 gifts, of a natural slant, administered by the U.S. National Park Service: Yellowstone National Park, Wyoming; Yosemite National Park, California; Mount Rainier National Park, Washington; Crater Lake National Park, Oregon; Rocky Mountain National Park, Colorado; Denali National Park and Preserve, Alaska; Grand Canyon National Park, Arizona; Arches National Park, Utah; Everglades National Park, Florida; Great Smoky Mountains National Park, North Carolina-Tennessee; Wind Cave National Park, South Dakota; Rainbow Bridge National Monument, Utah; Redwood National Park, California; Hawaii Volcanoes National Park, Hawaii; and Grand Staircase-Escalante National Monument, Utah.[9] Again, these represent just a few pieces of our natural legacy. Other countries are likewise blessed with their natural and cultural gifts.

The National Park System concept, as suggested by Adolf Murie,"represents a far-reaching cultural achievement."[10] Consider our loss had these places of cultural and natural wonder not been set aside. Remember, too, that this is just a sampling of places, out of more than 370, administered by one agency. The balance of the fabric of our natural and cultural heritage is set aside in a spectrum of other settings addressed in the Introduction. All together these monuments, large and small, make up a physical encyclopedia of our heritage. These are timeless and priceless gifts indeed.

Interpretation of Place as a Gift

The interpretive site itself offers inspiration. In addition, interpretation of the site may offer more insight, a deeper understanding, a more enriching experience. Interpretation offers a revelation of the cultural or natural beauty of the place (see Box 1).

Box 1
The Gift of Interpretation

Cabrillo National Monument, on Point Loma in California, commemorates the ocean voyage of Juan Rodríguez Cabrillo who "discovered" what is now the west coast of the United States. Cabrillo entered a port, which he named San Miguel, on September 28, 1542. Cabrillo had landed, just 50 years after Columbus found the "new world," in present-day San Diego.

On the 452nd anniversary of Cabrillo's landing, an interpretive drama was presented at the park titled "The Last Voyage." The theater performance was the work (the gift) of director William Virchis, who offered an introduction. The dramatic performance itself was entertaining and inspiring, but it was the introduction that captured so many of the principles espoused in this book.

Virchis related the topic to the knowledge and experiences of park visitors, he revealed meanings in an original manner, he presented Cabrillo's voyage in the context of a whole, he inspired and provoked and challenged, and he left the audience with his 30-minute creation of interpretation as an art form—theater.

Virchis was passionate. He loved the subject of his interpretation. He loved the medium in which the interpretation would be shared. And he loved the people who came to enjoy it. You could tell. As he spoke you felt fortunate to brush what Barry Lopez calls "one of life's deep, coursing threads."

Virchis started on a personal note. He told the audience a little about himself—how he, like Cabrillo, had come north from Mexico. He elucidated his own awareness of different cultural points of view and then noted that the clashing of cultures (Spanish explorers and Kumeyaay natives) would be a theme in the upcoming presentation. Discerning another culture is like "holding a prism before your eyes"—there is a distorted image of what we would otherwise see, based on our own preconceptions.

To provide a sense of a whole, Virchis placed Cabrillo's expedition in the larger context of the Iberian Conquest. Cabrillo was trained under Hernán Cortés and was a member of the invasion of Tenochtitlán: Mexico City. Cabrillo later became a builder of ships.

As a consequence of Cabrillo's shipbuilding and his navigation to the north, and a long line of events hence, we now have San Diego. Here, Virchis explained, is an example of how one event changed the world, "like when man landed on the moon." Virchis disclosed that this place, right here, is where California started. "Just think," he said, "what this looked like [452 years ago to the day] in the eyes of Cabrillo." Just a moment's walk outside the auditorium the visitor has seen, beyond the ultramarine of the harbor, the bustling sixth largest city in the United States. But—imagine for a moment—what did Cabrillo see?

Virchis explained that he comes from a tradition of storytelling, drama, and living life to its fullest. His culture seeks to experience the world.

Our presence on this planet is a wonderful and mysterious voyage. Like Cabrillo, we too are capable of going beyond everyday types of experiences—the mundane—to stretch ourselves to make new discoveries, to know better the intricacies of this world.

As a soldier under the leadership of Cortés, Cabrillo had been badly wounded. Yet he survived. Then, to the north of San Diego, he suffered a relatively minor fall. His wound festered and became gangrenous. Cabrillo died shortly thereafter.

"The Last Voyage," Virchis concluded as the actors assembled on stage, was about irony. He said, "If you can't make the most of today, you may as well give up on tomorrow." These are strong words, used only under proper circumstances, but in this instance they were appropriate. What Virchis meant was that, like Cabrillo, we don't know how long we have. His message was this: life is a Gift and we must celebrate every day.

Cultural beauty includes those meaningful things which humans have created. For example, an Anasazi cliff dwelling at Mesa Verde National Park, Thomas Jefferson's Monticello, or the beauty of a broom at a restored Shaker village.

Cultural beauty also includes the dignity and integrity which humans have shown themselves capable. Our national story includes men and women who have exhibited great courage in the face of adversity, great moral fortitude, and admirable inner beauty. Places that commemorate this drama of human conduct include several listed above in honor of Abraham Lincoln, George Washington, and Martin Luther King, Jr., for example. Interpreters translate artifacts, places, events, and deeds so that visitors may better understand and appreciate cultural beauty.

Likewise, interpretation of natural beauty consists of the revelation of the order of nature. Aldo Leopold referred to this concept as the heightened "perception of the natural processes by which the land and the living things upon it have achieved their characteristic forms and by which they maintain their existence."[11] In pursuing an interpretation of natural beauty Tilden asked, "What are the forces that created what one sees, and feels, as beautiful?"[12] Consider Crater Lake (volcanism), Yosemite (glaciation), and Grand Canyon (erosion).

Creating the Gift

At one level, the interpreter *has* a gift. That gift is the interpreter's talent and "although a talent can be perfected through an effort of the will, no effort in the world can cause its initial appearance."[13] The good interpreter has a talent for presenting interpretive stories compellingly.

In addition, the inspiration an artist receives can be perceived as a gift. As an artist (interpreter) works, an idea pops into his or her mind—some aspect of one's artistic creation (interpretation) is bestowed upon the creator. D. H. Lawrence observed, "Not I, not I, but the wind that blows through me."[14]

Robert Finch, a nature writer, stays attuned to the creative impulse which often reveals itself in a sudden change: "right in the middle of things—from what you expected to find to what you do find."[15]

Gary Snyder, writer and poet, concurs: "You get a good poem and you don't know where it came from. 'Did I say that?' And so all you feel is: you feel humility and you feel gratitude. And you'd feel a little uncomfortable, I think, if you capitalized too much on that without admitting at some point that you got it from the Muse, or whoever, wherever, or however."[16]

Note that these two elements—talent and inspiration—are gifts associated with the *creation* of the work. These elements represent the gift at the level of the artist or the "inner life of art."[17]

Giving the Gift

Interpreters, like many artists, are not known for their accumulation of material wealth. They are in their profession for reasons other than financial gain. The challenge and joy of the work itself is rewarding, along with the knowledge that one is giving a gift that cannot be measured monetarily.

The notion of gift, addressed above in terms of its "inner life," can be extended to its "outer life" as well. The "outer life" is when the gift is given and received. Even when a fee is involved, when we are truly touched by a work of art something is bestowed upon us which has nothing to do with the price.[18]

Our response to the art (this may be the place itself, the interpretation of the place, or a combination of the two) may illumine our world, foster our recognition of beauty, generate an energetic optimism, stimulate our sense of truth, revive the soul, set us on a courageous course of action, or simply overwhelm the senses. In the presence of meaningful art, we feel as if we have been touched by a resonating chord. At its absolute best, this is what all art, including interpretation, is about. Art communicates what cannot be said in mere words. It brings us to a point beyond the complacent and the mundane where our minds and spirits soar.

Keeping the Gift in Motion

According to Hyde, "the spirit of a gift is kept alive by its constant donation." [19] This means that the gift must not be removed from circulation. For example, some tribal cultures distinguish between gifts and capital. It is considered immoral to hoard or invest gifts, to get rich at someone else's expense.

Protecting a place of cultural or natural significance ensures that the gift will be available for all people and to future generations. Unless the site is somehow exploited or otherwise compromised, its gift properties are constantly available. The first and most important lesson is: Do not destroy the gift.

Another way to look at circulating the gift is in how each of us has been inspired by people who introduced us to our passion, our life's work. We have all had mentors who shared the gift of nature or culture in the broadest sense. These mentors may have been grade school teachers or university professors. They may have been colleagues or supervisors. They may have been parents or writers. Under their tutelage we learned valuable things. With this foundation of knowledge, and motivation to learn more, we made our own discoveries.

Our mentors taught us about nature or history and they taught us how, by their example, to inspire others just as they had inspired us. By perpetuating the example of our mentors we keep the gift in motion. Those who are now motivated by our words and actions continue to keep the gift alive as they share it with others. What is given is supposed to be given away again, not to the originator of the gift, but to someone else!

In tribal societies, such as the Kula of the South Sea islands near the eastern tip of New Guinea, this mode of circular giving involves tangible gifts—necklaces or armshells. Hyde notes, "When I give to someone from whom I do not receive (and yet I do receive elsewhere), it is as if the gift goes around a corner before it comes back. I have to give blindly. And I will feel a sort of blind gratitude as well." [20]

The gift of the interpreter is less tangible, but just as real. We have the privilege of receiving gifts and the obligation of passing them along. The gift originates from another person (a mentor).

A gift may also be perceived to come from Nature or the Creator: watching the behavior of a wolverine or seeing the alpenglow of a mountain, at sunset, as a full moon rises above it, reflected in a lake. If we open ourselves up to receive them, we are provided gifts that entertain, inspire, enrich and restore us. These gifts may also be passed along; that is communicated to an audience in such a way that they comprehend the wonder of what was observed and seek out similar experiences.

The Maori, natives of New Zealand, enlarge the circle beyond the body of the tribe to include nature and the gods. In the traditional hunting ritual the forest provides food for the hunters, the hunters give to the priests, and the priests give back to the forest and the deities—giving thanks in return for the sustenance the forest provides. Here we find a spiritual dimension of gifts beyond the scope of this book. Yet we note that this passage into the unknown and mystical is invigorating. We are exhilarated when gifts "arise from pools we cannot fathom." [21] Without a knowledge of boundaries we find that gifts are inexhaustible.

A Profession of Giving

The joy of the gift, for the interpreter, is in the giving. The profession is a noble one in that we are serving others by providing them life-enriching gifts. We do so with very little expected in return—mostly out of joy from giving the gifts.

We continue to learn and be inspired (receive) and we continue to interpret (give) from our wealth of knowledge and experience. Our gift is in helping others to see and in so doing we gain resolution in our own vision. As Mills wrote, "The essence of [interpretation] is to travel gracefully rather than to arrive." [22]

As interpreters, we are blessed with gifts and it is our blessing to share them with others.

All the earth

worships Thee;

they sing praises

to Thee,

sing praises to

Thy name.

—Psalms 66:4

Notes

Preface Notes

1. Mills, E., 1920, *Adventures of a Nature Guide and Essays in Interpretation*, p. 6.
2. Ibid, p. 12.
3. Ibid, p. 111.
4. Tilden, F., 1977, *Interpreting Our Heritage*. (The preface to the second edition is also included in the third edition, p. xix.)
5. Grater, R., 1976, *The Interpreter's Handbook: Methods, Skills, and Techniques*.
6. Sharpe, G., 1976, *Interpreting the Environment*.
7. Lewis, W., 1980, *Interpreting for Park Visitors*.
8. Grinder, A. and E. McCoy, 1985, *The Good Guide*.
9. Machlis, G. and D. Field, Eds., 1984, *On Interpretation*.
10. Machlis, G., Ed., 1986, *Interpretive Views*.
11. See, for example, Zehr, J., Gross, M. and R. Zimmerman, 1990, *Creating Environmental Publications: A Guide to Writing and Designing for Interpreters and Environmental Educators* and Trapp, S., Gross, M., and R. Zimmerman, 1991, *Signs, Trails, and Wayside Exhibits: Connecting People and Places*.
12. Ham, S., 1992, *Environmental Interpretation*.
13. Veverka, J., 1994, *Interpretive Master Planning*.
14. Knudson, D., Cable, T. and L. Beck, 1995, *Interpretation of Cultural and Natural Resources*.
15. Acorn Naturalists, 1997, *Acorn Naturalists 1997 Catalog*.

Introduction Notes

1. Leopold, A., 1949, *A Sand County Almanac*.
2. Tilden, F., 1977, *Interpreting Our Heritage*.
3. Mills, E., 1920, *Adventures of a Nature Guide and Essays in Interpretation*, p. 130.
4. Tilden, F., Undated, *The Fifth Essence*, pp. 56-7.
5. Mills, p. 128.
6. Tilden, F., 1983, *The National Parks*, pp. 29-31.
7. Mills, p. 128.
8. See Beck, L. and T. Cable, 1995, "Resolving the Interpreter's Identity Problem."

9.   Ibid. In the 1970s there was a movement within the interpretive profession proposing a slightly different spelling of the word interpreter ("interpretor") to distinguish the field from that of translators of foreign languages. Interest in the new spelling seemed to wane during the 1980s and into the 1990s. Then the altered spelling was resurrected in the mid-1990s in a text (*Interpretive Master Planning*) and a new interpretive communication journal (*The InterpEdge*). Although the altered spelling at first glance seems harmless enough, this is a complex issue. Most important is that "interpretor" cannot be found in the dictionary. So, only those who already know, somehow, that the new spelling refers to interpreters of cultural and natural history will understand the use. Everyone else will assume that the word is misspelled. Moreover, there is but a subtle difference in how the two spellings are (apparently) pronounced—there is very little verbal distinction.

10.   Tilden, 1977, p. 4.

11.   Ibid, p. 9.

12.   Mills, p. 126.

13.   Ibid, p. 158.

14.   Tilden, 1977, p. 9.

15.   Mills, p. 6.

16.   Ibid, p. 130.

17.   Tilden, 1977, p. 9.

18.   Mills, p. 170.

19.   Tilden, 1977, p. 9.

20.   Mills, p. 170.

21.   Tilden, 1977, p. 9.

22.   Mills, p. 129.

23.   Tilden, 1977, p. 9

24.   Mills, p. 120.

25.   Dahlen, D., Larsen, D., Weber, S. and R. Fudge, 1996, "The Process of Interpretation: Fulfilling the Mission Through Interpretive Competencies" and presentations by the authors at the 1996 National Association for Interpretation Annual Conference.

26.   Ibid.

Chapter One Notes

1.   Wurman, R.S., 1989, *Information Anxiety*, p. 138.

2.   Tilden, F., 1977, *Interpreting Our Heritage*.

3.   Piaget, J., quoted in Romey, W.D., 1968, *Inquiry Techniques for Teaching Science*, p. 158.

4.   Hammitt, W., 1981, "A Theoretical Foundation for Tilden's Interpretive Principles."

5. Knopf, R., 1981, "Cognitive Map Formation as a Tool for Facilitating Information Transfer in Interpretive Programming."

6. Hammitt, p. 10.

7. Sylwester, R. and Joo-Yun Cho, 1992/1993, "What Brain Research Says About Paying Attention."

8. Ibid, p. 72.

9. Tilden, F.

10. Silverman, L.H., In Press, "Personalizing the Past: A Review of the Literature with Implications for Historical Interpretation."

11. Anderson, J. and D. Blahna, 1995, "Who Are These People, and What do They Want? Assessment of Interpreters' Knowledge of Their Audience."

12. Ibid.

13. Hood, M., 1991, "Significant Issues in Museum Audience Research."

14. Loomis, R., 1996, "IIow Do We Know What the Visitor Knows? Learning From Interpretation."

15. Vance, C. and D. Schroeder, 1991, "Matching Visitor Learning Style with Exhibit Type: Implications for Learning in Informal Settings."

16. Bixler, R., Carlisle, C., Hammitt, W. and M. Floyd, 1994, "Observed Fears and Discomforts Among Urban Students on School Field Trips to Wildland Areas."

17. Csikszentmihalyi, M. and K. Hermanson, 1995, "Intrinsic Motivation in Museums: What Makes Visitors Want to Learn?"

18. Becker, C. L., 1932, "Everyman His Own Historian."

19. Thelen, D., 1991, "History Making in America."

20. Silverman.

21. Ibid.

22. Romey, W.D., 1968, *Inquiry Techniques for Teaching Science*.

23. Everhart, W., 1988, "Some Thoughts for Those Who Charm and Inform," p. T6.

24. France, A., quoted in Tilden, F., "Foreword to the Second Edition," by George Hartzog.

Chapter Two Notes

1. Mills, E., 1920, *Adventures of a Nature Guide and Essays in Interpretation*, p. 180.

2. Ibid, p. 126.

3. Tilden, F., 1977, *Interpreting Our Heritage*.

4. Ibid, p. 18.

5. Wurman, R.S., 1989, *Information Anxiety*.

6. Person, J.E., Jr., 1993, *Statistical Forecasts of the U.S.*, p. 174.

7. Adams, S., 1996, *Dilbert*, August 18, 1996.

8. Wurman, p. 201

9.   Ibid, p. 202.
10.   Ibid, p. 203.
11.   The discussion is based on Sylwester, R. and Joo-Yun Cho,1992/1993,"What Brain Research Says About Paying Attention."
12.   Ibid, pp. 74-75
13.   Csikszentmihalyi, M., 1990, *Flow: The Psychology of Optimal Experience*, pp. 123-24.
14.   Burroughs, J., 1912, Quoted in Cable, T., 1992, "To Enjoy Understandingly."
15.   Mills, E., p. 126.
16.   Dickinson, E., Quoted in Campbell, J.R., 1972, *In Touch with Students*.
17.   Hedge, A., 1995, "Human-Factor Considerations in the Design of Museums to Optimize Their Impact on Learning."

Chapter Three Notes

1.   Mills, E., 1920, *Adventures of a Nature Guide and Essays in Interpretation*, p. 180
2.   Tilden, F., 1977, *Interpreting Our Heritage*, p. 26.
3.   Ibid, p. 29.
4.   Mills, p. 180 and Tilden, pp. 26-7.
5.   Compiled from Ham, S., 1992, *Environmental Interpretation*, pp. 10, 11, 14; Kawasaki, G., 1991, *Selling the Dream*, p. 104; and Knudson, D., Cable, T., and L. Beck, 1995, *Interpretation of Cultural and Natural Resources*, p. 314.
6.   Sartre, J-P., 1965, *Nausea*.
7.   Jackson, P.W., 1995, "On the Place of Narrative in Teaching."
8.   Rifkin, J., 1991, *Biosphere Politics*.
9.   Caduto, M. and Bruchac, J., 1988, *Teacher's Guide to Keepers of the Earth*.
10.   Strauss, S., 1988, "Storytelling and the Natural World."
11.   Tilden, p. 28.
12.   Ibid.
13.   Beck, L., 1989, "Conversation with a Tramp: Lee Stetson on Interpretation."
14.   Ibid, p. 7
15.   Kawasaki, G., 1991, *Selling the Dream*.
16.   See Knudson, D., Cable, T., and L. Beck, 1995, *Interpretation of Cultural and Natural Resources*, Ch. 14, Arts in Interpretation.
17.   Coles, R., 1989, *The Call of Stories: Teaching and the Moral Imagination*.
18.   Williams, T.T., 1984, *Pieces of White Shell*. Also see, 1996, "An Interview with Terry Tempest Williams."
19.   Lopez, B., 1988, *Crossing Open Ground*.

Chapter Four Notes

1. Beck, L., 1989, "Conversations with Barry Lopez: Musings on Interpretation."
2. Ibid.
3. Williams, T.T., 1996, "Make us Uncomfortable." p. 9.
4. Abbey, E., 1968, *Desert Solitaire*, p. 233.
5. Tilden, F., 1977, *Interpreting Our Heritage*, p. 38
6. Beck.
7. Zeufle, M., 1994, "The Interface of Religious Beliefs and Environmental Values with the Interpretive Profession."
8. Knapp, D., 1995, "Moving Beyond Tilden."
9. Leopold, A., 1949, *A Sand County Almanac*, pp. 223-224.
10. Senge, P., 1990, *The Fifth Discipline*.
11. Kawasaki, G., 1991, *Selling the Dream*.
12. Olson, S., 1982, *Reflections From the North Country*.
13. McKibben, B., 1990, "The Courage to Look for Trouble," p. 15.
14. Ibid.
15. Wilson, E. O., 1992, *The Diversity of Life*, p. 351.

Chapter Five Notes

1. Olson, S., 1982, *Reflections from the North Country*, p. 112.
2. Commoner, B., 1971, *The Closing Circle*, p. 29.
3. Miller, G., 1956, "The Magical Number Seven, Plus or Minus Two: Some Limits On Our Capacity for Processing Information."
4. Tilden, F., 1977, *Interpreting Our Heritage*, p. 40.
5. Ham, S., 1992, *Environmental Interpretation*. See this source for an excellent discussion of thematic interpretation.
6. Thorndyke, P.W., 1977, "Cognitive Structures in Comprehension and Memory of Narrative Discourse."
7. Knudson, D., Cable, T., and L. Beck, 1995, *Interpretation of Cultural and Natural Resources*.
8. Lundberg, A., 1997, "Toward a Thesis-Based Interpretation," p. 16.
9. Ibid, pp. 16-17.
10. Ibid, p. 17.
11. Maslow, A., 1987, *Motivation and Personality*.
12. Tilden, p. 46.
13. Abbey, E., 1968, *Desert Solitaire*, p. 235.
14. Borun, M., Massey, C. and T. Lutter, 1993, "Naive Knowledge and the Design of Science Museum Exhibits."
15. Werling, D.P., 1995, "Regional Model Heritage Education."
16. Frome, M., 1982, "To Sin by Silence ..."
17. Ibid. Cited in Frome, p. 41.
18. Tilden, p. 40.

Chapter Six Notes

1.   Mills, 1920, *Adventures of a Nature Guide and Essays in Interpretation*, p. 233.
2.   Ibid, p. 130.
3.   Tilden, 1977, *Interpreting Our Heritage*, p. 47.
4.   Machlis, G. and D. Field, 1992, *On Interpretation*, p. 66.
5.   Ibid.
6.   Knudson, D., Cable, T., and L. Beck, 1995, *Interpretation of Cultural and Natural Resources*. (Chapter 5)
7.   Louv, R., 1991, *Childhood's Future*.
8.   Chawla, L., 1988, "Children's Concern for the Natural Environment," p. 19.
9.   Dubos, R., cited in Tanner, T., 1974, *Ecology, Environment, and Education*.
10.   Chawla, p. 19.
11.   Nabhan, G. and S. Trimble, 1994, *The Geography of Childhood*.
12.   Louv, p. 178.
13.   Williams, T., 1988, "Why Johnny Shoots Stop Signs," p. 120.
14.   Kingsolver, B., 1995, *High Tide in Tuscon*, p. 241.
15.   Bixler, R., Carlisle, C., Hammitt, W., and M. Floyd, 1994, "Observed Fears and Discomforts Among Urban Students on Field Trips to Wildland Areas."
16.   Williams, p. 120. Quote by Marshal Case, National Audubon's vice-president for education.
17.   Fogg, C. and L. Hartmann, 1985, "Interpretation for the Very Young." The discussion concerning Austin Nature Center programs for children is derived from this article.
18.   Ibid, p. 24.
19.   Bixler, et. al.
20.   The discussion concerning "Babes in the Woods" was derived from a program outline of the same title from the Missouri Department of Conservation. (Unpublished Document)
21.   Ibid, p. 13.
22.   Summarized from Tilden's Chapter 7 in *Interpreting Our Heritage* and Mill's *Adventures of a Nature Guide and Essays in Interpretation*.
23.   The discussion is a summary of a section titled "Children and Social Groups" from "Getting Connected: An Approach to Children's Interpretation" in Machlis, G. and D. Field, pp. 69-71.
24.   The discussion is a summary of a section titled "Interpretive Approaches" in Machlis, G. and D. Field, pp. 71-73.
25.   Machlis, G. and D. Field, p. 72.
26.   Ibid.
27.   Tilden, p. 48.
28.   Mills, p. 236.
29.   Compiled from Burr Oak Woods Conservation Nature Center, Blue Springs, Missouri, 1996 and 1997 program schedules. (Unpublished Documents)
30.   White, L. and M. Johns, 1996, "Inspiring Teens: Learning By Doing," p. 7.
31.   Ibid, p. 8.
32.   Baumer, M., 1996, "Youth Volunteer Naturalists—Something to Believe In," p. 7.
33.   Ibid.

34.   McGuire, F., Boyd, R. and R.Tedrick, 1996, *Leisure and Aging*.
35.   Ibid.
36.   Bultena, G., Field, D, and R. Renninger, 1992, "Interpretation for the Elderly."
37.   Manheimer, R., 1995, *The Second Middle Age*.

Chapter Seven Notes

1.   Warder, D. S. and R. Joulie, 1990, "Historic Site Interpretation: Past, Present and Future Research."
2   Luzander, J.C.F. and J. Spellman, 1996, "Living History: Hobby or Profession?" p. 241.
3.   Warder and Joulie.
4   Ibid.
5.   Luzander and Spellman, p. 241.
6.   Anderson, J., 1984, *Time Machines: The World of Living History*, p. 189.
7.   Ibid, pp. 189-192.
8   Peterson, D., 1988, "There is no Living History, There are no Time Machines," p. 28.
9.   Ibid.
10.   Mellish, X., 1996, "For Someone Who Died in 1826, He Gives a Lifelike Performance."
11.   Ibid.
12.   Peterson, p. 28.
13.   Golda, J., 1996, "The Conquistadors: The Best and Worst of Human Nature."
14.   See also the essay, "The Passing Wisdom of Birds" in *Crossing Open Ground* by Barry Lopez and *The Rediscovery of North America* by Barry Lopez.
15.   Golda. Quote by Kirkpatrick Sale, *The Conquest of Paradise*.
16.   Golda, p. 3.
17.   Harrison, E., 1993, "Can Walt Disney Interpret History?"
18.   Ibid, p. 2
19.   Ibid, p. 2
20.   Bigley, J.D., 1991, "Living History and Battle Reenactment The Dilemma of Selective Interpretation."
21.   Ibid, pp. 16-17.
22.   Doerner, J. and A. Heinlein, 1996, "American Battlefields: Compelling Stories and Interpretive Challenge."
23.   Bigley, p. 16.
24.   Bigley.
25.   Visitor's Guide, United States Holocaust Memorial Museum.
26.   Luzander and Spellman, p. 242.
27.   Tilden, F., 1977, *Interpreting Our Heritage*, p. 70.

Chapter Eight Notes

1.   Tilden, F., 1977, *Interpreting Our Heritage*, p. 95.
2   Ibid.
3.   Sydney Harris, quoted in Peter, L.J., 1977, *Peter's Quotations: Ideas for Our Time*, p. 64.
4   Statement attributed to Ritz Carleton of hotel fame.

5.   Tilden, p. 96.

6.   Thoreau, H. D., quoted in Peter, p. 64.

7.   Routman, E., 1994, "Considering High Tech Exhibits?"

8.   Ibid.

9.   Ibid.

10.   For example, a 2-year study by the U.S. Forest Service of nine interpretive centers found that less than 1 percent of the people read the entire exhibit text and of this one percent about 90 percent were experts that already were knowledgeable about the subjects. Yet, this same study found that 65 percent of the people interacted with audience participation games. And, any touchable item increased participation at an exhibit to 90 percent. (USDA Forest Service 1989, cited in Veverka 1994). Other studies indicating that in general participatory or interactive displays are superior to passive exhibits include: Melton (1972), Thier and Linn (1976), Peart (1984), Bitgood and Benefield (1986), Rosenfield and Terkel (1982), Koran, et. al. (1986) and Javlekar (1989). Moscardo (1988) reviewed the literature and concluded that visitors pay very little attention to exhibits (about 8 seconds average) and very little is learned or remembered from exhibits. However, Moscardo concluded that interactive displays are successful in attracting and holding visitor attention. Bitgood (1991) compiled a useful bibliography of articles dealing with interactive exhibits.

11.   Van Rennes and Mark (1981), Hilke, et. al. (1988) and Worts (1990) found that interactive computer exhibits appeal to visitors and enhance their experiences. Curran (1992), based on her experiences at a Corps of Engineers interpretive facility, is one voice among many practitioners endorsing interactive computer exhibits. Studies showing that interactive computer exhibits can be effective educational tools include Routman and Korn (1993) and Klevans (1990). This latter study reported that an interactive computer exhibit about endangered species at the Texas Memorial Museum was effective in teaching children and creating or enhancing positive beliefs in other museum visitors. Screven (1990) reviewed the literature about computers in exhibit settings and provided a discussion of their utility.

12.   Routman, E. and R. Korn, 1993, "The Living World Revisited: Evaluation of High Tech Exhibits at the Saint Louis Zoo," p. 20.

13.   Routman.

14.   M. Baumer, Assistant Nature Center Manager, pers. comm. 8 July 1996.

15.   Stofan, J., 1995, "Crossing the Sea: Sea World's Distance Education."

16.   Erickson, D., 1993, "CD-I Advancing Interactive Video Systems."

17.   Osterbauer, R. and M. Martell, 1995, "High Tech Magic: Satellites to Schools."

18.   Stofan, J.

19.   Rasp, D., 1996, "Satellite Technology Brings Millions to the Edge of Creation."

20.   Olson, L. and M. Reynolds, 1991, "Geographic Information Systems Make Good Interpretive Signs."

21.   Johnson, W.C., 1996, "Habitats and Satellites."

22.   Tilden, p. 97.

Chapter Nine Notes

1.   Tilden, F., 1977, *Interpreting Our Heritage*, p. 80.

2.   Ibid, p. 78.

3.   Ibid, p. 82.

4.   For studies describing how the length of labels in museum exhibits negatively affects visitor attention see, for example: Bitgood, et. al. (1986) and Thompson and Bitgood (1988). These studies have found that signs and labels with short texts typically are read more frequently than those with longer texts. Miles (1989) cites a study which found that visitor departures from a 13-minute AV presentation followed an exponential curve when plotted against time, with 50 percent leaving within the first 35 seconds. This suggests that AV programs be kept short and that interpreters work to enhance holding power at the beginning of these presentations.

5.   Miller, G., 1956, "The Magical Number Seven, Plus or Minus Two: Some Limits on Our Capacity for Processing Information."

6.   Patterson and Bitgood (1988) reviewed the satiation literature and presented several studies supporting the concept of object satiation and museum fatigue.

7.   Bitgood, S., 1991, "The ABCs of label design."

8.   Bitgood, S. and S. Bishop, 1991, "The Role of a Current Visit, Prior Visits, and Gender on Visitor Perception of a Natural History Museum."

9.   Thompson, D. and S. Bitgood, 1988, "The Effects of Sign Length, Letter Size, and Proximity on Reading."

10.   Bitgood, S. and D. Patterson, 1993, "The Effect of Gallery Changes on Visitor Reading and Object Viewing Time."

11.   Bitgood, S., Patterson, D. and A. Benefield, 1988, "Exhibit Design and Visitor Behavior—Empirical Relationships."

12.   Serrell, B. and B. Becker, 1990, "Stuffed Birds on Sticks: Plans to Redo the Animal Halls at Field Museum," p. 266-267.

13.   Ibid.

14.   Whitman, W., quoted in Mills, S. (Ed.), 1990, *In Praise of Nature*.

15.   Cable, T. and V. Brack, 1985, "The Martin-mosquito Myth: Interpretative Propaganda?"

16.   The following information about myths from films and paintings is from personal communication with John Doerner, Chief Interpretation, Little Bighorn Battlefield National Monument, 23 July 1996.

17.   Several versions of the "speech" exist. See for example Jeffers, S., 1992, *Brother Eagle, Sister Sky*.

18.   Zuefle, M. and L. Beck, 1996, "Are We Ministers of Misinformation?" p. 6. See also Hargrove, E., 1989, "The Gospel of Chief Seattle is a Hoax," Jones, M. and R. Sawhill, 1992, "Just Too Good to Be True: Another Reason to Beware of False Eco-prophets," Meredith, J. and W. Steele, 1993, "The Truth of Chief Seattle," and Suzuki, D. and P. Knudtson, 1992, *Wisdom of the Elders: Sacred Native Stories of Nature*.

19.   Zuefle, M. and L. Beck, p. 6.

20.   Dillon, C., 1994, "Interpreting Myths and Misconceptions of U.S. History."

21.   Ibid.

22.   Ibid.

23.   Ibid.

Chapter Ten Notes

1.   For further information see: Knudson, D., Cable, T., and L. Beck, *Interpretation of Cultural and Natural Resources,* 1995, Chapter 12, Performance Interpretation; Veverka, J., 1994, *Interpretive Master Planning*, Chapter 6, Planning Conducted Interpretive Programs; Ham, S., 1992, *Environmental Interpretation*, Chapter 3, How to Prepare and Present a Talk; Lewis, W., 1980, *Interpreting for Park Visitors*, Chapter 3, Primary Elements of Interpretation and Chapter 5, Talks.

2.   Dillard, A., 1989, *The Writing Life*.

3.   Lewis, W., 1980, *Interpreting for Park Visitors*.

4.   National Association for Interpretation "Mission" in *Legacy*, 1997, 8(1):2.

5.   National Association for Interpretation "Membership Categories" in *Legacy*, 1997, 8(1):38.

6.   Knudson, D., Cable, T., and L. Beck.

7.   Vander Stoep, G., 1993, "Interpretive Competencies: Continuing the Discussion."

8.   Vander Stoep, G., 1994, "NAI Members Speak: Summary of Workshop Results on Interpretation Competencies."

9.   Ibid, p. 270.

Chapter Eleven Notes

1.   Tilden, F., 1977, *Interpreting Our Heritage*, p. 57.

2.   Ibid, p. 59.

3.   Ibid.

4.   Ibid.

5.   Kingsolver, B., 1995, *High Tide in Tuscon.*

6.   Tilden, p. 62.

7.   Johnson, S., quoted in Royal Bank of Canada, 1976, *The Communication of Ideas: A Collection of Monthly Letters*, p. 97.

8.   Dillard, A., 1989, *The Writing Life*, p. 68.

9.   Edison, T., quoted in Davidoff, H., 1952, *The Pocket Book of Quotations*, p. 110.

10.   Tilden, p. 59.

11.   Tilden.

12.   Ibid, p. 59

13.   Twain, M., quoted in Winokur, J., 1990, *WOW - Writers on Writing*, p. 314.

14.   Emerson, R.W., quoted in Winokur, p. 272.

15.   Fadimn, C., quoted in Winokur, p. 272.

16.   Montaigne, M., quoted in Winokur, p. 272.

17.   Tilden, p. 60

18.   Zinsser, W., 1990, *On Writing Well*, p. 187.

19.   Ibid.

20.   Tilden, p. 66.

21.   Tilden, p. 67.

22.   Bixler, R., 1996, "Beyond the Joke Book: Using Age-appropriate Humor."

23.   Perelman, S.J., quoted in Zinsser, p. 207.

24.   For an excellent example of humorous interpretive writing with just the right amount of wit and humor, see Quammen, D., 1985, *Natural Acts.*

25.   Zinsser, p. 224.

26.   Steinbeck, J., quoted in Winokur, p. 346.

27.   Tilden, p. 60.

Chapter Twelve Notes

1.   This and all subsequent references to the interpretation program at Johnson County Parks and Recreation Department are based on an interview with Bill McGowan, Interpretive Program Supervisor, 24 March 1997.

2.   Osterndorf, L., 1995, "Pulling Money Out of a Hat: The Magic of Fundraising."

3.   See Merriman (1983, 1984, 1987, 1992).

4.   Stobaugh, S., L. Youngblood Sloan and L. Gray, 1995, "The Magic Wand: Cooperative Ventures in the Interpretive Field."

5.   Albrecht, B.E. and L. Risch, 1995, "Magic Dividends from Partnership Investment."

6. Newman, A., 1993, "Volunteers Help Parks Weather Cutbacks."

7. Daly, M., 1991, "How to Organize an Effective Volunteer Program."

8. Ritter, D., Osterbauer, R., and K. Dahill, 1992, "Volunteers Managing Volunteers."

9. Gordon, N., 1985, "Docent Interpretive Program at Año Nuevo State Reserve."

10. American Red Cross, 1988, "Volunteer 2000," Washington, D.C.

11. From "Volunteering and Giving Among American Teenagers" a 1996 report of the Independent Sector, a Washington, D.C. nonprofit organization. Quoted in Plate. 1996. "America's Teens Ready, Willing to Volunteer."

12. Ibid.

13. Loosli, C., 1996, "Training Teenage Volunteer Interpreters."

14. Baumer, M., 1996, "Youth Volunteer Naturalists–Something to Believe In."

15. e.g., Cialdini (1996).

16. e.g., Cable and Udd (1988), Cable and Huddleston (1989).

17. e.g., Chapter 16 - "The Business of Interpretation" in Knudson, Cable and Beck (1995), Covel (1995) and Merriman (1996).

18. See detailed description of USDA Forest Service's TQM efforts in Knudson, Cable and Beck (1995).

19. Barry, J. and J. Runkles, 1995, "Total Quality Management: Another Tool for Improving Visitor Centers."

20. Sharpe, G. and G. Gensler, 1978, "Interpretation as a Management Tool."

21. Exceptions include Brown and Hunt (1969) who reported that interpretation effectively distributed use more evenly between roadside stops and Clark et. al. (1972) and LaHart and Bailey (1975) who reported decreased litter due to interpretation.

22. Hendee, J., 1972, "Challenging the Folklore of Environmental Education."

23. e.g., the following papers present research results documenting various management benefits of interpretation: Lime and Lucas (1977), Roggenbuck and Berrier, (1981); Ormrod and Trahan (1982), Christensen and Clark (1983), Oliver, et. al. (1985), Vander Stoep and Gramman (1987).

24. Cable applied the Theory of Reasoned Action to measure attitude changes at an interpretive site in Canada (Cable, et. al. 1987). Since then, researchers at Colorado State University have led the way in applying subsequent refinements and additional theories to studying attitude changes and linking them to behavior (e.g., Bright et. al., 1991; Manfredo and Bright, 1991).

25. Manfredo, M., 1992, *Influencing Human Behavior: Theory and Applications in Recreation, Tourism, and Natural Resources Management*.

26.   e.g., Ham and Krumpe (1996) present the Theory of Reasoned Action and the Theory of Planned Behavior to offer a rationale for determining interpretive messages designed to modify the behaviors of two audiences: on-site visitors and local communities.

27.   Machlis, G., 1989, "The Devil's Work in God's Country: Politics and Interpretation in the 1990s."

28.   Frome, M., 1982, "To sin by silence..."

29.   Bevilacqua, S., 1993, "Milestones, Millstones, and Stumbling Blocks."

30.   A study of nature center managers (Holtz, 1976) found that 99% hoped to change the public's environmental attitudes. As mentioned in Chapter Four, a survey of interpreters (Zuefle, 1994) revealed that 82% believed their role is to challenge the visitors' belief systems. For additional information, see Hooper and Weiss (1990).

31.   McAvoy, L. and D. Dustin, 1983, "Indirect versus Direct Regulation of Recreation Behavior."

32.   Dustin, D. and L. McAvoy, 1985, "Interpretation as a Management Tool: A Dissenting Opinion."

33.   e.g., Foley and Keith (1979), Peart (1980).

34.   Machlis, p. 5.

35.   Dabney, W., 1988, "Travels with Freeman."

36.   Dahlen, D., Larsen, D., Weber, S., and R. Fudge, 1996, "The Process of Interpretation: Fulfilling the Mission Through Interpretive Competencies."

Chapter Thirteen Notes

1.   Tilden, F., 1977, *Interpreting Our Heritage*.

2.   Ibid, p. 85.

3.   Mills, E., 1920, *Adventures of a Nature Guide and Essays in Interpretation*, p. 236.

4.   Marshall, quoted in Nash, R., 1982, *Wilderness and the American Mind*, p. 203.

5.   Teale, E.W., 1954, *The Wilderness World of John Muir*, p. 312.

6.   Lopez, B., 1986, *Arctic Dreams*. [Paperback frontispiece.]

7.   Marshall, R., 1930, "The Problem of the Wilderness."

8.   Ibid.

9.   Olson, S., 1982, *Reflections From the North Country*, p. 84.

10.   Ackerman, D., 1990, *A Natural History of the Senses*, xviii.

11.   Marshall.

12.   Runte, A., 1987, *National Parks: The American Experience*.

13.   Lopez, B., quoted in Beck, L., 1989, "Conversations with Barry Lopez," p. 4.

14.   Tilden, p. 108.

15.   Thoreau, H.D., quoted in Nash.

16.   Heat-Moon, W.L., 1991, *PrairyErth*.

17.   Whitman, W., quoted in Heat-Moon, p. 22.
18.   Leopold, A., 1949, *A Sand County Almanac*.
19.   Tuan, Y-F., 1993, *Passing Strange and Wonderful*.
20.   Lopez, B., 1988, *Crossing Open Ground*, p. 64.
21.   Tilden, p. 88.
22.   Mills, p. 106.
23.   Stegner, W., 1991, "The Gift of Wilderness," p. 121.
24.   Little, C., 1987. "Letting Leopold Down," p. 48.
25.   Muir, J., quoted in Wolfe, L.M., *The Life of John Muir*.
26.   Muir, J., quoted in Nash, p. 126.
27.   Saint-Exupéry, A., 1943, *The Little Prince*, p. 87.

Chapter Fourteen Notes

1.   Csikszentmihalyi, M., 1990, *Flow: The Psychology of Optimal Experience*.
2.   Ibid, p. 3.
3.   Hedge, A., 1995, "Human Factor Considerations in the Design of Museums to Optimize Their Impact on Learning."
4.   Csikszentmihalyi.
5.   Ibid, p. 62.
6.   Csikszentmihalyi.
7.   Dustin, D., McAvoy, L., and L. Beck, 1986, "Promoting Recreationist Self-Sufficiency."
8.   Csikszentmihalyi, M. and D. Kleiber, 1991, "Leisure and Self-Actualization."
9.   Csikszentmihalyi.
10.   Dustin, D., McAvoy, L., and L. Beck.
11.   Csikszentmihalyi, M. and K. Hermanson, 1995, "Intrinsic Motivation in Museums: What Makes Visitors Want to Learn?"
12.   Ibid.
13.   Hedge.
14.   Csikszentmihalyi.
15.   Mills, E., 1920, *Adventures of a Nature Guide and Essays in Interpretation*.
16.   Dahlen, D., Larsen, D., Weber, S., and R. Fudge. 1996. "The Process of Interpretation: Fulfilling the Mission Through Interpretive Competencies."
17.   Csikszentmihalyi, M., 1975, *Beyond Boredom and Anxiety*.
18.   These qualities are derived from the following document: *Chartering a Management Philosophy for the Forest Service*, signed by F. Dale Robertson, Chief, December 19, 1989.

Chapter Fifteen Notes

1.   Boyer, D., 1985, "Yosemite Forever?"
2.   Tilden, F., 1977, *Interpreting Our Heritage*.
3.   Meadows, D., Meadows, D. and J. Randers, 1992, *Beyond the Limits*.
4.   Beck, L., 1989, "Conversations with Barry Lopez."
5.   Lopez, B., 1988, *Crossing Open Ground*.
6.   Tilden, 1977, p. 90.
7.   Sax, J., 1980, *Mountains Without Handrails*.
8.   Beck, L., 1989.
9.   Buscaglia, L., 1982, *Living, Loving and Learning*.
10.   Jones, S., 1996, "Open Your Heart to More Love."
11.   Holmes, E., 1996, "Love in Everyday Living."
12.   Mills, E., 1920, *Adventures of a Nature Guide and Essays in Interpretation*, p. 12.

Conclusion Notes

1.   Mills, E., 1920, *Adventures of a Nature Guide and Essays in Interpretation*, p. 180.
2.   Hyde, L., 1983, *The Gift*.
3.   Yeats, W. B., "Adam's Curse," in 1992, *W. B. Yeats: Selected Poems*.
4.   Associated Press, December 9, 1995, "Park Rangers: We're Going to Disney World."
5.   Muir, J., In Nash, R., 1982, *Wilderness and the American Mind*, p. 161.
6.   Abbey, E., In Van Matre, S., 1983, *The Earth Speaks*, p. 57.
7.   Sawhill, J., 1995, "The Art of Giving."
8.   Ridenour, J., 1994, *The National Parks Compromised*. The 15 cultural sites are drawn from an appendix listing the units of the National Park System (pp. 219-242).
9.   Ibid. The 15 natural sites are similarly drawn from this appendix, except for Grand Staircase-Escalante National Monument, Utah, which was added to the system in 1996.
10.   Murie, A., 1962, *Mammals of Denali*. p. 1.
11.   Leopold, A., 1949, *A Sand County Almanac*. p. 173.
12.   Tilden, p. 111.
13.   Hyde, p. xii.
14.   D. H. Lawrence, quoted in Hyde, p. xii.
15.   Trimble, S., 1989, *Words From the Land*. p. 23.
16.   Snyder, G., quoted in Hyde, L., p. 149.
17.   Hyde, p. xii.
18.   Hyde.

19.   Ibid, p. xiv.
20.   Ibid, p. 16.
21.   Ibid, p. 20.
22.   Mills, p. 125.

Bibliography

Abbey, E. (1968). *Desert solitaire.* New York: Simon & Schuster.

Ackerman, D. (1990). *A natural history of the senses.* New York: Random House.

Acorn Naturalists. (1997). *Acorn naturalists 1997 catalog.* 17300 East 17th Street, #J-236, Tustin, CA 92680.

Adams, S. (1996). *Dilbert.* August 18, 1996.

Albrecht, B., & L. Risch. (1995). "Magic dividends from partnership investment." *Proceedings of the 1995 National Interpreters' Workshop:* 149-151.

American Red Cross. (1988). *Volunteer 2000.* Washington, D.C.

Anderson, J. 1984. *Time machines: The world of living history.* Nashville, TN: The American Association for State and Local History.

Anderson, J., & D. Blahna. (1995). "Who are these people, and what do they want?: Assessment of interpreters' knowledge of their audience." *Proceedings of the 1995 National Interpreters' Workshop:* 280-292.

Barry, J.P. (1993). "Anchoring safely in current: An example of using interpretation to solve a management problem." *Legacy. 4* (4):22.

Barry, J.P., & J. Runkles. (1995). "Total quality management: Another tool for improving visitor centers." *Proceedings of the 1995 National Interpreters' Workshop:* 241-244.

Baumer, M. (1996). "Youth volunteer naturalists–Something to believe in." *Missouri Conservationist.* June:4-7.

Beck, L. 1989. "Conversation with a tramp: Lee Stetson on interpretation." *Journal of Interpretation.* 13(6):6-7.

Beck, L. (1989). "Conversations with Barry Lopez: Musings on interpretation." *Journal of Interpretation.* 13(3):4-7.

Beck, L., & T. Cable. (1995). "Resolving the interpreter's identity problem." *Legacy.* 6(5):28-29.

Becker, C.L. (1932). "Everyman his own historian." *The American Historical Review.* 37(2):221-236.

Bevilacqua, S. (1993). "Milestones, millstones, and stumbling blocks." *Legacy.* 4(4):24-26.

Bigley, J.D. (1991). "Living history and battle reenactment— The dilemma of selective interpretation." *History News.* 46(6):1218.

Bitgood, S. (1991). "The ABCs of label design." *Visitor Studies: Theory, Research, and Practice, Volume 3. (Proceedings of the 1990 Visitors Studies Conference):* 115-129.

Bitgood, S. (1991). "Bibliography: Hands-on, participatory, and interactive exhibits." *Visitor Behavior* 6(4):14-17.

Bitgood, S., & A. Benefield. (1986). *A comparison of visitors across zoos.* Technical Report No. 86-30: Psychology Institute, Jackson State University, Jacksonville, AL.

Bitgood, S., Nichols, G., Pierce, M., Conroy, P., & D. Patterson. (1986). *Effect of label characteristics on visitor behavior.* Center for Social Design Technical Report No. 86-55: Jacksonville, AL.

Bitgood, S., Patterson, D., & A. Benefield. (1988). "Exhibit design and visitor behavior-empirical relationships." *Environment and Behavior.* 20(4):474-491.

Bitgood, S., & S. Bishop. (1991). "The role of a current visit, prior visits, and gender on visitor perception of a natural history museum." *IVLS Review: A Journal of Visitor Behavior.* 2(1):49-65.

Bitgood, S., & D. Patterson. (1993). "The effect of gallery changes on visitor reading and object viewing time." *Environment and Behavior.* 25(6):761-781.

Bixler, R. (1996). "Beyond the joke book: Using age-appropriate humor." *Legacy.* 7(1):34-38.

Bixler, R., Carlisle, C., Hammitt, W., & M. Floyd. (1994). "Observed fears and discomforts among urban students on field trips to wildland areas." *Journal of Environmental Education.* 26(1):24-33.

Borun, M., Massey, C., & T. Lutter. (1993). "Naive knowledge and the design of science museum exhibits." *Curator* 36(3):201-219.

Boyer, D. (1985). "Yosemite forever?" *National Geographic.* January.

Bright, A., Manfredo, M., & C. Basman. (1991). "Implications of persuasion theory for interpretation." *Proceedings of the 1991 National Interpreters' Workshop:* 40-45.

Brown, B. (1996). "Dollars and sense." *Proceedings of the 1996 National Interpreters' Workshop:* 83-85.

Brown, P., & J. Hunt. (1969). "The influence of information signs on visitor distribution and use." *Journal of Leisure Research.* 1(1):79-83.

Bultena, G., Field, D., & R. Renninger. (1992). "Interpretation for the Elderly." In Machlis, G., & D. Field (Eds.), *On Interpretation* (revised ed.). Corvallis, OR: Oregon State University Press.

Buscaglia, L. (1982). *Living, loving and learning.* Thorofare, New Jersey: Charles B. Slack.

Cable, T. (1992). "To enjoy understandingly." *Legacy.* 3(2):8-9.

Cable, T., & V. Brack, Jr. (1985). "The martin-mosquito myth: Interpretative propaganda?" *Journal of Interpretation.* 10:29-32.

Cable, T., Knudson, D., Udd, E., & D. Stewart. (1987). "Attitude changes as a result of exposure to interpretive messages." *Journal of Park and Recreation Administration.* 5(1):47-60.

Cable, T., & E. Udd. (1988). "Therapeutic benefits of a wildlife observation program." *Therapeutic Recreation Journal.* 4:65-70.

Cable T., & L. Huddleston. (1989). "Bird Therapy." *Kansas Wildlife & Parks,* May/June:39-42.

Caduto, M., & Bruchac, J. (1988). *Teacher's guide to keepers of the earth.* Golden, CO: Fulcrum.

Campbell, J. (1972). *In touch with students: A philosophy for teachers.* Columbia, MO: Educational Affairs Publishers.

Chawla, L. (1988). "Children's Concern for the Natural Environment." *Children's Environments Quarterly.* 5(3):13-20.

Christensen, H., & P. Clark. (1983). "Increasing public involvement to reduce depreciative behavior in recreation settings." *Leisure Sciences.* 5(4):359-379.

Cialdini, R. (1996). "Activating and aligning two kinds of norms in persuasive communications." *Journal of Interpretation Research.* 1(1):3-10.

Clark, R., Burgess, R., & J. Hendee. (1972). "The development of anti-litter behavior in a forest campground." *Journal of Applied Behavior Analysis.* 5(1):1-5.

Coles, R. (1989). *The call of stories: Teaching and the moral imagination.* Boston: Houghton Mifflin.

Commoner, B. (1971). *The closing circle.* New York, NY: Knopf.

Covel, J. (1995). "Enhancing interpretive services and products: Lessons from successful businesses." *Proceedings of the 1995 National Interpreters' Workshop:* 167-169.

Csikszentmihalyi, M. (1975). *Beyond boredom and anxiety.* San Francisco: Jossey-Bass.

Csikszentmihalyi, M. (1990). *Flow: The psychology of optimal experience.* New York: Harper & Row.

Csikszentmihalyi, M., & D. Kleiber. (1991). "Leisure and self-actualization." In Driver, B., Brown, P., & G. Peterson (Eds.), *Benefits of leisure.* State College, PA: Venture.

Csikszentmihalyi, M., & K. Hermanson. (1995). "Intrinsic motivation in museums: What makes visitors want to learn?" *Museum News.* May/June:35-37, 59-61.

Curran, M. (1992). "Let's interact: Developing an interactive video computer system to interpret your site." *Proceedings of the 1992 National Interpreters' Workshop:* 203-206.

Dabney, W. (1988). "Travels with Freeman," *Journal of Interpretation.* 12(1):T7-8.

Dahlen, D., Larsen, D., Weber, S., & R. Fudge. (1996). "The process of interpretation: Fulfilling the mission through interpretive competencies." *Proceedings of the 1996 National Interpreters' Workshop:* 106-108.

Daly, M. (1991). "How to organize an effective volunteer program" *Directions.* 2(3):1,3.

Davidoff, H. (Ed.). (1952). *The pocket book of quotations.* New York, NY: Simon and Schuster.

Dillard, A. (1989). *The writing life.* New York: Harper & Row.

Dillon, C. (1994). "Interpreting myths and misconceptions of U.S. History." *Legacy.* 5(1):10-11.

Doerner, J., & A. Heinlein. (1996.) "American battlefields: Compelling stories and interpretive challenge." *Proceedings of the 1996 National Interpreters' Workshop:* 223.

Dustin, D., & L. McAvoy. (1985). "Interpretation as a management tool: A dissenting opinion." *The Interpreter.* 16:18-20.

Dustin, D., McAvoy, L., & L. Beck. (1986). "Promoting recreationist self-sufficiency." *Journal of Park and Recreation Administration.* 4(4):43-52.

Erickson, D. (1993). "CD-1: Advancing interactive video systems." *Proceedings of the 1993 National Interpreters' Workshop:* 77-80.

Everhart, W.C. (1988). "Some thoughts for those who charm and inform." *Journal of Interpretation.* 12(1):T5-T7.

Fogg, C., & L. Hartmann. (1985. "Interpretation for the Very Young." *Journal of Interpretation.* 10(1):21-27.

Foley, J., & J. Keith. (1979). "Interpretation in Canadian national parks and related resources—To what end?" In *Conference II, Canadian National Parks Today and Tomorrow.* University of Waterloo, Ontario.

Frome, M. (1982). "To sin by silence ..." *Journal of Interpretation.* 7(2):41-45.

Golda, J. (1996). "The Conquistadors: The best and worst of human nature." *The Explorer.* 4(7):1-3.

Gordon, N. (1985). "Docent interpretive program at Año Nuevo State Reserve." *Trends.* 22(4):22-25.

Grater, R. (1976). *The interpreter's handbook: Methods, skills, and techniques.* Southwest Parks and Monument Association.

Grinder, A., & E. McCoy. (1985). *The good guide.* Scottsdale, AZ: Ironwood Press.

Ham, S. , & E. Krumpe. (1996). "Identifying audiences and messages for nonformal environmental education: A theoretical framework for interpreters." *Journal of Interpretation Research.* 1(1):11-23.

Ham, S. (1992). *Environmental interpretation: A practical guide for people with big ideas and small budgets.* Golden, CO: North American Press.

Hammitt, W. (1981). "A theoretical foundation for Tilden's interpretive principles." *Journal of Environmental Education.* 12(3):13-16.

Hargrove, E. (1989). "The gospel of Chief Seattle is a hoax." *Environmental Ethics.* 11:195-196.

Harrison, E. (1993). "Can Walt Disney interpret history?" *INTERPR8* (National Association for Interpretation–Region VIII Newsletter). Holiday Edition: 2-3.

Heat-Moon, W.L. (1991). *PrairyErth.* Boston: Houghton Mifflin.

Hedge, A. (1995). "Human factor considerations in the design of museums to optimize their impact on learning." In Falk, J., & L. Dierking (Eds.), *Public institutions for personal learning: Establishing a research agenda.* Washington, D.C.: American Association of Museums.

Hendee, J. (1972). "Challenging the folklore of environmental education." *Journal of Environmental Education,* 3(3):19-23.

Hilke, D., Hennings, E., & M. Springuel. (1988). "The impact of interactive computer software on visitors' experiences: A case study." *ILVS Review: A Journal of Visitor Behavior.* 1(1):34-39.

Holmes, E. (1996). "Love in everyday life." *Science of Mind.* 69(5):24-30.

Holtz, R. (1976). "Nature centers, environmental attitudes, and objectives." *Journal of Environmental Education.* 7(3):34-37.

Hood, M. (1991). "Significant issues in museum audience research." *Visitor Studies: Theory, Research, and Practice Volume 4. (Collected Papers from the Visitor Studies Conference):* 19-23.

Hooper, J. , & K. Weiss. (1990). "Interpretation as a management tool: A national study of interpretive professionals' views." *Proceedings of the 1990 National Interpreters' Workshop:* 350-357.

Hyde, L. (1983). *The gift: Imagination and the erotic life of property.* New York: Vintage.

Jackson, P.W. (1995). "On the place of narrative in teaching." In McEwan, H., & Egan, K. (Eds.), *Narrative in teaching, learning, and research.* New York: Teachers College Press.

Javlekar, V. (1989). "Learning scientific concepts in science centers." *Proceedings of the 1989 Visitor Studies Conference.* 22:168-179.

Jeffers, S. (1992). *Brother eagle, sister sky.* New York, NY: Dial.

Johnson, W. (1996). "Habitats and satellites." *Legacy.* 7(3):13-14.

Jones, S. (1996). "Open your heart to more love." *Science of Mind.* 69(5):6-12.

Jones, M., & R. Sawhill. (1992). "Just too good to be true: Another reason to beware of false eco-prophets." *Newsweek.* May 4:68.

Kawasaki, G. (1991). *Selling the Dream.* New York: HarperBusiness.

Klevans, M. (1990). "An evaluation of an interactive microcomputer exhibit in a museum setting." *Proceedings of the 1990 Visitor Studies Conference.* 3:237-254.

Kilgore, D. (1978). *How did Davy die?* College Station, TX: Texas A&M University Press.

Kingsolver, B. (1995). *High tide in Tucson.* New York, NY: HarperCollins.

Knapp, D. (1995). "Moving beyond Tilden: Producing behavior change goals for environmental interpretation." *Legacy.* 6(1):20-23.

Knopf, R. (1981). "Cognitive map formation as a tool for facilitating information transfer in interpretive programming." *Journal of Leisure Research.* 13(3):232-242.

Knudson, D., Cable, T., & L. Beck. (1995). *Interpretation of cultural and natural resources.* State College, PA: Venture.

Koran, J., Koran, M., & J. Longino. (1986). "The relationship of age, sex, attention, and holding power with two types of exhibits." *Curator.* 29(3):227-244.

LaHart, D., & J. Bailey. (1975). "Reducing children's littering on a nature trail." *Journal of Environmental Education.* 7(1):37-45.

Leopold, A. (1949). *A Sand County Almanac.* Oxford University Press.

Lewis, W. (1980). *Interpreting for park visitors.* Philadelphia, PA: Eastern Acorn Press.

Lime, D., & R. Lucas. (1977). "Good information improves the wilderness experience." *Naturalist.* 28(4):18-21.

Little, C. (1987). "Letting Leopold Down." *Wilderness.* 50(177): 45- 48.

Loomis, R. (1996). "How do we know what the visitor knows?: Learning from interpretation." *Journal of Interpretation Research 1(1):* 39- 45.

Loosli, C. (1996). "Training teenage volunteer interpreters. *Proceedings of the 1996 National Interpreters' Workshop:* 110-111.

Lopez, B. (1986). *Arctic dreams.* New York: Charles Scribner's Sons.

Lopez, B. (1988). *Crossing open ground.* New York: Charles Scribner's Sons.

Lopez, B. (1990). *Crow and weasel.* New York: Harper Collins.

Lopez, B. (1990). *The rediscovery of North America.* Lexington, KY: The University Press of Kentucky.

Louv, R. (1991). *Childhood's future.* New York: Doubleday.

Lundberg, A. (1997). "Toward a thesis-based interpretation." *Legacy.* 8(2):14-17, 30-31.

Luzander, J.C.F., & J. Spellman. (1996). "Living history: Hobby or profession?" *Proceedings of the 1996 National Interpreters' Workshop:* 241-243.

Machlis, G. (Ed.). (1986). *Interpretive Views.* Washington, D.C.: National Parks and Conservation Association.

Machlis, G. (1989). "The devil's work in God's country: Politics and interpretation in the 1990s." *Journal of Interpretation.* 13(5):4-5.

Machlis, G., & D. Field (Eds.). (1992). *On interpretation.* (Revised Ed.). Corvallis, OR: Oregon State University Press.

Machlis, G., & D. Field. (1992). "Getting connected: An approach to children's interpretation." In *On Interpretation.* (Revised Ed.). Corvallis, OR: Oregon State University Press.

Manfredo, M., & A. Bright. (1991). "A model for assessing the effects of communication on recreationists." *Journal of Leisure Research.* 23(1):1-20.

Manfredo, M. (Ed.). (1992). *Influencing human behavior: Theory and applications in recreation, tourism, and natural resources management.* Champaign, IL: Sagamore Publishing.

Manheimer, R. (1995). *The second middle age.* Detroit: Visible Ink.

Marshall, R. (1930). "The problem of the wilderness." *The Scientific Monthly.* Reprinted in *The Living Wilderness.* 40:31-35.

Maslow, A. (1987). *Motivation and personality* (Third ed.). New York: Harper & Row.

McGuire, F., Boyd, R., & R. Tedrick. (1996). *Leisure and aging.* Champaign, IL: Sagamore Publishing.

McKibben, B. (1990). "The courage to look for trouble." *Courier.* March: 14-15.

McAvoy, L., & D. Dustin. (1983). "Indirect versus direct regulation of recreation behavior." *Journal of Park and Recreation Administration.* 1(4):12-17.

Meadows, D., Meadows, D., & J. Randers. (1992). *Beyond the limits.* Post Mills, Vermont: Chelsea Green.

Mellish, X. (1996). "For someone who died in 1826, he gives a lifelike performance." *The Wall Street Journal.* Nov. 15, 1996. B1.

Melton, A. (1972). "Visitor behavior in museums: Some early research in environmental design." *Human Factors.* 14(5):393-403.

Meredith, J. , & W. Steele. (1993). "The truth of Chief Seattle. .." *Legacy.* 4(2):30-31.

Merriman, T. (1983). "Casino operation to support a nonprofit nature center: A case study." *Proceedings, National Workshop, Association of Interpretive Naturalists.* Purdue University, IN.

Merriman, T. (1984). "Interpretive fundraising events: Smurfing toward solvency." *Proceedings, National Workshop, Association of Interpretive Naturalists.* Callaway, GA.

Merriman, T. (1987). "Special events planning and management." *Proceedings, National Workshop, Association of Interpretive Naturalists.* St. Louis, MO.

Merriman, T. (1992). "Romantic fundraising." *Legacy.* 3(2):6-7.

Merriman, T. (1996). "Working toward a customer-centered interpretive business-A paradigm sheet." *Proceedings of the 1996 National Interpreters'Workshop:* 112-115.

Miles, R. (1989). "Audiovisuals, a suitable case for treatment." *Visitors studies: Theory, research, and practice, volume two. (Proceedings of the 1989 Visitors Studies Conference):* 245-251.

Miller, G. (1956). "The magical number seven, plus or minus two: Some limits on our capacity for processing information." *Psychological Review.* 63(2):81-97.

Mills, E. (1920). *Adventures of a nature guide and essays in interpretation.* Friendship, WI: New Past Press.

Mills, S. (Ed.). (1990). *In praise of nature.* Washington, D.C.: Island Press.

Moscardo, G. (1988). "Toward a cognitive model of visitor responses in interpretive centers." *The Journal of Environmental Education.* 20:(1)29-37.

Murie, A. (1962). *Mammals of Denali.* Alaska Natural History Association.

Nabhan, G., & S. Trimble. (1994). *The geography of childhood.* Boston: Beacon Press.

Nash, R. (1982). *Wilderness and the American mind.* New Haven: Yale University Press.

Newman, A. (1993). "Volunteers help parks weather cutbacks." *Wall Street Journal.* (May 19):B1,6.

Oliver, S., Roggenbuck, J., & A. Watson. (1985). "Education to reduce impacts in forest campgrounds." *Journal of Forestry.* 83:234-236.

Olson, S. (1982). *Reflections from the North Country.* New York: Knopf.

Olson, L., & M. Reynolds. (1991). "Geographic information systems make good interpretive signs." *Proceedings of the 1991 National Interpreters' Workshop:* 242-243.

Ormrod, R., & R. Trahan. (1982). "Can signs help visitors control their own behavior?" *Trends.* 19(4):25-27.

Osterbauer, R., & M. Martell. (1995). "High-tech magic: Satellites to schools." *Proceedings of the 1995 National Interpreters' Workshop:* 275-277.

Osterndorf, L. (1995). "Pulling money out of a hat: The magic of fundraising." *Proceedings of the 1995 National Interpreters' Workshop:* 140-142.

Patterson, D. , & Bitgood, S. (1988). "Some evolving principles of visitor behavior." *Proceedings of the First Annual Visitor Studies Conference.* Jackson State University, Jacksonville, AL. 40-50.

Peart, B. (1980). "An application of the Foley-Keith objectives framework to interpretation activities." *Journal of Interpretation.* 5(2):6-9.

Peart, B. (1984). "Impact of exhibit type on knowledge gain, attitude change and behavior." *Curator.* 27(2):220-237.

Person, J.E., Jr. (Ed.). (1993). *Statistical forecasts of the U.S.* Detroit: Gale Research, Inc.

Peter, L. (1977). *Peter's quotations: Ideas for our time.* New York. NY: Wm. Morrow.

Peterson, D. (1988). "There is no living history, there are no time machines." *History News.* September-October: 28-30.

Plate, T. (1996). "America's teens ready, willing to volunteer." *Los Angeles Times.*

Quammen, D. (1985). *Natural acts: A sidelong view of science and nature.* New York, NY: Avon Books.

Rasp, D. (1996). "Satellite technology brings millions to the edge of creation." *Legacy.* 7(4):30-31.

Ridenour, J. (1994). *The national parks compromised.* Merrillville, Indiana: ICS Books.

Rifkin, J. (1991). *Biosphere politics.* New York: Crown.

Ritter, D., Osterbauer, R., & K. Dahill. (1992). "Volunteers managing volunteers." *Legacy.* 3(3):9-11.

Roggenbuck, J. , & D. Berrier. (1981). "Communications to disperse wilderness campers." *Journal of Forestry.* 79:295-297.

Romey, W. (1968). *Inquiry techniques for teaching science.* Englewood Cliffs, NJ: Prentice-Hall.

Rosenfeld, S., & A. Terkel. (1982). "A naturalistic study of visitors at an interpretive mini-zoo." *Curator.* 25(3):187-212.

Routman, E., & R. Korn. (1993). "The living world revisited: Evaluation of high-tech exhibits at the Saint Louis Zoo." *Museumedia.* 3(4):2-5.

Routman, E. (1994). "Considering high-tech exhibits?" *Legacy.* 5(6):19:22.

Runte, A. (1987). *National parks: The American experience.* Lincoln: University of Nebraska Press.

Saint-Exupéry, A. (1943). *The Little Prince.* New York, NY: Harcourt Brace Jovanovich.

Sartre, J-P. (1965). *Nausea.* Harmondsworth, UK: Penguin.

Sawhill, J. (1995). "The art of giving," *Nature Conservancy.* November/December: 5.

Sax, J. (1980). *Mountains without handrails.* Ann Arbor: The University of Michigan Press.

Screven, C. 1990. "Computers in Exhibit Settings." *Visitor Studies: Theory, Research, and Practice, Volume Three (Proceedings of the 1990 Visitor Studies Conference):* 130-138.

Senge, P. (1990). *The fifth discipline.* New York: Doubleday.

Serrell, B., & B. Becker. (1990). "Stuffed birds on sticks: Plans to re-do the Animal Halls at Field Museum." *Visitor Studies: Theory, Research, and Practice Volume Three (Proceedings of the 1990 Visitor Studies Conference):* 263-267.

Sharpe, G. 1982. *Interpreting the environment.* (2nd ed.). New York: John Wiley & Sons.

Sharpe, G. , & G. Gensler. (1978). "Interpretation as a management tool." *Journal of Interpretation.* 3(2):3-9.

Sharpe, G. (1993). "Milestones, millstones, and stumbling blocks." *Legacy.* 4(4):24-26.

Silverman, L.H. (In press). "Personalizing the past: A review of literature with implications for historical interpretation." *Journal of Interpretation Research.* 2(1).

Stalder, M., & B. Cahill. (1992). "Bears, bears and more bears—Interpretation as a resource management tool: A success story!" *Proceedings of the 1992 National Interpreters' Workshop:* 40-43.

Stegner, W. (1991). "The gift of wilderness." In Willers, B. (Ed.), *Learning to listen to the land.* Washington, D.C.: Island Press.

Stobaugh, S., Sloan, L. Y., & L. Gray. (1995). "The magic wand: Cooperative ventures in the interpretive field." *Proceedings of the 1995 National Interpreters' Workshop:* 146-148.

Stofan, J. (1995). "Crossing the sea: Sea World's distance education." *Proceedings of the 1995 National Interpreters' Workshop:* 264-266.

Strauss, S. (1988). "Storytelling and the natural world." *Journal of Interpretation.* 12(1):4-7.

Suzuki, D. , & P. Knudson. (1992). *Wisdom of the elders: Sacred native stories of nature.* New York, NY: Bantam.

Sylwester, R., & Joo-Yun Cho. (1992/1993). "What brain research says about paying attention." *Educational Leadership.* 50(4):71-75.

Tanner, T. (1974). *Ecology, environment, and education.* Lincoln, Nebraska: Professional Educators Publications.

Teale, E. W. (1954). *The wilderness world of John Muir.* Boston: Houghton Mifflin.

Thelen, D. (1991). "History making in America." *Historian.* 53(4):631.

Thier, H., &M. Linn. (1976). "The value of interactive learning experiences in a museum." *Curator.* 15(3):248-254.

Thompson, D. , & S. Bitgood. (1988). "The effects of sign length, letter size, and proximity on reading." *Proceedings of the First Annual Visitors Studies Conference.* Jackson State University, Jacksonville, AL: 101-112.

Thorndyke, P. (1977). "Cognitive structures in comprehension and memory of narrative discourse." *Cognitive Psychology. 9(1)* :77-110.

Tilden, F. (Undated). *The fifth essence.* Washington, D.C.: The National Park Trust Fund Board.

Tilden, F. 1977. *Interpreting our heritage* (3rd Ed.). Chapel Hill: The University of North Carolina Press.

Tilden, F. (1983). *The national parks*. New York: Knopf.

Trapp, S., Gross, M., & R. Zimmerman. (1991). *Signs, trails, and wayside exhibits: Connecting people and places*. Stevens Point, WI: University of Wisconsin-Stevens Point Foundation Press.

Trimble, S. (1989). *Words from the land*. Salt Lake City: Peregrine Smith.

Tuan, Y-F. (1993). *Passing strange and wonderful: Aesthetics, nature, and culture*. Washington, D.C.: Island Press.

Vance, C., & D. Schroeder. (1991). "Matching visitor learning style with exhibit type: Implications for learning in informal settings." *Visitor studies: Theory, research, and practice, volume four (Proceedings of the 1991 Visitor Studies Conference):* 185-199.

Vander Stoep, G. (1993). "Interpretive competencies: Continuing the discussion." *Proceedings of the 1993 National Interpreters' Workshop:* 335-338.

Vander Stoep, G. (1994). "NAI members speak: Summary of workshop results on interpretation competencies." *Proceedings of the 1994 National Interpreters' Workshop:* 270-271.

Vander Stoep, G., & J. Gramann. (1987). "The effect of verbal appeals and incentives on depreciative behavior among youthful park visitors." *Journal of Leisure Research.* 9(2):69-83.

Van Matre, S. (1983). *The Earth speaks*. Warrenville, IL: Acclimatization Experiences Institute.

Van Rennes, E. , & C. Mark. (1981). "Bridging the visitor exhibit gap with computers." *Museum News.* 60(1):21-30.

Veverka, J. (1994). *Interpretive master planning*. Helena, Montana: Falcon Press.

Warder, D. S. , & R. Joulie. (1990). "Historic site interpretation: Past, present and future research." *Proceedings of the 1990 National Interpreters' Workshop:* 324-332.

Werling, D. (1995). "Regional model heritage education." *Legacy.* 6(5):16-17.

White, L., & M. Johns. (1996). "Inspiring teens: Learning by doing." *Legacy.* 7(3):6-8.

Williams, T. (1988). "Why Johnny shoots stop signs." *Audubon.* 90(5):112-121.

Williams, T.T. (1984). *Pieces of white shell*. New York: Charles Scribner's Sons.

Williams, T.T. (1996). "Make us uncomfortable," (Williams challenges park interpreters.) *The Exchange.* 13(2):7-10.

Williams, T.T. (1996). "An interview with Terry Tempest Williams." *Timeline.* Issue 25, January/February:10-14.

Wilson, E. (1992). *The diversity of life*. Cambridge: Harvard University Press.

Winokur, J. (1990). WOW— *Writers on writing*. Philadelphia, PA: Running Press.

Wolfe, L.M. (1973). *Son of the wilderness: The life of John Muir* Madison: The University of Wisconsin Press.

Worts, D. (1990). "The computer as catalyst: Experiences at the Art Gallery of Ontario." *ILVS Review: A Journal of Visitor Behavior. 1(2):* 91-108.

Wurman, R.S. (1989). *Information anxiety*. New York, NY: Doubleday.

Yeats, W.B. (1992). *Selected poems*. New York, NY: Random House.

Zehr, J., Gross, M., & R. Zimmerman. (1990). *Creating Environmental Publications*. Stevens Point, WI: University of Wisconsin-Stevens Point Foundation Press.

Zinsser,W.(1990). *On writing well* (fourth ed.). New York, NY: HarperCollins.

Zuefle, D.M., &L. Beck. (1996)."Are we ministers of misinformation?" *Legacy 7(1):4-6.*

Zuefle, D.M. (1994). *The interface of religious beliefs and environmental values with the interpretive profession:A multimethodological exploratory study.* Ph.D. Dissertation. Texas A&M Univ. College Station.

Index

Sagamore
Publishing   1 800 327 5557
                    $24.95
                        (College Bookstore)